TREASURES OF

LAKSHMI

TREASURES OF
LAKSHMI
THE GODDESS WHO GIVES

Edited by

NAMITA GOKHALE
& MALASHRI LAL

PENGUIN BOOKS
An imprint of Penguin Random House

PENGUIN BOOKS

USA | Canada | UK | Ireland | Australia
New Zealand | India | South Africa | China | Singapore

Penguin Books is part of the Penguin Random House group of companies whose addresses can be found at global.penguinrandomhouse.com

Published by Penguin Random House India Pvt. Ltd
4th Floor, Capital Tower 1, MG Road,
Gurugram 122 002, Haryana, India

Penguin Random House India

First published in Penguin Books by Penguin Random House India 2024

10 9 8 7 6 5 4 3 2 1

ISBN 9780143459866

Typeset in Adobe Garamond Pro by Manipal Technologies Limited, Manipal
Printed at Replika Press Pvt. Ltd, India

www.penguin.co.in

For Aman Nath, who has given visual identity to our anthologies on Sita, Radha and now Lakshmi. Gratitude for your friendship and engagement always.

CONTENTS

SECTION 2
EXPLORING LAKSHMI'S MYSTIQUE: CREATIVE INTERPRETATIONS

SECTION 3
WEAVING LAKSHMI'S TAPESTRY: CULTURAL INTERPRETATIONS

ACKNOWLEDGEMENTS

WE ARE GRATEFUL to the many friends who shared their intuitions and insights, research and writing on Lakshmi. Invariably, in conversations about the manifest power of the goddess, references would come up that were intriguing and less known, leading us into a fascinating range of material. To the contributors of essays, translations, poetry and stories, our gratitude for giving us their time, learning and wisdom. Heartfelt thanks to the publishers who allowed us to use valuable material in this anthology.

Menka Rai was the wind behind our sails as we set out to explore and navigate the myriad stories around Sri Lakshmi and their sources and inceptions; this book was made possible by her patience and dedication. Manasi Subramaniam guided us, and Moutushi Mukherjee and Saloni Mital worked diligently on different aspects of the text. Special thanks to Ahlawat Gunjan for the superb design values. Gratitude to Aman Nath for bringing our Goddess trilogy to life.

To the divine energies of the sacred feminine that blessed this book, our respect and reverence.

Namita Gokhale and Malashri Lal

HYMNS TO LAKSHMI

Origin of Shri in the Satapatha Brahmana

PRAJAPATI, WHO CREATED all the living beings through the power of his *tapas*, also created Shri, shining and resplendent. All the gods were in awe of her attributes and wanted everything for themselves. After the gods took her attributes, Prajapati asked her to do the Mitravinda sacrifice. She performed the rituals with devotion and established herself as the goddess of prosperity, wealth and abundance .

1. Prajāpati was in fervid devotion, while creating living beings. From him Śrī (fortune and beauty) came forth. She stood there resplendent, shining and trembling, setting their minds upon her.
2. They said to Prajāpati, 'Let us kill her and take all this from her.' He said, 'Surely, that Śrī is a woman, and people do not kill a woman, but rather take anything from her leaving her alive.'
3. Agni then took her food, Soma her royal power, Varuṇa her universal sovereignty, Mitra her noble rank, Savitri her dominion, Pūshan her wealth, Sarasvatī her prosperity and Tvashtri her beautiful forms.

4. Śrī said to Prajāpati, 'Surely, they have taken all this from me!' He said, 'Thou ask it back from them by sacrifice!'

(Translated by Julius Eggeling in 1900)

1. Vedic hymn – Shri Suktam, translated by Swami Krishnananda

Shri Suktam is a hymn to Goddess Shri in the Rigveda. It is the earliest hymn to the goddess where she is depicted as the all-powerful deity. It consists of sixteen hymns where the goddess is praised with devotion to bestow wealth, prosperity, abundance, beauty and blessings to lead an auspicious life. In the hymn, the goddess is specifically connected to the fertility of land as well as wealth.

चन्द्रां प्रभासां यशसा ज्वलन्तीं श्रियं लोके देवजुष्टामुदाराम्।
तां पद्मिनीमीं शरणमहं प्रपद्ये अलक्ष्मीर्मे नश्यतां त्वां वृणे॥
आदित्यवर्णे तपसोऽधिजातो वनस्पतिस्तव वृक्षोऽथ बिल्वः।
तस्य फलानि तपसा नुदन्त मायान्तरायाश्च बाह्या अलक्ष्मीः॥

For shelter in this world, I resort to that Lakshmi who is beautiful like the moon, who shines bright, who is blazing with renown, who is adored even by the gods, who is highly magnanimous and grand like the lotus. May my misfortunes perish, I surrender myself to Thee. O Thou, resplendent like the sun! By Thy power and glory have the plants, like the bael tree, grown up. May the fruits thereof destroy through Thy grace all inauspiciousness rising from the inner organs and ignorance from the outer senses.

आर्द्रां पुष्करिणीं पुष्टिं सुवर्णां हेममालिनीम्।
सूर्यां हिरण्मयीं लक्ष्मीं जातवेदो म आवह॥
आर्द्रां यः करिणीं यष्टिं पिङ्गलां पद्ममालिनीम्।
चन्द्रां हिरण्मयीं लक्ष्मीं जातवेदो म आवह॥

Invoke for me, O Agni, Lakshmi, who shines like gold, is brilliant like the sun, who is powerfully fragrant, who wields the rod of suzerainty, who is the form of supreme rulership, who is radiant with ornaments and is the goddess of wealth. Invoke for me, O Agni, Goddess Lakshmi, who shines like gold, blooms like the moon, who is fresh with anointment of fragrant scent, who is adorned with the lotuses lifted up by celestial elephants in the act of worship, who is the presiding deity of nourishment, who is yellow in colour and who wears garlands of lotuses.

ॐ महादेव्यै च विद्महे विष्णुपत्न्यै च धीमहि।
तन्नो लक्ष्मीः प्रचोदयात्॥

We commune with the great goddess and meditate on the consort of Vishnu. May that Lakshmi direct us.

2. Puranic hymn – Lakshmi Suktam: The Vishnu Mahapurana, translated by M.N. Dutt

The Lakshmi Suktam is uttered by Indra in the Vishnu Purana when Lakshmi emerges from the churning of the ocean and chooses Vishnu as her husband. The hymn invokes the goddess as the giver of not just wealth and prosperity but also knowledge and moksha.

I salute the lotus-spring mother of all beings—
unto Sri having lotus-like eyes and
reposing in the bosom of Vishnu.
Thou art Siddhi and thou art nectar,
and thou Swaha and Swadha.
O purifier of the worlds.
And thou art twilight and light and
lustre, and affluence, and intelligence,
and veneration, and Saraswati.
Thou art the learning of sacrifice;
thou art the worship of the Universe-form (of the most high);
thou art the occult learning, O beauteous one;
and thou art the knowledge of Brahma, O Goddess—
and thou art the bestower of the fruit of emancipation.
And thou art the science of dialectics;
and thou art the three Vedas;
and thou art the *Vartta;*
and thou art the knowledge of chastisement, etc.
O goddess, this universe is filled with thy gentle and terrific forms.

3. Saubhagya Lakshmi Upanishad, translated by A.G. Krishna Warrier

The Saubhagya Lakshmi Upanishad is a minor Upanishad, supposedly composed during the medieval period. It provides guidelines on worshipping the goddess, recitation of mantras as well as the benefits of worshipping her. The hymn highlights the various qualities, forms and aspects, and interprets the attributes of Lakshmi, such as the lotus.

I-4: Seated in the spotless lotus
Coloured as its pollen heaps
Bearing in her lotus palms

Lotus pair and symbolled promise
Of fear dispelled and boons bestowed;
With jewelled crown and ornaments diverse
Wondrously adorned—Let Shri,
Mother of the world entire,
Promote our fortunes ever.

I-9: Her seat: The seat of Rama (the goddess of prosperity) consists of eight petals, three circles, divisions comprising twelve houses and four sides. In the pericarp (are inscribed) the seed of Shri, keeping the goal in view. Worship the nine powers with the words 'prosperity', 'elevation', 'glory', 'creation', 'honour', 'humility', 'individuality', 'upliftment' and 'welfare' in the dative case, each having Om in the beginning and Namah (salutation) in the end.

I-11: Shri Lakshmi, the giver of boons, the spouse of Vishnu, the donor of wealth, of golden form, is decked with a garland of gold and a chaplet of silver. She has the sheen of gold, is in a fortress of gold and dwells in the lotus. She holds a lotus in her hand and loves the lotus. The pearl adorns her. She is the moon goddess and the sun goddess, is fond of bilva leaves and is mighty. She is enjoyment, release, prosperity, increase, true increase, the ploughing and the development. She is the giver of wealth and the mistress of wealth. She is faith, rich in enjoyments, the giver of enjoyments, the upholder, the ordainer—these and similar terms in the dative case, with Om in the beginning and Namah in the end, are the mantras.

4. Mahalakshmi Stotra by Indra from Brihatstotra Ratnakara, translated by Arthur and Ellen Avalon

The hymn belongs to a collection of *stotras* compiled in fourteenth century by a poet named Venkatesa. The compilation includes twelve chapters and 182 hymns dedicated to different deities. Written in Sanskrit, all the stotras are rich with poetic beauty, devotional inspiration and philosophical depth. This particular hymn is said to be recited by Lord Indra to worship Goddess Mahalakshmi to gain back his wealth which he lost due to a sage's curse.

महालक्ष्म्यष्टकम् ।

श्रीगणेशाय नमः ॥ इंद्र उवाच । नमस्तेऽस्तु महामाये
श्रीपीठे सुरपूजिते । शंखचक्रगदाहस्ते महालक्ष्मि नमो-
ऽस्तु ते ॥ १ ॥ नमस्ते गरुडारूढे कोलासुरभयंकरि ।
सर्वपापहरे देवि महालक्ष्मि० ॥२॥ सर्वज्ञे सर्ववरदे सर्व-
दुष्टभयंकरि । सर्वदुःखहरे देवि महालक्ष्मि० ॥ ३ ॥ सि-
द्धिबुद्धिप्रदे देवि भुक्तिमुक्तिप्रदायिनि । मंत्रमूर्ते सदा देवि
महालक्ष्मि० ॥ ४ ॥ आद्यंतरहिते देवि आद्यशक्ति महे-
श्वरि । योगजे योगसंभूते महालक्ष्मि० ॥५॥ स्थूलसूक्ष्म-
महारौद्रे महाशक्ति महोदरे । महापापहरे देवि महाल-
क्ष्मि० ॥६॥ पद्मासनस्थिते देवि परब्रह्मस्वरूपिणि । पर-
मेशि जगन्मातर्महालक्ष्मि० ॥७॥

O Mahālakshmi! I salute Thee,
Thou art *Mahāmayā* and *Shripitha.*
Worshipped art Thou by Devas,
Holder of conch, disc and mace
O Mahālakshmi! I salute Thee.

O Mahālakshmi! I salute Thee.
Mounted art Thou on the back of Garuda.
Thou art a terror most formidable to Asura Kola.
Thou removeth all sins.
O Devi Mahālakshmi! obeisance to Thee.

O Devi Mahālakshmi !
Thou art the giver of intelligence and success,
And of both worldly enjoyment and liberation.
Thou art the self of *Mantra.*
O Mahālakshmi! obeisance to Thee.

Thou art both gross and subtle.
Thou art terrible and a great power,
Great-bellied art Thou.
Thou removeth all great sins.
O Mahālakshmi! obeisance to Thee.

O Devi Mahālakshmi!
Thou art the supreme Brahman,
The ever-pervading *Atman.*
Thou art the great Lord
And Mother of the world.
O Mahālakshmi! salutation to Thee.

5. Kanakdhara Stotram – Adi Shankaracharya

The hymn was composed by Adi Shankaracharya in the eighth century. The story behind the composition of this stotram is that Adi Shankaracharya was once on a pilgrimage. He came across a poor woman who was very hospitable and offered him a single gooseberry as food. Moved by her kindness and generosity, Adi Shankaracharya composed the Kanakadhara Stotram as a prayer to Goddess Lakshmi to bless the woman with wealth and prosperity. The hymn invokes the blessings of the goddess for the devotee, stating that even a glance of the goddess could bring prosperity in the life of the devotee.

नमोऽस्तुहेमाम्बुजपीठिकायैनमोऽस्तु
भूमण्डलनायिकायै।
नमोऽस्तुदेवादिदयापरायैनमोऽस्तु
शार्ङ्गायुधवल्लभायै ॥१३॥

I prostrate before you, O goddess, who is seated
on the golden lotus, who is goddess of the earth, the
consort of Narayana, compassionate to the Devas.

नमोऽस्तुदेव्यैभृगुनन्दनायै
नमोऽस्तुविष्णोरुरसिस्थितायै
नमोऽस्तुलक्ष्म्यैकमलालयायै
नमोऽस्तुदामोदरवल्लभायै ॥१४॥

My obeisance to you, O daughter of Bhrigu, consort
of Damodara. O Lakshmi, seated on a lotus and adorning
the broad chest of Mahavishnu, my salutations to thee.

नमोऽस्तुकान्त्यैकमलेक्षणायै
नमोऽस्तुभूत्यैभुवनप्रसूत्यै।
नमोऽस्तुदेवादिभिरर्चितायैनमोऽस्तु
नन्दात्मजवल्लभायै ॥१५॥

O consort of Gopala, the son of Nanda, you
are worshipped by the devas. You are Jyoti
incarnate, I prostrate before thee. Your eyes
are like lotus petals. You have created the world
and you bestow prosperity. Please accept my
salutations.

सम्पत्कराणिसकलेन्द्रियनन्दनानिसाम्राज्यदानविभवानि
सरोरुहाक्षि।सरोरुहाणि
त्वद्वन्दनानिदुरितोद्धरणोद्यतानि
मामेवमातरनिशंकलयन्तुमान्ये ॥१६॥

May I always have the desire to prostrate before you
because a pranam to you is capable of bestowing all
prosperity and will bring happiness to all the senses.
Worshipping the lotus-eyed goddess not only removes
all miseries but it confers happiness and plenty.

यत्कटाक्षसमुपासनाविधिः सेवकस्य
सकलार्थसम्पदः ।
सन्तनोतिवचनाङ्गमानसैः
त्वांमुरारिहृदयेश्वरींभजे ॥१७॥

The devotee who worships your Kataksha (sidelong
glance) is blessed with wealth and prosperity. To you,
the queen who dominates the heart of Vishnu, my
pranamas, through word, thought and deed.

6. Agastya prayer to Lakshmi in Skanda Purana, 4.1.5, translated by G.V. Tagare

The hymn was sung by Sage Agastya when he was roaming on the banks of River Godavari. Before arriving at this site, he had left the city of Varanasi and was missing the place so much that he was constantly talking about the greatness of the city. While roaming about, he came across Goddess Mahalakshmi. He was dazzled by her lustre and began praying to her.

Agastya said:
(Prayer to Mahalakṣmi)
80. O mother Kamalā of large eyes resembling lotus, I bow down (to you), O mother of the universe, residing in the lotus-like heart of Śrī Viṣṇu! O Lakṣmī, fair in complexion like the inner kernel of a lotus, be pleased with me. O daughter of the Milk Ocean, you are the sole refuge of those who bow down always.

81. You are the glorious lustre in the abode of Upendra (Viṣṇu). O sole mother of Madana, you are the moonlight in the Moon, O goddess with a face captivating the mind like the Moon. You are the splendour in the Sun. You shine with all refulgence in all the three worlds. O Lakṣmī, the sole refuge of those who bow down always, be pleased with me.

82. You are the Saktī (the burning power) that always abides in fire; in collaboration with you, Vedhas (Brahmā) creates the different types of worlds. Viśvambhara (Viṣṇu) sustains and supports everything with your (assistance), O Lakṣmī the sole refuge of those who bow down always; be pleased with me.

83. O deity free from impurities, Hara annihilates only those things forsaken by you; (actually) you create, sustain and annihilate. You are *Parā* (the greatest) and the *Avarā* (the smallest). O pure one, Hari became worthy of being adored by securing you (as his consort). O Lakṣmī, the sole refuge of those who always bow down, be pleased with me.

84. O splendid deity, only he on whom your benign glance falls, becomes heroic with good qualities. He alone is a good scholar; he alone is blessed; he alone is worthy of honour through good ancestry, good conduct and artistic qualities. That man is the only clean one in the entire world.

85. Wherever you happen to stay for even a moment, whether in a man, an elephant, a horse, a group of women, grass, lake, temple, house, cooked food, jewel, bird, animal, bed or a plot of land, that alone becomes splendid and glorious, O deity identical with all; none else (can do so).

86. Only the things touched by you get purity. All the things forsaken by you are unclean, O Lakṣmī, O consort of Śrī Viṣṇu. O Kamalā residing in the lotus, wherever your name is (uttered), auspiciousness is there.

87. Where can there be misery unto those who always repeat the names of Lakṣmī, viz., Lakṣmī, Śri, Kamalā, Kamalālayā, Padmā, Ramā, Nalinayugmakarā, Mā, Kṣirodajā, Amṛt-akumbhakarā, Irā and Viṣṇupriyā.

7. Hymn in Odia Lakshmi Purana, translated by Lipipuspa Nayak

The hymn is from the sixteenth-century text Lakshmi Purana, composed by Balaram Das in Odisha. The text narrates the story of Goddess Lakshmi's visit to a Chandala woman, Shriya. When she went back to the temple–palace, her husband and his elder brother asked her to leave the house, as she had become impure by accepting the worship of a lower-caste woman. The story provides a new attribute to the goddess, who is shown as a deity considering all her worshippers equal.

Praise to you, O Lakshmi,
the cherished daughter of seven oceans.
I fold my hands before you a thousand times,
Lakshmi, the consort of Lord Vishnu
and the Goddess of His house.
Praise to you, Kamala, the epitome of kindness,
as day after day you rear matters and beings
which move and do not move, and the lowliest insects.
With your infinitesimal grace,
a poor person comes to infinite riches,
and outshines Kubera, the rich man of the three worlds.

Those who court animus towards you, Mother,
they strive in vain for a morsel of rice;
how much so ever they earn, they remain hungry.
If someone listens to this episode with attention,
or sings it aloud with divine devotion,
he is cured of his penury
as you, the goddess of great miracles, are always
pleased with him.

8. Om Jai Lakshmi Mata

This hymn is very popular and sung within families during pujas and kathas, especially in the northern and western parts of India. The hymn is sung during the aarti, which is the final ritual in worshipping the goddess. The origin of this hymn cannot be traced. The verses take the devotee through different aspects of living a fulfilled life blessed by goddess Lakshmi.

Om Jai Lakshmi Mata, Maiya Jai Lakshmi Mata
Tumko Nishidin Sevat, Hari Vishnu Dhaata
Om Jai Lakshmi Mata
Uma, Rama, Brahmani, Tum Hee Jag-Mata
Surya-Chandrama Dhyaavat, Naarad Rishi Gaata
Om Jai Lakshmi Mata
Durga Rup Niranjanee, Sukh-Sampatti Daata
Jo Koi Tumko Dhyaavat, Riddhi-Siddhi Dhan Paata
Om Jai Lakshmi Mata
Tum Paataal-Nivaasini, Tum Hee Shubh Daata
Karma-Prabhaav-Prakaashinee, Bhavnidhi Kee Traata
Om Jai Lakshmi Mata
Jis Ghar Mein Tum Rahti, Tahaan Sab Sadgun Aata
Sab Sambhav Ho Jaata, Man Nahin Ghabaraata
Om Jai Lakshmi Mata

Tum Bin Yagya Na Hote, Vastra Na Koi Paata
Khaan-Paan Ka Vaibhav, Sab Tumse Aata
Om Jai Lakshmi Mata
Shubh-Gun-Mandir Sundar, Ksherodadhi-Jaata
Ratna Chaturdash Tum Bin, Koi Nahin Paata
Om Jai Lakshmi Mata
Maha Lakshmiji Ki Aarti, Jo Koi Jan Gaata
Ur Anand Samata, Paap Utar Jaata
Om Jai Lakshmi Mata
Om Jai Lakshmi Mata, Maiya Jai Lakshmi Mata
Tumko Nishidin Sevat, Hari Vishnu Dhaata
Om Jai Lakshmi Mata

AN INTRODUCTION

MALASHRI LAL

Om Hiranya Varnaam Harineem Suvarna Rajata Srajaam |
Chandraam Hiranmayeem Lakshmeem Jaatavedo Ma Aa Vaha ||1||

—SHRI SUKTAM

EVERY MORNING IN Jaipur, I would wake up to the sight of the glowing whiteness of the Lakshmi Narayan temple set against the brooding brown hillock of Moti Doongri and its crumbling fort. The contrast was startling for many reasons. The feudal heritage of Rajasthan and its decay seemed symbolized by the ruins atop the hill, while ancient India's enduring mythology seemed reinterpreted once again in contemporary tones in the new 'Birla Mandir' erected in 1988. The inseparable pair, Lakshmi–Narayan, gracing the sanctum sanctorum, had several other intellectual traditions suggested in the images along the wall, those of Socrates, Zarathustra, Christ, Buddha and Confucius among others. Ganesh, the auspicious protector, adorned the *toran* at the main entrance, and the statues of the founders, Rukmani Devi Birla and Braj Mohan Birla, stood as devotees in an outer pavilion.

Somewhat fancifully, the tableau vivant inspired thoughts about Lakshmi's eternal relevance in every time and context, for she represents abundance from her early appearance in the Rig Veda (x.71.2) 'भद्रैषां लक्ष्मीर्निहिताधि वाचि', indicating auspicious fortune, until the present day when at each Deepavali her devotees eagerly await her visit. Lakshmi, though faithful to Narayan/Vishnu, her consort through several avatars or cycles of birth and rebirth, is nevertheless a fickle and wandering goddess encapsulating the idea of mutability in the human condition. It occurred to Namita Gokhale and me that Lakshmi, interpreted through civilizational tropes, from her symbolism of abundance in the past, has been construed in modern times as the goddess of material wealth—imaged on gold coins, blatantly advertised, and calendar art, flaunted commercially.

These thoughts surfaced in further discussions with Namita Gokhale, friend, writer and co-editor of former books with me, *In Search of Sita: Revisiting Mythology* (2009) and *Finding Radha: The Quest for Love* (2018); and we launched upon our present publication, *Treasures of Lakshmi,* that is the final volume of our Goddess trilogy. Our attempt has been to capture the rich heritage of Lakshmi, who is among the primal divine figures of the Hindu pantheon and has appeared in multiple texts denoting profuse interpretations. It remains important to acknowledge that Indian textual or narrative systems are not linear; therefore conflicting, contradictory stories are to be accepted for their plenitude rather than exclusivity. To our surprise, we found no collection on Lakshmi that anthologized the various traditions in which she played a key role or gathered her relevance in regional literature. Nor was there much creative writing that would imagine her as a protagonist in storytelling frameworks. Lakshmi's significant presence in social reality and her surprising absence from comprehensive literary scholarship fuelled our resolve to compile and edit this book, inviting friends and collaborators to search for Lakshmi in her glorious magnitude.

The story of origins is always shrouded in mystery, and its fascination lies in the variations that are presented for a major goddess such as Lakshmi. The churning of the ocean described in the Vishnu Purana is the popularly circulated vignette—that of *devas* and *asurs* at an extended cosmic war for extracting and taking control over Amrit, the elixir of immortality. Mount Meru is the gigantic spindle and the dreaded snake Ananta Sesha is the churning rope. For aeons, the contending armies exert themselves, and such stupendous energy is released in the cosmos that even celestial beings falter in their resolve. Finally, the resplendent Devi Lakshmi emerges seated on a thousand-petalled lotus, holding the Akshay Patra in her arms, the pot of abundance that carries both grains and gold. She brings with her the symbols of prosperity—Kamadhenu, the generous cow, Kalpataru, the wish-fulfilling tree, and Chintamani, the gem that can actualize dreams. Studied with care, every detail points to factors of well-being rather than the exclusive status of material wealth. Moreover, the vibrant interplay of water, animals, vegetation and forms of earthly life suggests a respectful, environmental interdependence that promises harmony.

Other stories proliferate around Lakshmi, or Shri, as she is also known, throughout Sanskrit texts, each adding attributes of glory and effulgence to her. Shri Suktam, appended to the Rig Veda, would place Lakshmi somewhere around 1000 BC as the earliest reference, but through the prayerful Vishnu Purana, the Skanda Purana containing a thousand names of Lakshmi, Saubhagya Lakshmi Upanishad, about wifely conduct, Adi Shankaracharya's Kanakdhara Stotram, the Ashtalakshmi Stotram, and other texts, the goddess continues as a major force in religious and spiritual thinking among Hindus over the centuries. She is the bestower of good fortune and the cornucopia of abundance, but it is not easy to hold her attention.

The paradoxes associated with Lakshmi are no less fascinating. In the elaborate tale of Samudramanthan, the churning ocean pushed out the inauspicious Alakshmi, the older sister, before Lakshmi manifested herself. In stories associated with the sisters, they are affectionate towards each other, and both need to be propitiated, Alakshmi being told respectfully to stay out of the home, while Lakshmi is invited indoors. Although they denote antithetical properties, for example, cleanliness vs dirt, wealth vs poverty, beauty vs ugliness, light vs darkness, the pair is a reminder of the dichotomies of everyday life and provides a cautionary tale about precarious balances. To emphasize this, Goddess Lakshmi is shown to be capricious and restless, wandering around in search of true devotees. In a charming folk narrative in Odiya by Balaram Dasa, Lakshmi favours a poor 'chandal' woman, thereby incurring the wrath of her husband Jagannath and brother-in-law Balaram. Lakshmi stands by her decision to help the good woman and withdraws her bounty from her own family—placing them in a situation without food or succour until they realize the folly of class and caste discrimination. Such narratives on the just distribution of wealth have a contemporary ring to them, and the common terms even today—Grihalakshmi and Alakshmi—are testimony to a timeless vocabulary.

The charm of Lakshmi is undoubtedly also pictorial, hence her depiction in art and sculpture abounds. The magnificent lotus seat, the elephants that flank her to anoint her with holy water, the wide-eyed owl accompanying her, the various symbols in her hand that are contextualized by region or tradition, all add up to a sumptuous visual feast. Her red sari, bejewelled crown and gold ornaments further the effect. However, in the process of such deification, the simpler Lakshmi of older traditions and her earthbound folk versions have been subdued. In addition, little recognition has been given to Lakshmi's contribution to Buddhism, Jainism and Tantra, where the powerful goddess appears at certain stages and is absorbed as a divine figure evolving from the foundational base of that practice.

These narratives build a matrix without geometry, a story without chronology. Lakshmi, the eternal consort of Vishnu, who sustains the universe, is shown as residing on his chest, sitting next to him or at his feet, indicating, as in other Hindu iconography, the irrevocable fusion of female and male energy in the cosmos—Ardhanareeshvara, Shiva–Parvati, Prakriti–Purush among others. Is there a philosophical purpose or an enduring exemplum speaking through the millennia? Lakshmi may be the key to unlocking some such secrets—the treasures of wisdom, beyond wealth.

Our book *Treasures of Lakshmi* opens with 'Hymns to Lakshmi' like a conch shell announcing an occasion. From the original Sanskrit—mellifluous and resonant—to modern times, the translations in English by various hands convey the changing perceptions of the goddess. The transcendent abstractions about prosperity and abundance in the ancient Shri Suktam leads later to the contemporary vocabulary of *Astha Lakshmi* (eight appearances), each with her specific attributes.

Within that vast framework, the first section unveils Lakshmi's essence in the 'divine interpretations' proffered by historians, economists, storytellers and mythologists. Bibek Debroy's nuanced reading of the symbols of the goddess and their etymological origins places a thoughtful system of inscription before us, referring readers to the Gayatri Mantra and the Bija Mantra particular to Lakshmi, among several other intricacies in the worship pattern. Jawhar Sircar describes Lakshmi as an 'amorphous Goddess' tracking her through texts and iconography, and probing a few regional variations. He draws out the paradox of the Samudramanthan legend saying, 'We have a disconnect between her origin from the sea and her firm habitat on placid water—that is churned in limited quantities by the two elephants.' In Devdutt Pattanaik's essay 'Decoding Lakshmi' we discover different interpretations of wealth that surface in the story: 'The battle of Devas and Asuras is the battle between spenders and hoarders, distributors and creators.' Meghnad Desai follows Lakshmi through her incarnations of Sita and Rukmini, and comments on her links with the agricultural cycle. He opens up the concept of the Grihalakshmi—the householder—the woman who is an asset to the domestic economy. Mahalakshmi, the figure explored by Renuka Narayanan in the legends of southern India, links her to the scholar–preachers Adi Shankara and Vedanta Desika. The puzzle about wealth being a blessing or a bane comes up in the comparison between Kubera and Lakshmi in the essay by Ashutosh Garg showing a sociological history of power games. Menka Rai looks into another segment of the goddess's influence to find her in the mythology and iconography of Buddhism and Jainism. Sunita Pant Bansal's personalized narrative about growing up in Kumaon describes the art of *aipan*, or 'Lakshmi yantras' with mystical patterns. In other words, in this section, the divine Lakshmi presides regally over multiple traditions and has an honoured place in every part of India.

These probing essays are followed by a second section of creative writing where the freewheeling imagination of an author can explore terrains beyond legend. In a way, this is part of the paradigm of telling and retelling by which mythology in India accretes a splendid multiplicity. What creatures of the deep ocean might Lakshmi have encountered before she surfaced in the Samudramanthan is the question embedded in Koral Dasgupta's short story. Among them is Kurma, the tortoise, Vishnu's avatar, holding guard over Lakshmi while she excitedly explores the depths. Bulbul Sharma recounts memories of Lakshmi Puja through a child's perspective of the elaborate preparations at home—the auspicious *ghot*, the chants and the storytelling while the young ones wait eagerly for the feast to follow. Bulbul Sharma's piece is an important reminder of Lakshmi *panchali* that enjoins householders 'to be kind to elderly relatives, and never unkind or envious of others'. Since all gods and goddesses have *vahanas* or vehicles, we requested Prasanna K. Dash to present stories about Lakshmi's owl, very popular in Bengal and figured in wooden artifacts designed by local artisans. Further, we retrieved a lovely novella, *Lokkhir Agaman* by Bonophul, the pen name of Balai Chand Mukhopadhyay (1899–1979), and Arunava Sinha has translated a spine-chilling extract for our book—about the sacred owl of Lakshmi and the magical transformations that the goddess can bring. This is followed by Rabindranath Tagore's poem 'Nagarlakshmi', published in *Katha* in 1899, translated for us by Reba Som. In this sensitively written poem, based on a Buddhist tale about a famine in Sravastipura, Lakshmi is the giver of victuals and her devotees are not always the wealthy. Contemporary poems by Sanjukta Dasgupta and Tamalika Chakraborty play upon the themes of materiality, opulence and the dazzle associated with the worship of the goddess, while the undercurrent is the insatiable greed of the modern world. 'Lakshmi' is also the girl child, today not a welcome arrival in many homes struggling with economic burdens and gender discrimination.

The third section, 'Weaving Lakshmi's Tapestry', is a valuable resource for researchers, as it is the first-ever selection and compilation from sacred texts of Hinduism, the Buddhist Jatakas and the Tantric traditions. Our purpose is to show the vast influence of Lakshmi, whether in the consciousness of believers or in the ambit of civilizational discourse. The resplendent grace of the Devi and her gentle benevolence made Lakshmi desirable for a multitude of reasons. To begin with, Lakshmi is the ideal image of munificence, whether it be grain, gold, cattle, food, shelter, justice or equity. The rightness of desire is what Lakshmi heeds, not necessarily the voice of the rich and the powerful. We are pleased to present verses from the Puranas translated by Bibek Debroy, Swami Vijnanananda, G.V. Tagare and others and to discover early translations of the Jataka Tales mentioning Lakshmi. Modern commentaries on iconography yield valuable insights on the diverse depictions that Lakshmi has inspired. The debate on Lakshmi's early presence in Buddhism and her later fading out when Tara and Vasudhara appear in the pantheon has no final arbiter. Lakshmi of the Tantric traditions is deeply researched through 'invocations' by Constantina Rhodes and the 'Kamalatmika' image by Menka Rai, and the allusions may come as a surprise. The environmental cohesion that Lakshmi portrays is evident in the owl, tortoise, lotus, elephants and other creatures of the earth who are associated with her. Among these, the pair of sacred elephants are the subject of Niharika Sankrityayan's essay and Alka Tyagi translates an ancient treatise on how to depict the image of Lakshmi. Bounteous as she is, the auspicious Lakshmi needs a counterpart so her worshippers do not lapse into a false security, hence Alakshmi, the destructive sister is dramatically portrayed by Tanashree Redij and P.P. Joglekar. Such dualism is integral to Indian mythology as a reminder on the impermanence of existence even as one craves for the blessings of sufficiency. Interestingly, Malashri Lal's essay, 'The Brand Rhetoric', shows the emergence of Lakshmi in the public sphere of government and corporate schemes as the harbinger of prosperity for the girl child and the entrepreneurial woman; for example, the cosmetic brand Lakmé originated in honour of Lakshmi.

The fourth section, 'Folk Interpretations', spans an enormous cultural space. The 'little traditions', as A.K. Ramanujan calls folk narratives, contain charming and sometimes disturbing stories about Lakshmi. 'Once Lakshmi converted Brahma into a cow and Shiva into a calf and sold them to a Chola king', begins a legend in *Bhavisyottara Purana* immediately leading to a curiosity about the outcome. Another legend, recalled by Sukumari Bhattacharji, speaks of the independent-minded goddess sometimes siding with a demon such as Bali; then Vishnu has to exercise his supreme power to win her back for the Gods. Religious studies scholar Nilima Chitgopekar traces the evolution of the tulsi shrub as a counterpart of Lakshmi: 'Worshipped as a goddess in her own right, one could say that Tulsi is a plant embodiment of the Devi,' she says. Balaram Dasa's *Lakshmi Purana,* a fifteenth-century text about a 'chandal' devotee, has been cited by modern commentators as an expression of the goddess's defiance of hierarchies. In Odisha this story remains popular, and we present an extract from a translation by Lipipuspa Nayak which vividly captures the cadences of the oral narration and the rituals accompanying it.

Bidyut Mohanty's book *Lakshmi the Rebel: Culture, Economy and Women's Agency* gathers inspirational accounts of Lakshmi in the *vrat kathas* from many parts of India, of which we have selected two—one translated from Marathi, the other from Bengali. The *vrat kathas* first establish the *vidhi,* or method of worshiping Lakshmi, then move into storytelling. Remembering that folk narratives are largely community based activities, these are revelatory examples of conduct codes for women. Largely, 'the worship is to assure four types of grants: Dharma, Artha, Kama, Moksha, but also Purushartha, Sat, Santaan, and Soubhagya,' explains Mohanty. In the story from Maharashtra, a wife teaches her husband a lesson by simply withholding salt from his food, implying that 'wealth' has a broader definition than gold. He had taunted her about what she might have brought as a gift from her natal home and her answer had been 'Sar' (salt), causing a sarcastic reaction from him. The simple domestic routine of a well-cooked meal restores the equilibrium in thinking mindfully about a divine blessing. Several traditional tales from rural areas present humility and gratitude as enduring virtues. From Bengal comes the story of Kojagori Lakshmi Puja which is a harvest related festival performed on a full-moon night. Based on the *Lokkhi Panchali*, there are several versions from which Mohanty's choice highlights the contrarieties inherent in Lakshmi and Alakshmi. In summary, a virtuous king helped out his subjects by purchasing any items left unsold in the market. To test his Dharma, Vishvamitra carved a statue of Alakshmi, which no one would buy, and the king remained faithful to his practice. When Alakshmi was given residence in the palace, all the forms of Lakshmi left him and devastation started. He had received a boon of understanding the language of plants and animals and realized that everyone declared him foolish in accepting Alakshmi, but in his own eyes he had a pledge to keep. By a twist of fortune, the queen performed the Kojagori Lakshmi Puja outside the palace and called for restoring her husband's wealth. The woman's piety was such that Alakshmi now had to leave the kingdom. Women, in such narratives, have the agency of worship but their wishes are focused on the family's well-being. N.A. Deshpande translates the Puranic myth of Alakshmi.

The goddess has a teaching voice in some of the folk tales—again perhaps due to the community engagement in her worship. A popular folk story for children, rendered by Sunita Pant Bansal, has a jealous servant girl who is very critical of her mistress, the queen, so Lakshmi changes their places. It's in dire circumstances that the errant girl realizes the value of the queen's generosity, *daan* (donation) being a revered virtue. In a Kannada story, presented by Partha Sarathi Gupta, Lakshmi tells Alakshmi, 'There will come a day when wisdom shall teach men the art of dodging your gaze.' However, the inauspicious sister cannot be wished away and keeps appearing in moralizing tales.

The enthralling aspect of such stories is that they evolve continuously and adapt to the times. It comes as a surprise to find the Astha Lakshmi Stotram, composed in 1970, within the time span of our personal memories, that Prof. R. Mahalakshmi presents in her book on Lakshmi. The attributes are meticulously described for Adi Lakshmi, Dhanya Lakshmi, Dhairya Lakshmi, Gaja Lakshmi, Santana Lakshmi, Vijaya Lakshmi, Vidya Lakshmi and Dhana Lakshmi. It appears almost like a litany about the evolution of the goddess, from primeval times to now, when materiality or Dhana Lakshmi has emerged as the main identity.

Swamini Atmaprajnananda Saraswati, a theologian steeped in the Sanskrit traditions, traces the thousand appellations (*sahasranama*) of Goddess Lakshmi showing certain clusters of meaning and the correlation between others. Aligned to this is Alka Tyagi's translation of 108 names of Lakshmi which comprise a common prayerful offering in Hindu homes. The lyrical cadence of Sanskrit and the intellectual understanding of the names by which the goddess is revered encourages a transition over the aeons during which the power of the divine feminine has prevailed.

Our book, *Treasures of Lakshmi*, hopes to restore the comprehensive picture of a goddess who presided over the beginnings of cosmic creation and who should continue to be venerated as the benefactor of the most liberal definitions of 'prosperity'. Whether it is Lakshmi's 108 names or a sahasranama of a thousand appellations, her blessings are multidimensional and eternal.

I end with words by A.K. Coomaraswamy:

'Sri Lakshmi is essentially Aditi, Prakriti, Maya, Apsaras, Urvashi, the Waters, all the possibilities of existence substantially and maternally personified.'

SECTION 1

UNVEILING LAKSHMI'S ESSENCE: DIVINE INTERPRETATIONS

'As the tutelary deity of the rice-growing agriculture of native India she is called The One Possessing Dung (*karisini*). Her two sons are Mud (*kardama*) and Moisture (*ciklita*), personifications of the ingredients of a rich soil. She is honey-like (*madhavi*) and is said to grant gold cows, horses and slaves. She wears garlands of silver and gold. She bestows health, long life, prosperity, offspring and fame. Fame personified is another of her sons. She is made of gold (*hiranyamayī*), of golden hue (*hiranyavarna*), imperishable, beautiful and valuable as gold. She is called *harivallabha* and *visnupatni,* The Beloved Spouse of Vishnu.'

Heinrich Zimmer, *Myths and Symbols in Indian Art and Civilization*

1

LAKSHMI UNVEILED: A JOURNEY INTO ABUNDANCE

BIBEK DEBROY

LAKSHMI—THE WORD, LIKE many words in Sanskrit, has multiple meanings. Among other things, it means good fortune, prosperity and success. It means beauty and charm. And it also means the beautiful goddess of wealth and prosperity. Who is Devi Lakshmi? That depends on the devotee and the text. At one level, she is Devi herself. At another, she is one of Devi's manifestations as Maha Lakshmi, the other two being Maha Saraswati and Maha Kali. She is Shri or Rama, the beautiful one, Vishnu's consort. She is the one who manifested herself when the ocean of milk was churned by the Devas and the Asuras for Amrit. The use of the word 'manifestation' is important. Lakshmi, or generally Devi, isn't born. She is always there, omnipresent, though not always visible and manifest.

There is a Devi Sukta in the Rig Veda. The word *sukta* means 'good saying', but it is specifically used for a hymn of praise. This is the 125th sukta in the tenth mandala (collection) of the Rig Veda. But it praises Devi, not Lakshmi in particular. Shri is specifically praised in the Shri Sukta. This is from the appendices of the Rig Veda, known as the Khila portions, which have clearly been composed later than the main text of the Rig Veda. This portion requests Agni, the fire god, to invoke Lakshmi for the devotee:

> 'Through her, I will obtain gold, cattle, horses and men.'
> 'There is a tender golden glow around her. She is seated on a lotus. Her complexion is like that of a lotus.'
> 'Through her favours, let the Alakshmi in me be destroyed.'

The Shri Sukta is one of the earliest textual references to Shri or Lakshmi, and the bits within quotes are exact translations of parts of the Shri Sukta. This is of course a textual reference. Archaeological excavations also show that Lakshmi has been worshipped for thousands of years.

Lakshmi's iconography will typically depict her that way, golden in complexion. The word 'padma' means lotus. Hence, Padma is one of Lakshmi's names. She is Padmasana, seated on a lotus. The word 'kamala' also means lotus. Hence, Kamala is another one of Lakshmi's names. She is Kamalasana, seated on a lotus. Alakshmi, described as Lakshmi's older sister, is Lakshmi's antithesis. Lakshmi stands for prosperity and Alakshmi for adversity. Lakshmi is the goddess of good fortune, Alakshmi is the goddess of misfortune. But one must realize that Lakshmi has many forms and her iconography will also differ. Usually, she has four arms. But Lakshmi with eighteen arms is not unknown either.

There is also the concept of Ashta Lakshmi, or eight different forms of Lakshmi. These are known as Adi Lakshmi, Dhan Lakshmi, Dhanya Lakshmi, Gaja Lakshmi, Santana Lakshmi,

Dhairya Lakshmi, Vijaya Lakshmi and Vidya Lakshmi, all capturing different forms of wealth and fortune. As I said, the iconography for each of these is different, as are their mounts. Adi Lakshmi (primordial Lakshmi) will have four hands, Dhan Lakshmi six (*dhan* means wealth), Dhanya Lakshmi eight (*dhanya* means grain), Gaja Lakshmi four (*gaja* means elephant, but indicates animals, a source of wealth), Santana Lakshmi (eternal Lakshmi) six, Dhairya Lakshmi eight (*dhairya* means patience and fortitude), Vijaya Lakshmi eight (*vijaya* means victory) and Vidya Lakshmi four (*vidya* means learning). But the iconography, attire and what the hands hold are not always standard. There are other forms of Lakshmi too—Saubhagya Lakshmi, who grants good fortune; Rajya Lakshmi, the one who bestows the prosperity of a kingdom; and Vara Lakshmi, the one who grants boons.

Hence, if we think of the owl as Lakshmi's mount, that is not invariably true. To take one example, *samkhya* philosophy talks of three *gunas*: sattva, representing purity; rajas, representing passion; and tamas, representing darkness. When Lakshmi represents sattva guna, her mount is Garuda. When Lakshmi represents rajas guna, her mount is an elephant. When Lakshmi represents tamas guna, her mount is an owl. It is not unusual to find Lakshmi mounted on a lion too.

When she possesses four arms, they symbolically represent the four *purusharthas* or objectives of human existence: dharma, artha, kama and moksha. In the usual iconography, she will be attired in red and be seated on a lotus (or standing on it). Two of the four hands will be in the *abhaya* and *varada* mudras. A mudra is a position of the hands. In both these mudras, the palm faces outwards, towards the front. Abhaya mudra is the one that signifies granting freedom from fear, and the hand will face upwards. Varada mudra is the one that signifies the granting of boons, and the hand will face downwards. Images of most deities will have the hands in abhaya and varada mudras, and Lakshmi is no exception. What of the other two hands? This being Lakshmi, one hand will hold a lotus. And the other hand will often hold a pot, indicating wealth and prosperity.

The stories and suktas we hear about Lakshmi are often from the Puranas. An example of such a *stotram* (hymn of praise) or sukta is Kamala Stotram from the Vishnu Purana. It is beautiful and speaks of Kamala being a personification of the sound 'OUM'. She is a form of the five elements of fire, earth, water, wind and space. This stotram calls her Chandi, Durga, Kalika and Koushiki. She is full of yoga. She is eternal and primordial knowledge. She is responsible for the creation, preservation and destruction of the universe. We are told that Shiva told Parvati about this stotram.

There are eighteen Maha Puranas or major Puranas, believed to have been composed by Krishna Dvaipayana Veda Vyasa after he composed the Mahabharata and Hari Vamsha. Devi features prominently in the Markandeya Purana, in that part of the Markandeya Purana known as Devi-Mahatmya, or Durga-Saptashati, or Chandi. There is a stotram in this section and it has a refrain most people are familiar with: '*Ya Devi sarvabhuteshu.*' There are several shlokas with that refrain and one of them says, '*Ya Devi Sarvabhuteshu Lakshmi-rupena samsthita.*' This is a stotram. Hence, it is a prayer addressed to Devi. A translation of that bit is: 'To that Devi, who is established in all beings in the form of Lakshmi.' As I said, Lakshmi is one of Devi's manifestations. Most of us are familiar with the standard Gayatri Mantra. But some of us may not know that there are Gayatri Mantras addressed to specific divinities. There is one addressed to Lakshmi too. '*OUM. Shri Mahalakshmai cha vidmahe Vishnupatnai cha dhimahi tanno Lakshmi prachodayat.*' If one is familiar with the basic Gayatri Mantra and knows that Lakshmi is Vishnu's wife, this does not require a translation.

The Devi Bhagavata Purana is entirely about Devi. Most of us have heard of Shakti *peethas*. After Daksha's sacrifice, when Sati immolated herself, parts of her body fell down in various parts of the country and became Shakti peethas. The Devi Bhagavata Purana gives us the names of 108 such Shakti peethas (sometimes, a different number, like fifty-one, is given). In each case, there is a specific geographical region and the name of the Devi who resides there. Accordingly, Kamala resides in Kamalalaya, Maha Lakshmi in Karavira and Lakshmi Mata in Siddhavana. Where are these places today? Such questions are often impossible to answer. Plus, it depends a bit on the text. There are tantra texts of much later vintage, say 500 years ago. *Tantrachudamani* is an example of this. It has a section on the determination of peethas, where Devi herself speaks about fifty-one Shakti peethas, the parts of her body that fell down after being severed by Vishnu's chakra, and the Bhairava (Shiva) who has established himself in these places. We are told that the neck fell down in Shrishaila (in present-day Andhra Pradesh)—Devi is named Maha Lakshmi there, and Bhairava's name is Bhimalochana. However, there is also a stotram about eighteen Shakti peethas, attributed to Adi Shankaracharya. This mentions Maha Lakshmi in Kolhapura. The text matters.

I should mention the Skanda Purana, one of the Maha Puranas. It is quite common for texts to have 1000 names for a deity. The Skanda Purana gives us 1000 names for Lakshmi. The sage Sanatkumara told the sage Gargya about these names. This is known as the Lakshmi Sahasranama. Listing 1000 names will be boring, but there are several names there that we are not that familiar with. Some of them also describe Lakshmi physically. For example, her face is like a blooming lotus. Her eyes are like the petals of lotuses. Her face is like the full moon. Her complexion is like that of pure crystal. Her three eyes are the sun, the moon and the fire. This bit also mentions Lakshmi's Beej Mantra. *Beej* is a seed and a Beej Mantra is somewhat esoteric and secret, difficult to explain. The expression carries within it the seed of the mantra. Lakshmi's Beej Mantra is '*aim hreem shreem*'. (There are other Lakshmi Beej Mantras too.) A very simple—and not quite correct—way of stating this is to say that 'aim' stands for Saraswati, 'hreem' stands for Kali and 'shreem' stands for Lakshmi.

I mentioned the churning of the ocean earlier. That occurs in many texts and many Puranas. The Devas and the Asuras fought incessantly. On one such occasion, the Devas were defeated and the three worlds (heaven, earth and the nether regions) were taken over by the king of the demons, Bali. The gods sought Vishnu's help. Vishnu suggested that the ocean be churned. This churning of the ocean is known as Samudramanthan. When the ocean was churned, it would yield Amrit, the nectar that confers immortality. However, the gods didn't possess the capacity to do this alone and sought the help of their cousins, the demons. There was an agreement that they would divide up whatever the ocean yielded. However, the churning of the ocean required a churning rod and a churning rope. Mount Mandara became the churning rod. Vasuki, the king of the serpents, became the churning rope. With Vasuki coiled around Mount Mandara, the churning could begin. But one still needed something for Mandara to rest on, something that could be the base. Vishnu assumed the form of a turtle and the churning started. As a result of this churning, fourteen different treasures arose from the ocean. One of these was Lakshmi, the goddess of wealth, Vishnu's wife. She arose, holding a lotus in her hand. Lakshmi is described as Vishnu's wife, Saraswati is described as Brahma's wife and Kali/Parvati/Sati is described as Shiva's wife.

'Navaratri' simply means 'nine nights'. Sometimes, people use the term 'Navaratra'. A lunar fortnight is known as *paksha*, and auspicious days are reckoned in accordance with the lunar day, *tithi*, which does not necessarily correspond to a solar day. When the moon waxes and increases every day, it is the bright lunar fortnight, known as Shukla Paksha. This ends in Purnima or

Purnamasi, the night of the full moon. After that, when the moon wanes and diminishes every day, it is the dark lunar fortnight, known as Krishna Paksha, culminating in Amavasya, the night of the new moon. Therefore, every month there is a Shukla Paksha and a Krishna Paksha. In general, Shukla Paksha is propitious for worshipping Devas and Krishna Paksha for ancestors. The nine nights of Navaratri are spread across the first lunar tithi to the ninth: *pratipada*, *dvitiya*, *tritiya*, *chaturthi*, *panchami*, *shashthi*, *saptami*, *ashtami* and *navami*. Out of the twelve Navaratris, Sharada or Ashvina Navaratri (in September–October) is special. At that time, Devi is worshipped, such as Durga in the eastern parts of the country. Sometimes, Nava Durgas, or nine different forms of Durga, are also worshipped. There is more than one listing of Nava Durgas. In one of these listings, Lakshmi is the name of one of the Nava Durgas.

In our traditions, there is something special about all transitions in time: day to night and night to day (*sandhya*), Shukla Paksha to Krishna Paksha and vice versa, the sun moving from one sign of the zodiac (*rashi*) to another (*sankranti*), the transition from *uttarayana* (the northwards movement of the sun) to *dakshinayana* (the southern movement of the sun) and vice versa. Therefore, it is understandable that there should be something special about Purnima and Amavasya. Festivals are occasions for celebrating and there are celebrations when there is wealth and prosperity. Historically, prosperity has been linked to harvests. That's the reason there are so many festivals in the months of September and October. The Gregorian months of September and October (Ashvina and Kartika, according to Indian calendars) are more special than most. That cycle of celebration starts with the worship of Devi, ending with Vijaya Dashami (the tenth lunar tithi, the day of victory). But it doesn't end there.

We then have a clutch of three tithis in Krishna Paksha: Trayodashi, Chaturdashi and Amavasya, the first two being the thirteenth and fourteenth lunar tithis. That Trayodashi is popularly known as Dhanteras, a variation of Dhan Trayodashi. Since dhan means wealth, Dhan Trayodashi is a celebration of wealth and prosperity. Beliefs and customs differ, often locally. It is sometimes believed that along with Lakshmi, Dhanavantari, the physician of the gods, manifested himself from the churning of the ocean that day. The day of Lakshmi Puja is not uniform throughout the country. For example, in eastern parts, Lakshmi Puja is on the tithi of Purnima that follows Vijaya Dashami. This is known as Kojagari Lakshmi Puja. Literally, the expression means, 'Who is awake?' On that full-moon night, Lakshmi moves around, entering a house where the resident is awake and avoiding the one where the owner is asleep. If you want wealth and prosperity, you had better be awake.

But in some parts, Lakshmi is worshipped on Dhan Trayodashi, as is Dhanavantari. Because of Dhanavantari, this Trayodashi has now become 'National Ayurveda Day'. The next day is Chaturdashi. This Chaturdashi is known as Naraka Chaturdashi or Bhuta Chaturdashi. Before being killed by Krishna, Narakasura sought the boon that he should be worshipped with lights on this day, and it was granted. This brings us to the night of Amavasya. In some parts of India, this is the day of Lakshmi Puja. In other parts, this is the day of Kali Puja. Both Lakshmi and Kali are Devi's forms. We also know the day as Deepavali or Diwali. *Deepa* is a lamp, with an allusion to the lamp of knowledge (*jnana*) driving away the darkness of ignorance. India is a country with many festivals. Usually, they are localized. If one is looking for a pan-Indian festival, that would be those days in September and October associated with harvests, wealth and prosperity—and the worship of Lakshmi.

There are many aspects to Lakshmi. These are only some of them.

2

LAKSHMI: THE GODDESS WHO DEFINES INDIA

JAWHAR SIRCAR

The Approach

OF ALL THE Hindu deities, Shiva may be the most complex, but Lakshmi is certainly one of the most amorphous—when one attempts to capture her within a definitive framework. She is undoubtedly one of the oldest deities, and one can claim, quite confidently, that she has survived for three full millennia, even as 'superior' Vedic gods and goddesses like Brihaspati, Brahmansthapati, Indra, Varuna, Mitra, the Adityas, Agni, the Ushas, Vayu, Savitur, Pushan, the Ashwins and others have just disappeared, some rather too early. Many of their traits have been subsumed in other deities, and some, like Agni, are invoked through ritual, in their material form, but they are not worshipped on a daily basis.

One has to appreciate that in Indic religions a deity is not just an image or an idol—some deities do not even possess a human or an anthropomorphic form. Deities represent some 'power' or an overwhelming characteristic, like Surya stands for the sun and all that he represents or emanates—daylight, heat, life-giving energy, radiation, the seasons and so on. This god is invoked only or mainly for these qualities. A deity is, in fact, a metaphor for a life force or a necessity.

Lakshmi is a metaphor not only for wealth and economic prosperity but also for the fickleness that invariably accompanies wealth. More than that, this deity stands for auspiciousness, which explains why 'Shri', the oldest name for Lakshmi—which stands for 'the decorous'—is prefixed to names and events to convey both propriety and prosperity. In fact, Lakshmi's story really begins when she is merged with the late Vedic deity 'Shri'. Scholars feel that although Vedic civilization mentions her for the first time around 1000 BCE, her prototype may have continued to exist among the post-Harappan people, whose emphasis on material prosperity far exceeded that of the Vedic people. No image of any proto-Lakshmi has, however, been located, but we are yet to understand fully the evidence collected so far. It is only natural to expect that since wealth must have been the highest priority in a trade-based, material-rich civilization like that of the Harappans, there may have been a deity dedicated to wealth. If validated, this would indicate that Lakshmi in whatever form enjoys one of the longest continuums among all deities.

Every Indic deity is not necessarily what she or he began as—they adjust, evolve, modify, reshape, accommodate, accustom and acclimatize. The failure to adapt is fraught with the danger of obsolescence, as Brahma has shown by disappearing altogether, except at Pushkar. Like 'corporations', deities change their appeal to reach out to larger target audiences. They go through mergers with deities that already exist or local deities to acquire their strengths, immunities and characteristics. Shiva appears to have absorbed the Harappan god of animals—Pashupati, as some call him—who is in a yogic meditation pose. He then acquires the characteristics of the Vedic Rudra with his mighty roar—the frightening hurricane or tempest—via the 'Shri Rudram' hymn of the Yajur Veda. Bare-bodied in the icy Himalayas, clad only in tiger-skin, covered often in ashes, with his *trishul* (trident) and the hourglass drum, the *damaru*, Shiva appears in his classic iconic form. But, at the same time, he is equally well known in his aniconic, phallic shape as the omnipotent lingam.

Vishnu, on the other hand, maintains his core self but appropriates a lot of floating legends about super-gods through his ten (actually, nine, so far) incarnations—the Dashavatara. The point is that Lakshmi could also continue to thrive, with equal popularity, through different ages as she absorbs contradictory legends. A keen observer would be able to trace the pre-Vedic characteristics from later accretions. She has her own course of adaptations as Vishnu's wife through his different incarnations as Vamana, Parashurama, Rama and Krishna. She is there by his side as Padma or Kamala, Dharani, Sita and Rukmini. Then, there are eight Lakshmis to represent liberation, wealth, blessings, animals, children, valour, knowledge and victory.

We have deliberately used the term 'Indic' as Lakshmi may have been 'Hindu' to begin with but was revered by Buddhists and Jains as well. In fact, her first proper representation was at the celebrated Buddhist stupas of Sanchi and Bharhut in the two centuries preceding Christ. There are holy Jain texts that say that before an exalted soul like a Tirthankara was born, his mother dreamt of several auspicious creatures, including the goddess Shri, which became a synonym of Lakshmi. We may recall that Buddhism and Jainism loosened socio-economic strata and shackles, promoting, thereby, the entrepreneurial spirit. It is only natural, therefore, that the goddess of wealth, Lakshmi, would be coveted and respected by both anti-Vedic religions that encouraged mercantilism.

Let us now approach the Lakshmi story along four different routes and then try to make sense of our findings at a later stage. We could begin with her origin legends; then move to the textual mentions of her; take a look at her iconographic descriptions; and finally try to understand the civilizational traits conveyed through the symbols surrounding her. Obviously, it is difficult to keep the four approaches completely and clinically distinct, as in Indic religions the barriers between legend and text and iconography are much too fluid. Nevertheless, it may be useful to adopt this quadri-linear approach when grappling with subjects that are so amorphous by nature.

Origin Legends

The Vishnu Purana describes the arrival of Shri in the Samudramanthan or the legend of the churning of the ocean in search of the nectar of immortality thus:

> Then, seated on a lotus,
> Beauty's bright goddess, peerless Shri arose
> Out of the waves; and with her, robed in white,
> Came forth Dhanwantari, the gods' physician.

This grand appearance of Lakshmi is greeted with great joy and wonder, and the sea of milk presents her with a wreath of unfading flowers while the artist of the gods decorates her with lovely ornaments. There is, indeed, some amount of rivalry among the gods for her affections, but she chooses Vishnu and positions herself on his chest, seated on a lotus. A struggle ensues between the Devas and the Asuras for the possession of the nectar of immortality and when peace finally reigns and order is restored, Sakra eulogizes Lakshmi on behalf of the much-relieved gods:

I offer my obeisances unto the Goddess who is the abode of lotuses,
who holds the lotus, whose eyes resemble the petals of a lotus, whose
face is a lotus, and who is dear to the Lord who has a lotus navel.

You are Siddhi (superhuman power), Ambrosia, Svaha (auspicious) and
Svadha (spontaneity), O purifier of the worlds. You are twilight, night,
effulgence, opulence, intelligence, faith and Sarasvati.*

Shri or Lakshmi is thus assigned—as the spouse of Vishnu, the 'great preserver of the universe'—the additional task of ensuring economic growth and social stability. This version of the legend is repeated in many a text, Puranic or otherwise. Let us note how the Griffith's Ramayan† reiterates the same tale:

When many a year had fled,
Up floated, on her lotus bed,
A maiden fair, and tender-eyed,
In the young flush of beauty's pride.

Queen of the gods, she leapt to land,
A lotus in her perfect hand,
And fondly, of the lotus sprung,
To lotus-bearing Vishnu clung.
Her, gods above and men below
As beauty's Queen and Fortune know.

---

* Horace Hayman Wilson, *The Vishnu*, 1840, p. 79. Translated at sacred-texts.com.

† Ralph T.H. Griffith, *The Ramayan of Válmíki*, 1870, p. 204. Translated into English verse.

The Vishnu Purana was composed over a fairly long period between the fifth century BCE and the tenth century CE, over which the original kernel could grow and expand its coverage. It could, thus, absorb many of the known or acceptable legends and beliefs concerning Vishnu and his consort. The Ramayana and the Mahabharata are believed to have been completed between 300 BCE and 300 CE, and these two epics and the Puranas represented the Brahminical upsurge and retort to the sweeping popularity of Buddhism and Jainism. This was after the decline of the strong pro-Buddhist late Maurya age. The Puranas appear to be the product of centuries of ideological craftsmanship that often grappled with obtuse and complex issues concerning deities and their existentialist problems. They could be viewed as Brahminical schools and projects that usually completed their task of compiling all existing stories concerning specific deities and extolling their virtues, while linking the Purana and its deities to the wider universe of other well-known Puranas. It may be noted that none of the early Maha Puranas are dedicated to any goddess and it is only the appendix of the Markandeya Purana that contains the earliest comprehensive Puranic validation of the mother goddess. Of course, even the older Puranas, like Vishnu's, extol the virtues of individual goddesses, but mainly in the context of male deities.

While the Samudramanthan origin is generally accepted as the primary legend concerning the arrival of Lakshmi on earth, the same Vishnu Purana contains another story that says that she was the daughter of the sage Bhrigu and Khyati, and it was only later that she reappeared as the goddess who emerged gloriously out of the ocean. John Dowson quotes yet another legend where she is addressed as *kshiraabdi tanaya*—daughter of the sea of milk—and she is represented as floating on a lotus at the time of creation.* What we may need to note is that the overwhelming

---

* John Dowson, *A Classical Dictionary of Hindu Mythology and Religion, Geography, History, and Literature* (New Delhi: Rupa Books, 1991), p. 176.

section believes that she arose from the ocean, which is fine, but that she is on a lotus. This is interesting as this flower and plant are rooted to static pools of water, usually found in the 'interior' of India, not on the coast and certainly not in the middle of the ocean. We have, therefore, a disconnect between her origin from the sea and her firm habitat on placid water—which is churned in limited quantities by the two elephants. It appears that by this time Vedic civilization had come to terms with the habitat of the wet-rice-cultivating peoples of India.

Textual Evidence

Many are surprised to learn that the core Rig Veda does not mention Lakshmi at all, though it does cite a 'Shri'. This text was composed between the thirteenth century BCE and approximately the eleventh century BCE. This represents the earliest phase of the Vedic people and their language, Sanskrit, and the divide with those they demeaned as demons was quite obvious. All we can say from this evidence is that at that stage of social development there did not appear to be any great need for the acquisition and concentration of wealth—which forms the core of Lakshmi's existence and blessings. From other sections of Vedic literature it is clear that what mattered the most was cattle and cattle wealth. It was basically a pastoral society, on the move all the time, perhaps to locate new fields for their animals to graze on. There is a marked distaste for the dark-skinned settled peoples of India and a pronounced antipathy for both technology and accumulated riches. These are spelt out in as many words in scattered sections of the Rig Veda where the technological advancements of the non-Vedic people are viewed as magic, mirage and trickery. Wealth other than that of cattle had little use in the Vedic world.

Zimmer feels, however, that though Vedic society represented 'strictly patriarchal warrior herdsmen and the installation of patriarchal gods', the mother goddess (of the Indus civilization) 'maintained her supremacy, nevertheless . . . in the hearts of the native population'.* As we shall see, the evolution of Shri from the Vedic goddess of auspiciousness to Lakshmi, the deity of corn and bounty in post-Vedic settlements, she filled a big gap. She emerged as the corn goddess, like Core of the Greeks, Demeter of the Romans, the Egyptians' Isis, the Sumerians' Innana, Ishtar of the Babylonians and Anahita of the ancient Persians. Even the Vikings had their Freia.

Shri–Lakshmi is the Hindu form of the timeless mother goddess who nurtures and nourishes all life, but it is only in the later Vedic and post-Vedic periods that we get the early signs of the divide with other ethnic groups of India being bridged. The first mention of Shri that we get is Shri Sukta, which is a *khilasukta*, that is, a supplementary sukta (set of mantras) to the Rig Veda. It is the earliest hymn comprising multiple verses that invoke Lakshmi as the goddess of wealth and prosperity. It appears between the fifth and sixth cantos or mandalas of the *Bashkalashakha* or recession of the Rig Veda. The Shri Sukta has fifteen mantras or *riks*, and the very fact that it is also available in sources other than the Rig Veda prove that these are the primary texts related to the worship of Goddess Lakshmi. Many of these have several additional verses, sometimes going up to twenty-two, thus making a total of up to thirty-seven verses. The most common additions made to the fifteen mantras are the 'Aphalashruti' (recompense for chanting the hymn) and the 'Lakshmi Gayatri Mantra'. Even the additional verses that the Shri Sukta carries are actually supplementary to it, and as said, the sukta itself is supplementary to the Rig Veda. Isidor Scheftelowitz† takes pains to explain how separate strata are

* Heinrich Robert Zimmer, *Myths and Symbols in Indian Art and Civilization* (New Jersey: Princeton, 1946), p. 99.

† Isidor Scheftelowitz, *Shri Sukta* (Berlin: Deutsche Morgenlandische Gesellschaft, 1921), pp. 37–50.

discernible on the basis of stylistic and linguistic differences in the Shri Sukta. Verses 1–2 and 13–17 are addressed to Lakshmi, while verses 3–12 are invocations to Shri—at a time when there are reasons to believe that they were distinct but analogous deities. In short, the Shri Sukta coalesced the earlier Shri and the later Lakshmi. The various interpolations and layers represent the different attempts by different schools of thought. We discover, as we move along, that the Atharva Veda mentions her on multiple occasions and the Shatapatha Brahmana cites her in book XI at 4:3:1.

As we examine more texts, we see how some of the additional verses of the late Vedic period are so similar to those stated in the Puranas and the epics, even though these were composed well over a thousand years after the Rig Veda. This is the strength of Brahminical Hinduism that keeps relentlessly forging interrelationships between textual materials of different ages to lend legitimacy to each other. This is the highly 'referenced continuum' which forms the solid scriptural foundation of the religion which overrides its internal self-contradictions by cross-linking and reiterating common tales separated by a millennium, if not more.

Iconography

Though the literature of the Vedas and the subsequent period displays a remarkable flair for art, detail and splendour, we get no material form as sculpture or craft or paintings. In fact, the first attempts at representing human or divine images manifest themselves in the shape of the *yaksha* or its female counterpart, the *yakshi* or *yakshini*. They represent a class of generally benevolent but sometimes mischievous nature spirits who are said to be the custodians of hidden treasures. From their short height and often-unwholesome looks they appear to represent the indigenous people as viewed by those who composed Vedic and post-Vedic literature, commonly classified as 'Aryans'. Even this development was rather late, in the fourth and third centuries BCE. This is well after the establishment and mass popularity of Buddhism and Jainism as challengers of Vedic and post-Vedic Brahminism. Jainism has a yakshi for each of its twenty-four Tirthankaras, and Indic religions often paid homage to yakshas as tutelary deities of a city, district, lake or well. They were worshipped by the masses, mainly indigenous, with nagas (serpent deities), feminine fertility deities and mother goddesses. It appears that yaksha worship coexisted with the priest-conducted sacrifices of the Vedic period.

In art, the yakshas are among the earliest deities to be depicted in the form of sculptures for worship, veneration or propitiation. It is later, only in the second century BCE, that we get the first major representations of a Hindu deity—Lakshmi, not in any Hindu temple (none have been discovered from that period), but on the highly decorative gates and railings of the Buddhist stupas at Bharhut and Sanchi in central India. It is more or less during the same period that we also come across the icon of Balaram of Mathura and we get the first stirrings of idol worship in India—some 2200 years ago, not earlier. The sculpture of a yakshi found at the Buddhist site of Amaravati and the one standing on a lotus at Basrah in Bihar appear to be the forerunners of Lakshmi.

The imagery of Lakshmi in literature, as we have seen, is that of 'an exceptionally beautiful woman, standing or sometimes sitting on a lotus with four hands—two of which hold lotus flowers and the lower left in the upright *mudra* or posture or benediction or blessing'.* She is also seen holding a padma (lotus), *shankh* (conch shell), Amrit-*kalash* (pot of nectar) and a bilva fruit. The 'Lakshmi Sahasranama' and the 'Devi Mahatmya'

---

* Stephen Knapp, *Hindu Gods and Goddesses* (Delhi: Jaico Books, 2012), p. 138.

identify her with the great Devi and describe Lakshmi as having eighteen hands, holding a rosary, an axe, a mace, an arrow, a thunderbolt, a lotus, a pitcher, a rod, a sakti, a sword, a shield, a conch, a bell, a wine cup, a trident, a noose and a discus in her eighteen hands. The most common symbols of wealth and auspiciousness that are closely associated with Lakshmi are the pot, a pile of gems, a throne, a fly-whisk, a conch, a fish, a parasol, nagas, yakshas, a footstool, a horse, an elephant, a cow and the wish-fulfilling tree. Her standard pose, Gaja Lakshmi, is that of Lakshmi with two elephants which constantly pour pitchers of water over her. She is occasionally accompanied by an owl that can see through darkness while the elephants symbolize work, activity and strength. There are, of course, several variations, especially in the different regions.

There are several contenders for the oldest sculpture of Lakshmi. We get a Gaja Lakshmi from Sonkh in Mathura that is dated to the pre-Kushan era, while a terracotta plaque with images of Lakshmi dating to the second century BCE was located in Atranjikhera in Burhanabad, Uttar Pradesh. Other archaeological sites with ancient Lakshmi terracotta figurines from the first millennium BCE include Vaisali, Sravasti, Kausambi, Campa and Chandraketugadh. A Lakshmi statuette has been found in Pompeii, Italy, that is dated to before the eruption of Vesuvius in 79 CE, which is very interesting indeed. In addition, we come across Lakshmi quite frequently in the ancient coins of various Hindu kingdoms from Afghanistan and north-western India. Gaja Lakshmi has been found on the coins of Scytho–Parthian kings Azes II and Azilises; she also appears on Shunga Empire King Jyesthamitra-era coins of the period between the second and first centuries BCE. These surely prove that Lakshmi images were in circulation in the first century BCE—much before most other deities. This itself is a remarkable fact worth pondering over.

Making Sense of Symbols

This is the most interesting part, and we shall avoid metaphysics altogether—like saying that her four hands indicate dharma (righteousness), artha (wealth), kama (sensual pleasures) and moksha (final liberation). Instead, let us ponder over what we see and try to decipher their purport. The first fact that stares at us is her connection with the ocean from which she arose, as Jaladhija, daughter of the ocean. For a civilization that has developed inland, rather than based on sea trade, this is rather unusual. True, the Malabar and Coromandel coasts have produced seafarers, as have other enclaves like Gujarat and Odisha, but oceanic trade can hardly be considered as central to existence as, for instance, in Britain and Portugal. In fact, crossing the oceans had been taboo for long periods. Yet, almost all the origin tales of many a civilization, whether highly advanced or markedly less so, have been centred on vast, unconquered waters—to highlight both the unknown and the limits of man's existence. Much of the action of Hindu mythology, the great Samudramanthan, has to take place on this centre-stage and we may view it as such.

The rest of Lakshmi's symbolism is rooted not only very far away from the oceans but around static water. The lotus and the water from which it springs is necessarily calm and has little motion, which is another way of saying it is stagnant and often marshy. But this landscape does represent stability, unlike, say, Saraswati, who personifies a flowing stream. The utter placidity of the lake from which arises the lotus is far removed from turbulent rivers or tumultuous oceans. In fact, this is the geography in which thrived the nagas, snakes or snake-like amphibians that Vedic civilization chastised a lot and was not only careful to stay away from but deliberately avoided. It was the territory of their foes who slinked away into the marshes and waters, confusing the dry-land-loving Vedic people who cursed them. Thus, the most beauteous of its products, the lotus, is a crown jewel on which sits Lakshmi—symbolizing a mastery over the watery landscape or the acceptance of it. The appropriation of the very Indian symbol, the lotus, by Vishnu and his consort, Lakshmi, is almost an act of finality seen in the manner in which they dominate. Lakshmi uses it not only to sit or stand, but both hold lotuses in their hands as well. It is not that the Vedic Aryans were averse to the lotus—they were enraptured by its beauty and say so in their literature. But the habitat in which it prospered the most—across the Yamuna and the Saraswati, in the marshy areas of the Ganga valley, was terra incognita to them some two millennia before Christ. Later, Buddha and Bodhisatvas like Padmapani-Avalokiteshvara also coveted this lotus symbol, and Padma Sambhava or Guru Rinpoche, who introduced Buddhism to Tibet, has strong associations with the lotus. Many an Indic deity like Saraswati may be seen seated on lotuses, but the association of the lotus with Vishnu–Lakshmi is complete.

Sukumari Bhattacharji says that 'Lakshmi becomes the tutelary goddess of a primarily rice-growing agricultural population'. This explains why the waters are basically stationary and yet they are shaken into controlled motion by the two elephants which keep pouring pitchers of water over Lakshmi. The importance of waters in agriculture was definitely realized by the later Vedic people as we come across invocations like these in the Yajur Veda: 'The waters divine do thou pour full of sweetness to avert disease from men, from their place let arise plants with fair leaves'. But the concept of settled agriculture and the importance of the abundance of water for rice cultivation dawns a little later. 'Lakshmi is Karisini (the cow-dung goddess, and cow dung is manure),' explains Bhattacharya, 'her sons are Kardama (mud) and Ciklita (moisture)—things essentially linked up with agriculture. Gupta art represents Lakshmi with the cornucopia and the lotus as metaphors for plenty and beauty. Suniti Kumar Chatterji also connects Lakshmi quite definitively with the goddess of bounty in other parts of the ancient work. He says that Shri is 'derived from the same root from which the Latin Ceres, the corn-goddess is derived'.

There is no doubt that the Indian nation was formed only after the Vedic Aryans crossed over to the *doab* of the Ganga and Yamuna and settled down, on whatever terms, with the indigenous folk of India—when the agricultures of the dry-land wheat cohabited with the rice of the wetlands. This was when water in abundance became a civilizational trait, and the lake, the lotus and the serpent were not only accepted but deified. The lotus, thus, is not only an object of beauty, it represents the very treaty of Hindustan—for the flat lotus and inverted lotus were accepted and utilized to the fullest by subsequent rulers, from the Afghan, Turki and Mughal to the British, in their wondrous art of India.

Connections to the Yakshi Cult

It is often said that Lakshmi has associations with the Yakshi cult that was the forerunner of formal image-worship in India. Even after Indic gods and goddesses started appearing in iconic shapes, Yakshi sculptures of wood, stone, metal, terracotta and other material ran parallel to formal images of deities for almost two millennia, till about the sixteenth century. As the earliest of Indic deities to be found in image form, her sculpture is bound to have some carryovers from Yakshi imagery, as is evident in the stylistic forms of yakshis at Amaravati and Basrah. The Yaksha cult was basically a worship of pre-Aryan folk deities for boons or protection and appeared in different styles—from beautiful, big-breasted women to short, fat, squatty doorkeepers. With such strong appeal, some of them, like Kubera, the god of riches, found their way into the Hindu and Buddhist pantheons.

Interestingly, adorning most Buddhist shrines are images of Kubera, the pot-bellied yaksha king and later the treasurer of the gods, very closely associated with Lakshmi. Ganesha, too, has iconographic signs like a copious belly that reveal his connection with the outer fringe of Ganas and Yakshas. Ananda Coomaraswamy insists that 'Ganesha is undoubtedly a Yaksha type, by his big belly and general character: but he is not cited by name in any lists. There is a frieze in the University Museology of Philadelphia known as the 'Trinity of Fortune' that displays Ganesha, Kubera and Lakshmi. As said before, the two of them have definite and strong Yakshi origins, and the third may have had some such trait. Lakshmi would ultimately occupy Kubera's space in the realm of prosperity, and relegate Ganesha's position a lot, by reaching the status of 'top-of-the-mind recall' where wealth is concerned. We have mentioned that Jains have yakshis as female attendants for each Tirthankara and they were housed in their temples.

Yet, it is difficult to pin the yakshi label on Lakshmi. Coomaraswamy sums it up, saying, 'It is beyond doubt that Yakshinis were extensively worshipped, in part as beneficent, in part as malevolent beings.' He goes on to list the Sapta-Matrika (seven mothers), sixty-four Yoginis, the Dakinis of Kali, the Bengali Sitala and even Minakshi of Madurai as either yakshis or having yakshi lineage. But he does not list Lakshmi, proving that until further evidence can be gathered, she has no yakshi origins, though she may have had associations with Kubera and Ganesha.

The Concept of Alakshmi

The Shri Sukta entreats Lakshmi to banish her sister Alakshmi, or misfortune, who is associated with need, hunger, thirst and poverty. Though Alakshmi is not mentioned by name in Vedic, Upanishadic or early Puranic literature, she appears to embody all the characteristics of the Rig Vedic goddess Nirrti, the evil one. She is modelled on the mirror image of Lakshmi except that every benevolent characteristic is replaced by the opposite, malevolence. The cosmology of Vishnu and the Padma include her and say that when the Samudramanthan churned out various deities and objects, Alakshmi arrived before Lakshmi. She is, therefore, known as Jyestha, the elder one, but since the gods knew her evil designs, they sent Alakshmi to reside among malignant persons and spread grief and poverty among them. She is seen as the asura of inauspiciousness that emerges whenever one is not careful. This is the moot point that the auspicious and the terrible are separated by a thin divide.

Since the Sanskritic way of life could not be ensured without a normative whip, Alakshmi was created to keep the women of the house in their place. Any transgression from the rules of strict purity and hygiene was considered Alakshmi and invited ruin. Even quarrels among brothers were said to be caused by Alakshmi, an attribute that was invariably bestowed upon one or more women, namely, daughters-in-law. She or they were accused of bringing in rivalries and jealousies into the household which thus ruined the male lineages or *kula*. Viewed from this angle, it was the epitome of patriarchy that ensured through an invisible surveillance that its values were enforced, using the threat of social ostracism.

We get glimpses of the Vedic way of life from the Padma Purana in its indictment of Alakshmi:

> Always remain, causing misery, in the houses of those men who speak cruel and false words and the mean men who eat at dusk . . . Your stay will be there where there are skulls, hair, ashes, bones, and chaff fire. Always remain, causing grief and poverty in the houses of those mean men who eat without washing their feet . . . in the houses of those who clean their

> teeth with sand, salt, or charcoal. O, you eldest one, causing filth, your stay will be in the houses of those mean men who eat mushrooms and a left-over coconut, men of sinful thoughts, who eat sesamum-flour, bottle-gourd, garlic, shoots of young plants, a species of *kadamba*. Always stay in that house which is bereft of sacrifices to preceptors and gods, and bereft of gifts to guests, and where the sound of [the recital of] the Vedas is absent. Stay where brāhmaṇas, good men and old men are not honoured.

The Linga Purana suggests a divide along the lines of caste and culture by extolling Shri as the embodiment of patriarchal righteousness and relegating the lazy and rebellious Alakshmi to outside the pale of Vedic virtues.

Through Alakshmi, we get the don'ts of the Indic way of life and its obsession with hygiene and ritual purity. We also get glimpses of cultural dislikes like garlic (to which Manu added onion) and certain other food items like mushrooms—which was finally forsaken in the nineteenth-century provinces that were exposed to the European way of life and better reconciled to Muslim dishes, and in the twentieth century in the rest of India. In the Buddhist Jatakas, too, there are tales of men and women who request Goddess Lakshmi to drive away the goddess of misfortune, Kalakanni.

Thus, every form of social commitment was injected into the household, mainly on women who are branded as Alakshmi for the slightest transgression. Though the term could also be applied to men, we never hear of men being Alakshmi—as the gender of this noun is decisively feminine. We reiterate that the Indic view of life and hygiene and the ritually pure and impure was enforced quite unforgivingly on women of the household through the mortal dread of being termed as Alakshmi. Though Mircea Eliade and Kunal Chakrabarti have observed that at the theological level Brahminism saw no conflict between good and evil, it seems that in everyday existence women in the domestic sphere found it expedient to comply with the 'do's and don'ts' of so-called religious prescriptions.*

Regional Variations

Before ending, it may only be proper to mention that while Lakshmi is universally regarded as a prime deity across the length and breadth of India, there is no uniformity in her worship or even image. In the north and west of India, Lakshmi is worshipped on a grand scale on the darkest moon night, Amavasya, as on Diwali—when everything is lit up with lamps. For Gujarat, her worship marks the beginning of a new year. The south has, however, a tradition of worshipping Lakshmi during three of the nine nights of Navaratri, preceding Dussehra. The goddess is seated on a huge lotus in an asana posture and is flanked by Ganesha and Saraswati. In Bengal and the east, comprising Assam, Tripura and parts of Odisha, her worship is on Kojagori Purnima, the full-moon day of the lunar month of Ashwin. This is a week after the autumn Navaratri and Durga Puja, and here, Lakshmi is on the lotus as her seat or stool and her pot of wealth is very local—quite different from north and west India. It is placed firmly on her lap, her right arm wrapped around it, her owl near her feet. There is no image of her in standing position being bathed by two elephants on two sides as in other parts of India. In Andhra Pradesh, Karnataka, parts of Tamil Nadu, Maharashtra and Odisha, Vara Lakshmi Vratham is observed on the second Friday of Shukla Paksha in the month of Shravan. People observe a fast, and this day dedicated to Lakshmi has great significance in these states.

---

* Kunal Chakrabarti, *Lakshmi's Other: Brahmanical Construction of a Negative Goddess* (Kolkata: Bangiya Itihas Samiti, 2018).

This is just a glimpse of how diversity thrives amid unity in India, and has done for several millennia. Hinduism is basically the management of variations and contradictions.

3

DECODING LAKSHMI*

DEVDUTT PATTANAIK

A BOWL OF rice will provide equal satisfaction to a rich man and a poor man, to a saint and a sinner. A bowl of rice does not judge the person who consumes it. The same applies to a piece of cloth. A piece of cloth will provide comfort to whosoever drapes it, man or woman, irrespective of caste, creed or religion. And a house will provide the same quality of shelter to all, without any discrimination. We may judge a bowl of rice, a piece of cloth or a house, but the rice, the cloth and the house will never judge us. For rice, cloth and house are forms of Lakshmi, the goddess of wealth.

It annoys us to find Lakshmi with people we don't like, people whom we deem to be criminals and sinners. We believe that Lakshmi should abandon amoral and perverse people. But there she is, with them, and we find it exasperating, irritating and

* First published in *Deccan Herald*, Bangalore, on 16 October 2009.

so unfair. In mythology, all villains seem to be rich. Ravana lived in the city of gold and Duryodhana lived like a king till the day he died. Contrast this with Rama, who had to live, for no fault of his, in the forest for fourteen years, and the Pandavas, who were born in the forest and had to live in the forest, in abject poverty, for most of their lives. Why is it so? Does Lakshmi like bad people? Or is she just indifferent to the notions of ethics and morals and propriety and virtue that matter so much to us?

Ancient Indian seers spent a lot of time contemplating the nature of wealth. And they compiled this knowledge through the stories, symbols and rituals of Lakshmi. Lakshmi embodies the principles of artha, economic and political activity. She is one of the four goals of life, said the seers, the other three goals being: dharma, social order; kama, pleasurable pursuits; and moksha, spiritual practice.

Some scriptures say that Lakshmi follows Vishnu, who is the upholder of dharma, and her son is Kamadeva, the god of pleasure. Is that wishful thinking? After all, Lakshmi is often seen in the company of Vishnu's enemies—the demonic Asuras, whose city located under the earth was called Hiranyapura, the city of gold, that precious metal so closely associated with Lakshmi. And everyone knows that Lakshmi's arrival need not always be pleasurable. Her arrival is followed by quarrels and strife. So what is this mystery?

To understand Lakshmi, we have to understand where wealth comes from. Wealth in its most primal form comes from under the ground. Plants come from under the ground. Minerals come from under the ground. Water comes from under the ground. Even petrol comes from under the ground. Lakshmi is therefore called Patala-nivasini, she who resides in the subterranean realm. Patala is also the realm inhabited by the Asuras. The king of the Asuras is called Puloman, and his guru is Shukra of the Bhargava clan. And this brings us to two names of Lakshmi—Pulomi and

Bhargavi, which means daughter of Puloman, and daughter of Bhrigu, daughter of the demons and/or their guru! It makes sense, since wealth comes from under the ground, she owes her origin to those who rule the realm under (*tala*) our feet (*pa*). In some scriptures, Lakshmi is called Varuna's daughter; Varuna being the god of the sea. Varuna, incidentally, is also addressed as Asura in Vedic texts. The term Asura applies to all forces that lock wealth. The sea locks wealth, the subterranean realms lock wealth, trees lock wealth—until it is harnessed and released. Those who release this wealth are called Devas. And Devas live above the ground as fire (Agni), wind (Vayu), sun (Surya), moon (Chandra) and rain (Indra).

Children's books often translate the word Asura as demon. And the word demon has a moral judgement. But this moral judgement is missing in Indian literature. Asuras are the children of Brahma, just like Devas. The two sets of beings have different mothers. Diti is the mother of the Asuras and Aditi is the mother of the Devas. The former live under the ground and the latter live above the ground. The former create wealth while the latter yank her out. This makes Lakshmi Asura-putri (daughter of the Asuras) and Deva-patni (wife of the Devas). Indra's consort, Sachi, is a form of Lakshmi.

Equating Asuras with demons is a legacy of early European scholars, blindly adopted by later Indian academicians. Since Asuras were enemies of Devas, and since Devas were worshipped and hence considered gods, Asuras became demons, a natural conclusion for people who were obsessed with force-fitting everything into the binary framework of good and evil.

The reason why Devas were worshipped was not moral, it was material; they released wealth and made it available to all—they released rain from clouds, trees from seeds, water from earth, metals from rocks. Asuras were not worshipped because they hoarded wealth, locked it away from humans. They had to be killed if Lakshmi had to be released. The sun god's sunlight, the wind god's air and the rain god's water made the plants come out. The fire god's heat released metal from rocks. Without violence, wealth could not be secured: the field had to be ploughed, crops had to be cut, grains had to be threshed, rocks had to be broken and smelted . . . in other words, 'war' had to be declared on the Asuras and their daughter had to be taken forcibly.

Indra and the Devas live a life of luxury surrounded by wine and women and music and dance. Indra is very blessed. Unlike humans, who have to work for a living, he can get anything he desires by simply wishing for it, for in his realm, Amravati, exists the wish-fulfilling tree, Kalpataru; the wish-fulfilling cow, Kamadhenu; and the wish-fulfilling gem, Chintamani; and even the elixir of immortality, Amrit. That is why Indra's abode is called Swarga or paradise. Still, Indra is extremely insecure. He fears he will lose his wealth. For unlike the Asuras, he does not know how to create wealth; he can only procure and distribute wealth. A sage's curse can cause Lakshmi to leave his side in an instant. And this invariably happens, thanks to the megalomania stirred by wealth.

Once again Indra leads the Devas to fight and kill the Asuras and get Lakshmi back. The Asuras can keep creating Lakshmi because they are blessed with something the gods do not possess—Sanjivani Vidya, the secret of regeneration. This can bring the dead back to life, in other words make the barren land fertile. This is a gift obtained for the Asuras by their guru, Shukra, a devotee of Shiva. So the Asuras keep generating wealth and the Devas keep snatching wealth away from them. Which is why everywhere during harvest time we narrate stories of demons being killed—on Dussehra, Mahish-Asura is killed by Durga; on Diwali, Narak-Asura is killed by Krishna; and on Onam, Bali-Asura is killed by Vaman.

The battle of the Devas and the Asuras is a battle between spenders and hoarders, distributors and creators. It begins with a defeat of the Devas and the loss of Lakshmi, and ends with a victory of the Devas and the return of Lakshmi. That it is never-ending indicates it is not a battle of good over evil. It is a fertility cycle.

The funny thing is, neither the Devas nor the Asuras are happy. They try hard to hold on to Lakshmi but she slips away. In folk tradition Lakshmi is described as being squint—one never knows where she is actually going. She is also called Chanchala, the whimsical one, eternally restless. They say one should never keep the image of Lakshmi standing in the house; she will get tired and run away. One is advised to keep images of Lakshmi comfortably seated, preferably next to Saraswati, goddess of knowledge.

While Lakshmi brings prosperity into a household, Saraswati brings peace. The two goddesses are described as quarrelling sisters. Lakshmi loves to go to places where Saraswati resides. But her arrival marks the end of wisdom and peace. With wealth come quarrels, bickering over money matters, annoying Saraswati, who runs away, which is why they say prosperity and peace rarely coexist. The only god who can bring them together is Ganesha. In some scriptures, he is described as their brother. In others, Lakshmi and Saraswati are forms of Riddhi and Siddhi, wives of Ganesha.

Typically, everyone chases Lakshmi. As for Lakshmi, she is drawn to only one god, Vishnu, who is not a Deva but greater than all Devas, who is actually God (spelt with an upper case) or Bhagavan. Vishnu is the only one who got the Devas and the Asuras to cooperate and serve as the force and counterforce of a churn that got Lakshmi and other magical treasures to rise from the ocean of milk.

Vishnu is typically shown siding with the Devas. He offers Amrit, the nectar of immortality, only to the Devas, and he fights alongside them in the battles against the Asuras. This seems unfair until one steps back and observes Vishnu's role as the preserver.

Brahma, as the creator of both Devas and Asuras, sides with both of them equally. Shiva, as the destroyer, is indifferent to both Devas and Asuras and will give them equal power. This equality does not result in movement or dynamism; it produces a stagnant destructive statement. Vishnu creates an imbalance that causes the forces of the cosmos to flow, for day to follow night, summer to follow winter. He balances the Sanjivani Vidya given to the Asuras by Shiva with Amrit which is reserved only for the Devas. So while one group can regenerate themselves after being killed, the other group is immortal. One group keeps dying and being reborn while the other group stays alive forever. When the Asuras are killed, the Devas win and Lakshmi is with them. When the Asuras are brought back to life by Shukra, the Devas lose and Lakshmi is back with her fathers.

While Indra seeks Lakshmi for himself, Vishnu does not. Vishnu seeks to create order in the cosmos by the rhythm of nature and order in society by rules and regulations. The story goes that when the earth complained that the kings of the earth were plundering her wealth in greed, Vishnu promised to take care of her by instituting the code of civilized conduct known as dharma. The earth turned into a cow and Vishnu became her cowherd and caretaker, Gopala. He protected her with dharma and she, in exchange, gave artha and kama.

Dharma is all about balance—taking only as much as one needs and sharing the excess. Parashurama kills Kartaviryarjuna, who steals the cows which are given as gifts to sages. Rama kills Ravana, who disregards the laws of marriage. Krishna kills the Kauravas, who are unable to share wealth with their own family. This makes Vishnu a deity intent on making the world a better place. Perhaps that is why Lakshmi sits coyly at his feet. He is Shrinivas, the eternal abode of Lakshmi.

4

LAKSHMI: THE GODDESS WHO GIVES

MEGHNAD DESAI

Introduction

THERE ARE MANY gods and goddesses in the Sanatan Dharma (Hinduism is a newer word, proposed as recently as the nineteenth century). Aldous Huxley translated it as 'the perennial philosophy'. In the Rig Veda, the gods which feature in the hymns are Indra, Agni, Varuna and Surya, who become minor gods by the time of post-Buddha India. It is said that when Alexander arrived in the Indian subcontinent in the fourth century BCE, there was worship of a god similar to Heracles, who has been later identified as Krishna.

The Vishnu Purana is dated by its most recent translator, Professor Bibek Debroy, as being from the period 450 BCE to 300 BCE, definitely a post-Buddha document.* You see

* Bibek Debroy, trans., *Vishnu Purana* (Gurugram: Penguin Random House India, 2021), p. xxi. All citations from the Vishnu Purana will be from this excellent translation.

immediately that the Vishnu Purana is post-Vedic and even post-Vedantic. Vishnu replaces the abstract universal principle of Brahman: 'He is the supreme Brahman.'* The irresistible conjecture is that faced with the concrete persona of Buddha and the rapid spread of Buddhism, the Sanatan Dharmists retaliated with a personal but immensely powerful god: Vishnu.

So, sometime in the second half of the last millennium BCE, there is a shift to the modern Trimurti structure with Brahma, Vishnu and Mahesh. The old Rig Vedic gods are demoted and a new set emerges which takes over. The Vishnu Purana has stories about all three deities but constantly reiterates the supreme position of Vishnu.

Then, Brahma somehow gets displaced. (We need not go into this episode.) There are few, if any, temples dedicated to him, relative to the other two male gods. Somewhere, then, the mother goddess, Durga/Kali/Amba, becomes as important in the Trinity as Vishnu and Shiva. There is some discussion of Durga being a pre-Aryan goddess, but this may be controverted. Saraswati is the only other goddess worshipped in her own right and not as the consort of a male god.

The point is that while the pantheon of deities is crowded, there are only three at the top—two male gods and one female goddess. (Of course, attributing gender to gods and goddesses is tricky. Shiva doubles up as Ardhanareeshwar.) Lakshmi, the subject of this essay, is not in the top Trinity. She appears as the consort of Vishnu and is worshipped especially on the thirteenth night of the waning moon cycle, two nights before Diwali. The occasion is called Dhanteras in Gujarati, being the one night dedicated to the goddess of prosperity. No other goddess has a Diwali slot.

---

* Debroy, Chapter 1 (2). In Chapter 3 (18), 'Buddha and the Heretics', there is a character called Mayamohan who seduces various Asuras to abandon the path of the Vedas.

But as Shri, Lakshmi is ubiquitous. We append the labels 'Shri', 'Shriman', 'Shrimati', indicating someone favoured or due to be favoured by the goddess Lakshmi. Widows (in Gujarati at least) are addressed as 'Gangaswaroop', definitely not Shrimati. Fortune for a woman resides in having a husband around.

It is in the Vishnu Purana—a massive document running to almost 600 pages in Bibek Debroy's book—that we encounter Lakshmi's story. Purana storytelling is, of course, not straightforward or linear. It wanders, often telling the same story more than once with different nuances. You are supposed to listen and retain the details.

Lakshmi is first mentioned along with the story of Sati (Parvati) in Chapter 1 (8) titled 'Rudra's Account'.* In the Vishnu Purana, Parashara is talking to Maitreya and telling him the long story of Vishnu. Rudra occurs in the Rig Veda and is called Shiva later on. Rudra marries Sati. But then Daksha's anger comes in the way and Sati gives up her body. However, she is born again as the daughter of Himavat and Mena as Uma. 'In this form, the illustrious Hara married her again.'

The first casual mention of Lakshmi follows. 'Bhrigu's wife Khyati gave birth to the divinities, Dhatri and Vidhatri, and to Shri, the wife of Narayana, the god of the gods.' Maitreya asks how that can be, since Lakshmi emerged from the churning of the ocean. So, in a way, Lakshmi's story is presumed to be known, but of course given the style of a Purana it has to be told again. Parashara launches into a laudatory description of Shri, but more so of Vishnu, whose female companion Shri is. Vishnu is praised to the utmost, while Lakshmi has glory as Vishnu's other.

Chapter 1 (9) is devoted to the story of the emergence of Lakshmi from the churning of the ocean, Samudramanthan.† It

---

* Debroy, pp. 36–39.

† Debroy, pp. 39–52.

is a fascinating account as to how Shri emerges from the ocean-churning process. The story starts in somewhat dramatic fashion with the sage Durvasa 'observing the vow of acting like a lunatic'. He has a divine garland made of santanaka flowers, which grow in Indra's gardens. The sage throws the garland at Indra, who is riding the Airavata. Indra puts it on the Airavata, who throws it off. Durvasa is enraged by this disrespect and curses Indra and the gods that they will lose their prosperity. He says, 'All mobile and immobile entities dread the arousal of Lakshmi's wrath. But because you take yourself to be the king of the gods, in your pride, you have slighted her and me.'* In this way, the story of Lakshmi is laid out. (Though she is first mentioned in 'Rudra's Account', that is a passing reference in which Lakshmi is included along with other characters.)

The curse is severe. 'All the herbs and plants decayed and died. There were no sacrifices and ascetics no longer performed austerities. The minds of people no longer turned towards Dharma donations. All the worlds were devoid of spirit. The senses were overwhelmed by avarice . . . Trifling objects came to be desired. Where there is Lakshmi, there is spirit. When there is spirit, the elements follow. When there is no Shri, how can there be spirit.'†

This short introduction to Lakshmi mentions several aspects. She is good for the herbs and plants which have decayed in her absence. But more than that, she exists as a known spirit with proven powers. Brahma tells the gods what to do: call upon Vishnu. He is clearly way superior to Indra, mere king of the gods. The low ranking of the Rig Veda gods relative to Vishnu, where he is just a minor presence, is now confirmed.

So the ocean-churning solution is proposed by Vishnu with the well-known placing of gods and demons on opposite

* Debroy, pp. 40–41.

† Debroy, pp. 41–42.

sides. Vishnu shows great cunning as he sets up the process. He is a tortoise. First to emerge is surabhi, 'the store of oblations, worshipped by the gods'. This seems to be liquor, with Varuni, the goddess of liquor, her eyes rolling around in intoxication. This is followed by the parijata tree, the apsaras and the moon. Then follows Dhanavantari carrying a *kamandal* full of Amrit.

It is at this stage that Shri emerges from the ocean, holding a lotus in her hand. 'Her beauty was dazzling and she was sitting on a full-blown lotus.'* She is greeted with a recital of the Shri Sukta by the gods. Apsaras dance and the waters of the Ganga and other rivers come to bathe her. 'While all the gods looked on, she took her place on Hari's chest.' Amrit is duly snatched away from the demons and given to the gods by Vishnu. Indra then launches into a long narration of praise for Lakshmi.

Even so, this is a man's world. Indra says, 'When you glance favourably towards them, men always obtain wives, sons, houses, well-wishers, grain, wealth and other things.' (The wish for sons rather than daughters is constant in the hymns of the Rig Veda. How they found wives without anyone wanting daughters is anyone's guess.) '. . . Do not forsake our treasury, our cattle pens, our homes, our garments, our bodies or our wives.'† Note, wives come last.

No doubt, Lakshmi has powers. The praise continues. 'Even if a man does not possess any qualities, [if noticed by Lakshmi] his lineage obtains prosperity.'‡ Indra then climaxes by asking Lakshmi for boons. The first is that she will not abandon the three worlds. The second is that she will not forsake anyone who worships her by reciting the *strotram* in praise of her. She grants both.

---

* Debroy, p. 48.

† Debroy, p. 50.

‡ Debroy, pp. 50–51.

The Vishnu Purana tells us again that Shri was the daughter of Bhrigu and his wife, Khyati. Thus, she has a human origin before she emerges again from the ocean at the time of its churning. Is her emerging from the Samudramanthan an analogy of marriage of the young woman who gets divine status only after being churned up to marry her denoted husband? Then, whenever Vishnu takes human birth, she accompanies him as his consort. In the Vamana incarnation she was Padma; Dharani to Parashuram, Sita to Rama, Rukmini to Krishna. 'She assumes a body just like his.'*

Interpretation

The Lakshmi section thus occurs early on in the Vishnu Purana, and that seems to be it. But there remain some (unorthodox) questions to be answered. Why was she born of human beings (Bhrigu and Khyati) and then made to be born again, emerging from the ocean? Was it because she had to be married to Vishnu to attain divine status?

This reminds us of Sita, who is the human consort of Rama, the human avatar of Vishnu. Sita is found abandoned in a field being ploughed by Janaka. We never know who her mother, let alone her father, is. She is born but then becomes an abandoned child, buried underground on farmland. Why? Anyway, because she was found buried in the earth or for another reason, she treats the earth as her mother. She gets to marry Ramachandra in a *swayamvara*. But her purity is tested twice by her husband. Finally, she disappears back into the earth from where she had emerged. Why this suspicion of Sita?

The Vishnu Purana has fascinating variations on the ways people are born. Janaka himself is said to be born† from his

* Debroy, p. 52.

† Debroy, Chapter 4 (5), 'Kings of Mithila', pp. 301–03.

father Nimi's body. 'The King was without a son and the sages were scared of there being no king. Therefore, they kneaded his body, like kindling. A son was born. Since he was born in this way, he came to have the name of Janaka. Since his father was Videha, he was also known as Vaideha. Since he was produced through churning [manthana, as a footnote explains], he was known as Mithi.'*

As Rukmini, Lakshmi is hardly visible, later displaced by Radha as Krishna's constant 'other'. As Dharani, the wife of Parashuram, she is not well known. As Vishnu's consort, she is invoked for the instrumental reason that she brings prosperity to men who will worship her.

It is normally thought that the Ramayana precedes the Mahabharata, inasmuch as such things can be historically dated. Consider the women in the Mahabharata. Satyavati is able to entice Shantanu despite having been a 'single mother', with Vyasa being the son of Parashara. She is also a working woman plying her boat on the river. Yet, she lays down tough conditions for Shantanu to agree to. When needed, she harnesses her first-born, Vyasa, to cajole her daughters-in-law, Ambika and Ambalika, to give heirs with his cooperation. This is a far more 'liberated' status than Sita or Lakshmi achieve. Obviously, things went backwards for women later. But perhaps Lakshmi is still a help to her sisters.

A clue may be found in the expression *grihalakshmi*. Describing the housewife as the Lakshmi of the house (the house itself being a sign of prosperity) may be taken as a sign that 'Lakshmi' is used as a way of honouring the woman as a wife. This is my interpretation and no doubt it can be debated. Parvati is the only other consort of a god of the Trinity, but she has a turbulent life, finds her father being hostile to Shiva, self-destructs and reappears as Uma in some accounts. Shiva shows devotion to his consort, which is

---

* Debroy, pp. 392–93.

far in excess of Vishnu's devotion to Lakshmi. So Lakshmi is the compromise, a woman who is an asset as a housewife. We could say that it is only as a wife that Shri attains divine status. The same, therefore, applies to all women. Lakshmi is thus meant to give dignity to married women (not yet widowed). By associating prosperity with Lakshmi, it makes the married woman a guarantor of prosperity for the household, hence grihalakshmi. It is not being a woman but being a married woman with a living husband that makes the woman Lakshmi.

5

LAKSHMI'S SOUTHERN SOJOURN

RENUKA NARAYANAN

PERHAPS WHAT WE miss seeing today in popular calendar images of Maha Lakshmi showering gold coins is the compassion in her gaze. And if we look again at Raja Ravi Varma's images of Sita, the avatar of Maha Lakshmi, we will see her soft gaze and gentle hand reaching out in blessing.

Valmiki highlights this tender quality of Sita's innate compassion in the Ramayana. Trijata, the only pleasant *rakshasi* in the Ashokavana, has a vivid dream in which she sees Rama conquering Lanka. When she warns the horde of nasty rakshasis not to torment Sita further since Rama will come to finish them off, Sita's reaction is remarkable. She tells Trijata, 'They are only employees, poor things, who are following Ravana's orders. I will protect them! Tell them they will come to no harm.'

Queenly? Goddess-like? It's all of a piece if we consider the history of Maha Lakshmi in Indian culture. Let's look at south

India, for instance, where she is loved as the ultimate embodiment of compassion and not only as the giver of gold.

Interestingly, however, the most famous story in south India about Maha Lakshmi tells of how she bestowed gold out of compassion. It is the story of the Kanakadhara Sthavam or Stotram, the 'Litany of the Shower of Gold'. Its protagonist is none other than Adi Shankara, the ancient reformer and philosopher born in Kerala who rescued the Hindu religion from the chaos into which it had descended in his time. He reconstituted the faith across India, and many of his reforms are followed even today while his Advaita philosophy is still widely upheld.

Adi Shankara believed that the individual soul or Jivatma was not separate but part of the Supersoul, the Paramatma. The journey of human life was therefore the struggle of the Jivatma to be reunited with the Paramatma. Nobody could fight against malignant fate except by working off bad karmas in this present life. But—and this 'but' is deeply entrenched in the culture—only Maha Lakshmi had the power to rewrite a person's destiny through her compassion.

The story goes that as a young bhikshu, or student, of barely eight, Shankara went out, as was the custom, to beg for alms from householders. One morning he stopped outside a rundown house with holes in the thatch and a generally unkempt air. Standing outside, he called in his bright, boyish voice, '*Bhavati bhiksham dehi*,' meaning 'Whoever's at home, please give me food'. Inside lived a desperately poor woman—let's call her Hemavati—who had been starving for several days. She was horrified to hear a bhikshu calling for alms and deeply embarrassed that she had to fail in her social duty. She peered out and felt even worse when she saw such a little boy.

'Alas, young bhikshu,' she called out tremulously to the waiting child. 'I have nothing to give you. I have had no food myself for several days.'

'Have you nothing at all for me?' asked the clear child-voice gently.

'Wait, let me take one last look,' Hemavati found herself saying. She turned over her empty pots, bins and baskets. There lay a single shrivelled amla, or Indian gooseberry, at the bottom of the last basket. Hemavati pounced on it and took it to the door. Opening the door only a little to hide her ragged state, she put out her right hand with the amla. 'I am so sorry, child, I have nothing at all but this. Please take it if you don't mind such paltry alms. It would make me very happy,' she said, deeply ashamed, and dropped the amla in the boy's alms bowl.

Instead of going away, the boy looked at the amla with a troubled face. Hemavati heard him draw a deep breath and saw him step back, raising his arms aloft in salute to the sky. He shut his eyes as though praying and spontaneously began to sing a hymn of praise to Maha Lakshmi. Twenty-one beautiful verses poured from him, describing the goddess in whom he saw all the goddesses as one.

'Let her garland of glances that protects Lord Vishnu fall on me as well,' he sang. 'Gracious goddess, giver of love, giver of joy, giver of wealth and the right to rule kingdoms, be merciful as the cool breeze. Shower a rain of wealth on this parched land.'

A gentle breeze blew when the boy finished his litany and a great concentration of light appeared before him, so bright that it stood out even in daylight.

'You have pleased me greatly with your sweet song,' Hemavati heard a thrillingly melodious feminine voice say. 'Ask something of me, child.'

'Gracious Mother! Please make this poor lady prosperous, I beseech you,' said the boy.

'I may not do so, son, for she never gave anybody a thing in charity in her last life,' said the celestial voice.

'Why, Mother, look how she gave away the gooseberry, the very last thing she had in her house. She was starving for days and could have kept it for herself—the first bit of solid food that she accidentally found while looking to feed me. But she gave it away in alms, did she not? Mother, you know very well that you alone have the power to erase and change the destiny written by Lord Brahma on each person's head,' cajoled the child.

Hemavati heard an amused laugh.

'So be it,' said the goddess and the column of light faded.

The next moment, a hail of hard gooseberries fell through the holes in Hemavati's roof, each made of solid gold. She would be rich beyond imagination now. She rushed out to thank Shankara, penitently promising to feed the poor henceforth. As Shankara walked away with a beaming smile, she looked at his disappearing figure in awe: what a bold, tender-hearted little bhikshu to address the goddess on another's behalf, and in such verse as to make her appear, and then to bandy words with her like that and get his way!

This legend had a profound impact on south Indian culture, and the Kanakadhara Sthavam is part of the daily prayers in many households even today. A famous recording by Bharat Ratna M.S. Subbulakshmi, the great Carnatic singer, was released in 2003 in the album *Sri Venkateswara Balaji Pancharatnamala: Vol. 4.* It is about eight minutes long and is easily found on YouTube. Even if people don't know the prayer well they tend to recognize this beautiful and hugely popular verse:

Sarasija-Nilaye Saroja-Haste
Dhavalatama-Amshuka-Gandha-Maalya-Shobhe
Bhagavati Hari-Vallabhe Manojnye
Tri-Bhuvana-Bhuti-Kari Prasida Mahyam.

—Kanakadhara Sthavam, Shloka 18

In this verse, Shankara incorporates the mantra in the Shri Sukta from the Rig Veda where Maha Lakshmi is addressed as 'Sarasija-Nilaye', meaning the one who is seated on a lotus, and 'Saroja-Haste', meaning holding a lotus in her hand. In the next lines, Maha Lakshmi is called 'Dhavalatama-Amshuka-Gandha-Maalya-Shobhe', meaning the one whose radiance is soothing and whose fragrance is like sandalwood. She is the dear consort of Maha Vishnu (Hari-Vallabhe) and the mother of the three worlds (Tri-Bhuvana), by whose grace all three worlds attain happiness. So not only is there a beautiful continuity from the Rig Veda, the most ancient of the world's scriptures, but also Shankara's affirmation of Maha Lakshmi's power as the ultimate giver.

In the post-Shankara period, Indian religion and culture received a rude shock from foreign invasions. In the thirteenth–fourteenth centuries a learned sanyasi, Madhava Vidyaranya (1296–1386), realized the need to protect south India from the marauding captors of Delhi. He inspired the two brothers Harihara and Bukkaraya to build a city and establish a Hindu kingdom. Thus was the Vijayanagar empire born in 1336, and it grew into a bulwark against Delhi for 300 years. This led to a cultural, socio-economic and architectural revival in south India like nowhere else in India.

Vidyaranya Swami was a staunch Advaitin, or follower of Adi Shankara's Advaita philosophy. He mentored three generations of Vijayanagar kings and became the Shankaracharya of the Sringeri Mutt. His philosophical work *Panchadashi* is still very much in vogue, read and discussed in spiritual circles.

With this background, there is no way that Vidyaranya Swami would not have prayed to Maha Lakshmi along with Harihara and Bukkaraya from Adi Shankara's Kanakadhara Sthavam, especially 'Gracious goddess, giver of the right to rule kingdoms', invoking her compassion for his just and worthy cause. He was duly rewarded, as history testifies.

Another great scholar of the time, Vedanta Desika (1268–1369), was born near Kanchipuram in the northern Tamil country. He was a child prodigy, a polymath, polyglot, philosopher and mathematician. Sitting in his little village he solved the 'Knight's Tour Problem' in chess that Europe took several more centuries to work out—till the seventeenth century, in fact. The problem was to have a knight traverse across all squares on a chessboard without visiting any square twice. The 'Padhuka Sahasram' by Vedanta Desika presents a solution to the problem.

In 1311, the northern invader Malik Kafur, representing Alauddin Khilji, attacked Srirangam, which was then renowned for its wealth. Kafur's army entered the Srirangam temple via its northern enclosure. The unarmed Shri Vaishnavas within the temple were easily overpowered and the temple's riches were stolen. The temple was attacked and plundered again by the armies of Mohammed bin Tughlaq in 1323. Desika, says tradition, lay hidden among the dead bodies of Shri Vaishnavas at Srirangam who were killed by the invaders. He managed to smuggle out rare documents and escaped to Karnataka, having successfully hidden the image of Maha Lakshmi, worshipped at Srirangam as Ranganayaki, from desecration.

However, Desika did not give up his life of creativity and scholarly inquiry. He remained an ardent devotee of Maha Vishnu and Maha Lakshmi. In fact, he, too, gave Maha Lakshmi the credit for being able to reverse the Lord's decisions through her mercy and control his actions by her overpowering quality of compassion. This view of Maha Lakshmi as the primary force behind the Lord's powers is articulated at length in Desika's seminal work 'Daya Satakam', a poetic work on her and Maha Vishnu as Lord Balaji at Tirupati. Its verses are still recited today as 'the religion of *daya* (compassion)' which Desika propagated as the *kula* guru, or spiritual leader, of Shri Vaishnavas in the south.

We have seen the adoration of and adherence to Maha Lakshmi by three outstanding historical figures. She was and remains equally beloved among the common people. Women have a tender relationship of their own with her as the giver of happiness. This is expressed not only through daily prayers but formally once a year through the occasion of Vara Lakshmi Vratham.

Vara Lakshmi Vratham, also called Vara Lakshmi Puja, is a ceremony to propitiate Maha Lakshmi as 'Vara Lakshmi', the manifestation of Lakshmi who grants boons (*varam*). It is primarily performed by married Hindu women in south India for the welfare and happiness of their families, particularly in the Telugu and Tamil regions. This occasion is observed on the Friday before the day of the full moon, or Purnima, in the lunar month of Shravan (July–August), considered a holy month across India. Families that observe Vara Lakshmi Vratham cherish a silver mask of Maha Lakshmi that is used during the puja and pass it down the generations. The daily prayer, 'Maha Lakshmi Ashtakam', or eight verses in her praise, is chanted with extra fervour. This prayer comes from the Padma Purana, one of the eighteen major Puranas, and hails her all-knowing and merciful nature.

To give you a glimpse of Vara Lakshmi Vratham as it is still observed in south India, perhaps I can do no better than describe the happy scene that it was in childhood. My mother had a silver mask of Lakshmi smaller than her palm. She tied this to a coconut and placed it face-first in a narrow-necked *kalash*, or traditional brass pot, about a foot high. She tied a little Kanjivaram silk skirt over the pot so that the installation looked like a doll in a skirt. She fixed a long plait of flowers to the doll's back and placed it under a high, rectangular table on which she draped a 'canopy'. It was a Benarasi stole in iridescent *mayil kazhuthu* or peacock-neck blue. A large mirror was placed at the back to show the decorated plait.

The ritual prayers were done early in the morning to formally install the goddess in our home. We little girls had to hold a small brass plate with auspicious red lime water in it and wave it clockwise thrice at our front door, singing '*Raave ma intiki*', Telugu for 'Come to my house, Goddess'. Though ours was a Tamil household, this was the traditional song in our home for Vara Lakshmi Vratham, as in many other homes. Since the major south Indian languages are all present in Carnatic music, this cultural fluidity was considered normal. We enjoyed the *naivedyam* or offering of special foods, which included vadai and payasam.

My mother had little cards printed in her name and those of her daughters, inviting ladies of her acquaintance to *manjal–kumkum* (haldi–kumkum), to come and accept lucky turmeric and vermilion at our house. The ladies would arrive in the evening, bow to Maha Lakshmi's installation, and sit around on carpets and grass mats in our emptied living room. Everyone wore traditional saris in pleasant colours, bindis and jewellery, while my little sister and I wore *paavadai-chokka*, the south Indian skirt and blouse worn on festival days by young girls. The room smelt very pleasantly of flowers, incense and the redolence of the morning's puja ingredients.

As the elder daughter of the house, I had four duties every year at Vara Lakshmi Vratham. First, to carry around a salver with bowls of turmeric paste, sandalwood paste and vermilion paste. After every single lady had anointed herself, my second duty was to take around a small metal basket of flowers. It was filled with strings of jasmine and red roses for each lady to tuck into her hair. My third duty was to make several rounds with a tray of shundal. These were tiny brown chickpeas, boiled and spiced with curry leaves and coconut. My follow-up duty afterwards was to collect the dried leaf bowls in which the shundal was served.

The ladies chatted away and took turns to sing Carnatic songs to the goddess, praising her beauty and tender nature.

They looked like goddesses themselves in their pretty saris, foreheads aglow with lucky marks and pretty bangles on their wrists. This, too, was homage to Maha Lakshmi whose 'sixteen adornments', called *solah shringar* in the north, include flowers, make-up and jewellery.

I had to look alert and spring to my fourth duty when the ladies began to leave. On a table near the door was a pile of little cloth pouches, one for each lady and a few extra. Each pouch held a small mirror, a comb, a little round box of kumkum, a piece of turmeric root, a few fresh betel leaves with areca nuts and a pure cotton blouse piece for a sari in lucky crimson or ochre. My task was to keep handing these pouches to my mother when she put out her hand.

Such were the pleasant occasions of Vara Lakshmi Vratham, events that are still conducted in many south Indian homes, even among the diaspora. It is a slice of secret India, invisible to the outside world, centred as it is on domestic ritual and prayer. The Lakshmi masks are precious heirlooms, some of them centuries old. But then, love and reverence for Maha Lakshmi as the personification of compassion and generosity are millennia old, so it is not to be wondered at.

6

THE REAL DEITY OF WEALTH: KUBERA AND LAKSHMI

ASHUTOSH GARG

ONE OF THE many interesting aspects of Hinduism is that among the surprisingly large pantheon of Hindu gods and goddesses, it is always easy to find a deity who can grant us anything we wish for. For example, Saraswati gives knowledge, Hanuman blesses us with fearlessness, Durga is the giver of power while Ganesha is invoked to remove obstacles. Similarly, people desirous of acquiring wealth usually worship Lakshmi. However, at times it is not unusual to invoke Kubera either.

Wealth has been one of the foremost requirements in every era and continues to be so, even today. However, the irony here lies in the fact that people in Kaliyug treat wealth as a primary need and yet they are completely oblivious to the life of the primary deities of wealth: Lakshmi and Kubera. One might notice that in matters of wealth, people now prefer Lakshmi to Kubera.

The question here is, if Kubera is also considered the deity of wealth, why has the worship of Lakshmi become more popular? Is it because Kubera's jurisdiction is limited to material wealth whereas Lakshmi is considered to be the presiding deity of not only wealth but also prosperity and abundance, which gives her an edge over Kubera in terms of influence? Or is it due to the fact that Kubera's sheen has waned over time? If so, what could be the reason for this? If we are to find satisfactory answers to these questions, it is pertinent to have a look at the status of Kubera and Lakshmi in Hindu scriptures. Let's talk about Kubera first.

Kubera: The God of Wealth

As we glance through various scriptures, contradictory imageries of Kubera appear which make it difficult to formulate a definite opinion about this god of wealth. It is interesting that Kubera finds mention in certain Vedic texts not as the god of wealth but as the lord of evil spirits. In *Manusmriti*, Kubera has the status of a Dikpaal (guardian of the direction). However, after the composition of the Puranas, an altogether different image of Kubera emerged.

The Shiva Purana describes the story of Kubera's previous birth, according to which Gunanidhi, the son of a Brahmin called Yajnadatta, fell into mischief and started stealing. One night Gunanidhi was running out of a Shiva temple after stealing fruits and sweets. Just then, he saw that the lamp inside the temple was about to be extinguished. Gunanidhi immediately tore his cloth, made a wick out of it and lit the lamp again. As a result of this good karma, he was born into the house of a king where he did many more good deeds. He went on to accumulate a lot of good karma and was finally blessed to be born as Kubera in the house of Vishrava, a descendant of Lord Brahma.

It is said that at the time of birth, Kubera had only eight teeth in his mouth. He was chubby, short, physically weak and impatient by nature. His short-tempered attitude caused him to pronounce curses but also got him into trouble for which others pronounced curses on him as well. Despite his physical disabilities and temperamental failings, Kubera did severe penance and pleased Lord Brahma to obtain important titles like Dhaneshwar (lord of wealth) and Uttar Dikpaal (guardian of the north). Kubera's significance rose as he joined the prestigious Ashta Dikpaals (a group of eight guardians of the directions) and rose on an equal footing with Indra, Yama, Varuna, Vayu and Agni. Further, Kubera was blessed with the divine Pushpak Viman and the golden city of Lanka. According to Valmiki's Ramayana, Ravana was born from the demoness Kaikesi, the second wife of the sage Vishrava, which makes Kubera and Ravana half-brothers! Later, Ravana, out of jealousy, snatched the Pushpak Viman and Lanka from Kubera. Yet, Kubera didn't despair and built another city named Alkapuri in the region of Kailasa, the abode of Lord Shiva. There, again, through severe penance, Kubera managed to please Lord Shiva, who blessed him with the title of Yaksharaj (the lord of yakshas).

In the Mahabharata and several other texts, Kubera has been depicted prominently in the role of a Dikpaal. Another popular image of Kubera is that of treasurer. The famous yaksha and yakshini statues installed at the gates of the Reserve Bank of India in Delhi indicate that the onus of safeguarding wealth lies on the yakshas. Kubera, being the king of yakshas, is entrusted with the task of distribution and protection of wealth. All the above details reveal Kubera's ambitious and enterprising nature.

Notwithstanding the above, it is undeniable that Kubera is after all a human being who attained the status of a deity through grit, penance and good karma. And, being a human, he is prone to all kinds of human-like shortcomings.

As far as humans are concerned, nobody is perfect. We are all a mix of good and bad shades. And so is Kubera. His pure and holy form seen in ancient Hindu texts undoubtedly earned him a lot of respect, and society accepted him as worthy of worship. However, as times changed and socio-economic patterns altered, certain unfortunate incidents came to the fore which seriously tarnished Kubera's image. Some grey shades came to be associated with his personality. Let us see what these untoward incidents are which sullied the fame of the god of wealth.

As Kaliyug progressed, man's intellect became fickle, and he revelled more in vice than virtue. Out of six major enemies—lust, anger, greed, attachment, pride and jealousy—greed turned out to be the most damaging. It benumbed man's intelligence; his ethics and behaviour began to be governed by the power of wealth; dissatisfaction increased to a level where despite having enough money people discovered illegal ways to earn more. This ill-gotten wealth was no longer simply money; it earned a new name and came to be known as black money.

With this new form of money coming into being, a parallel economy started flourishing. People began to hoard currency, immovable property, gold, silver and other valuables. The roots of black money spread across the globe, and the market dealing in it came to be known as the black market. Spiralling inflation led to traders making manifold profits, skyrocketing prices and starvation. Keeping up this illegal trade and black money forced man to indiscriminately exploit nature. The poor became poorer while the coffers of the rich brimmed with wealth. The network of anarchy and social inequality widened unchecked. Then came the time when black marketers and hoarders of black money came to be called 'dhankubera' (deity of wealth)! Man became a slave of money as wealth took over the minds and hearts of millions. Kubera, the real god of wealth, had made *nara* (man) his vehicle and thus earned a name for himself: Naravahan (one who rides man)!

In the context of Kubera, the immortal poem 'Meghdoot,' composed by the Sanskrit poet Kalidasa, is an important document that lends historicity to Kubera's existence. Through 'Meghdoot', the relevance of Kubera was reinstated in Kaliyug, and his declining charisma got a boost. However, after Kubera's name came to be associated with black money, the distinction which he had earned through hard work and penance turned into infamy.

There is a possibility that these incidents showed Kubera in a poor light and led to a decline in his worship while Lakshmi emerged as a preferred substitute. As the glory of Kubera further diminished, he was almost completely replaced by Lakshmi, who has now become extremely popular as the primary goddess of wealth.

Lakshmi

Though it is difficult to cover the greatness of Lakshmi in its entirety, it would be relevant to look at the origin and role of the goddess in respect of wealth, glory and abundance in order to fully understand her glory in Hindu culture.

The rise of Lakshmi in the Hindu pantheon is not a recent phenomenon. Many references related to Lakshmi are found in Vedic texts and the Shatapatha Brahmana, wherein she is depicted as a symbol of prosperity and good fortune. In almost all religious texts, Lakshmi is described as the goddess of abundance, fortune, power, luxury, beauty, fertility and auspiciousness and, of course, wealth. These auspicious elements have always been on man's wish list, and this is why Lakshmi, the giver of prosperity, has continued to gain fame and popularity.

Lakshmi's significance can also be gauged from the fact that Shri—another holy name of Lakshmi—is widely used. In Hindu society, there is an old tradition of prefixing 'Shri' before the names of respectable persons. The word 'Shri' is also a symbol of prosperity and auspiciousness. This explains why married men and women are addressed as 'Shriman' and 'Shrimati' as marriage infuses familial and worldly wealth into the ecosystem which is considered no less than a blessing of Lakshmi. Just as the spiritual secret of life is hidden in the syllable 'Om', similarly the term 'Shri' subsumes the material aspect of this cosmos.

Talking about the origin of Lakshmi, it is said that after the curse of the sage Durvasa, when the glory of Indra and other Devas waned, Vishnu suggested they churn the ocean and extract nectar from it. The Devas along with the Asuras, their maternal cousins, churned the ocean and consequently fourteen gems appeared from it. Lakshmi (Shri) was one of them. These precious items were distributed among the Asuras and the Devas. However, Lakshmi decided to become the consort of Vishnu. Since then she is said to have resided in his heart. That is why Vishnu is also called Shrinivas (one who is the abode of Shri). Once, an enraged Maharishi Bhrigu kicked Vishnu's chest, forgetting that it was the very place where Shri resided. Annoyed with this incident, Lakshmi left Vishnu to live as Padma in south India. Vishnu took the form of Venkateshwar to please Padma and remarried her. Another interesting tale states that Kubera donated a lot of money to Venkateshwar to make his marriage with Padma successful. It is the place where the Tirupati temple is located. Even today, devotees offer huge donations to Tirupati's *hundi* (donation box) so that Lord Venkateshwar can repay the money lent to him by Kubera!

According to the Devi Bhagwat Purana, Lakshmi originated from the left side of the Supreme Being, after which she divided herself into Lakshmi and Radha. Both of them attained Vishnu in different forms. The Vishnu Purana states that during each of Vishnu's incarnations Lakshmi also incarnates with him—during the churning of the ocean, she took the form of Padma, in the Vamana avatar she became Kamala, with Parashurama she took the form of Dharani, with Rama's avatar she came as Sita, and when Vishnu became Krishna, she assumed the form of Rukmini.

According to a legend in the Lakshmi Purana composed in the fifteenth century by an Odiya poet, Lakshmi resided in the house of an untouchable woman. This angered her brothers Balaram and Jagannath, who forbade the goddess from entering the temple. As a result, extreme poverty and hunger took over the city of Puri. At last, Balaram and Jagannath admitted their mistake and sought forgiveness. This story outlines Lakshmi's wholehearted protest against caste-based discrimination and her outright support for women's empowerment in the then-conservative society. These stories tend to further strengthen the position of Lakshmi in modern society.

Lakshmi vs Kubera

Whether the origin of Lakshmi lies in the churning of the ocean or the left part of the Supreme Being, there is no gainsaying the fact that she has been wholeheartedly accepted as a goddess right from the beginning, whereas Kubera was born as a human (the son of Vishrava) and only later attained the status of a deity through penance. By casting a cursory glance at other references to Kubera, it is difficult to tell how society actually sees him—as yaksha, devta, lokpaal or man!

Lakshmi symbolizes internal prosperity and auspiciousness that includes purity of character, but Kubera is mainly related to material wealth. He achieved the status of a deity through penance, but in mythology his personality is shown to be full of vices. Contrary to this, Lakshmi, the goddess of wealth, is beautiful and gentle. If a woman in India needs to be praised, she is often described as a form of Lakshmi. Similarly, when a girl is born, people equate it with the arrival of Lakshmi. However, when a son is born, nobody says that Kubera has arrived!

Kubera has a terrible shortcoming: he is arrogantly proud of his wealth. A story in this context tells of how Kubera invites Shiva and Parvati to show off his new-found wealth and status. However, unable to leave Kailasa, Shiva and Parvati send their son, Ganesha. No sooner does Ganesha reach Kubera's palace than the latter begins to boast of his treasures. Bored of Kubera's ceaseless bragging, Ganesha asks for food and sits down to eat. Kubera offers food to Ganesha out of conceit but soon finds that nothing can satiate his hunger. Everything that the arrogant Kubera offers Ganesha disappears into the fathomless belly of the elephant god! Soon, Kubera's granaries and treasures begin to recede but Ganesha keeps asking for more. Kubera realizes something is wrong, so he rushes to seek Shiva's help and is told that Ganesha cannot be satisfied with pride. Shiva gives Kubera a bowl of rice and tells him to feed it to Ganesha with humility and reverence. Kubera does as instructed and seeks forgiveness for his conceit. Ganesha eats the bowl of rice and gladly gives out a loud burp, telling him that his tummy is full. Thus, Kubera learns a lesson in humility.

However, as far as Lakshmi is concerned no such incident that exudes arrogance is available in Hindu texts. This is another area where Lakshmi scores a point over Kubera.

Kubera acquired his wealth through luck. Apart from his penance to please Brahma, he did not make any other major effort to acquire his possessions. It is easy to find wealth and fortune, but it takes courage and skill to safeguard it. Here, Kubera loses points for he lacks both skill and courage. Taking advantage of his weakness, Ravana takes away Kubera's Pushpak Viman and Lanka without having to fight a war while Kubera watches helplessly.

No such weakness is seen in Lakshmi's character and temperament. Besides being the giver of wealth, Lakshmi is also the presiding deity of abundance and prosperity, yet she exhibits no demerits such as hatred, anger or arrogance. This proves that

Lakshmi is far more superior, pure and worthy of worship as compared to Kubera.

Another important question is, whether we worship Lakshmi or Kubera, where will this endless greed and attachment to wealth take us? Like a greedy bee who gets trapped in honey and dies, if we get trapped in the quagmire of greed, who will protect us? Well, the good news is that the answer to this question is also found in our scriptures.

Hindu texts clearly mention that whenever dharma is in danger, it is safeguarded by one who protects dharma and in turn dharma protects him. That's why they say, 'Dharma *rakshati rakshitah*!' (One who protects dharma is in turn protected by dharma.) But what is dharma?

Dharma is nothing but a restrained lifestyle and faithful observance of one's duty. Dharma is the foundation on which virtues such as kindness, forgiveness, sacrifice, modesty, humility, decorum, morality and patience find place. Those who lack these qualities are away from dharma and those who are away from dharma cannot be saved. Therefore, those who stay away from the ugly shadows of unrighteousness and black money will find protection. However, those who become possessed by greed are sure to meet a sad and unfortunate end.

The biggest advantage of Kaliyug is that the paths of downfall and liberation are both open to us. The direction we choose will depend on the kind of wealth we prefer to possess. Those who prefer pristine and sacred wealth are inspired to move on a virtuous path, but those who promote impure wealth will surely suffer. Therefore, it is for us to choose what we want.

(Note: A part of this essay is based on Ashutosh Garg's famous Hindi novel Kuber: Lanka Ka Poorv Raja.*)*

7

LAKSHMI IN BUDDHISM AND JAINISM

MENKA RAI

AS A REGION rich in diverse culture and religion, the subcontinent of India has seen the origin of numerous religious traditions over the centuries. This cultural diversity has fostered acculturation and accommodation of religious beliefs and ideas from one tradition to another. A notable manifestation of this trait is the adaptation of deities from one religion to another. This phenomenon is exemplified by the presence of Shri/Lakshmi in traditions which are outside the fold of Hinduism. Shri is initially mentioned in the Rig Veda and the Shatapatha Brahmana as an all-powerful deity. Over the years, with the advent of Buddhism and Jainism, she was also adopted as the deity of wealth and fortune in the new religious traditions. Additionally, many other deities and semi-divine beings such as Ganesha, Kubera, Indra, Krishna and more were embraced in Jainism and Buddhism, particularly in Mahayana and Vajrayana Buddhism.

Interestingly, these traditions initially began with the concept of 'godlessness', and no divine figures were worshipped in Jainism and Buddhism. However, over time, the followers started to worship deities belonging to Hinduism and other folk religions, who became visible in the texts and temples of their traditions. One possible reason for the adoption of divine and semi-divine figures is that the followers of the new traditions came from different religious and social groups. Along with their support for newly adopted religions, they also brought deities, worship patterns and other cultural attributes from their own traditions.

Shri/Lakshmi in Buddhism

The oldest known depictions of Lakshmi, dating back to the second century, are found in the Buddhist cave temples of Bharhut and Udaygiri, as well as the stupa at Sanchi.* The image is represented in these structures on gates and stone railings, in the form of Gaja Lakshmi. In the Sanchi stupa, Lakshmi is depicted at several places, as standing on a full-bloomed lotus and two elephants standing on lotuses flanking her on both sides, showering water on her from a kalash (pot) held in their trunks. The Gaja Lakshmi image from Bharhut was donated by a *bhikkhuni* (Buddhist nun), attesting to the fact that Shri was accepted as a Buddhist deity by then.†

In the earliest Pali literature, the term Siri (Shri) is used to refer to 'luck' or 'fortune' and Lakshmi is referred to as Lakkhi. Siri/Lakkhi is mentioned in many Jataka stories to refer to 'luck and fortune'

---

* Niranjan Ghosh, *Concept and Iconography of the Goddess of Abundance and Fortune in Three Religions of India* (University of Burdwan, 1957), p. 128.

† Miranda Shaw, *Buddhist Goddesses of India* (Oxford: Princeton University Press, 2006), p. 102.

and sometimes as the goddess of fortune. The Sudhabhojana Jataka mentions Siri as one of the four daughters of Sakka (Shakra/Indra).* In some texts, she is also referred to as the goddess of beauty and prosperity. In the Siri Jataka, the term 'lakhhika' is used to refer to someone who is favoured by luck (lakkhi). However, she is not always seen as the embodiment of fortune and wealth but also as a deity who symbolizes more than material wealth. In the same Jataka, Buddha explains to his disciple that the favour is earned through virtuous conduct in the previous life.† Therefore, it would mean that Siri is also the goddess of conduct who rewards those who are of meritorious behaviour. The Siri Kalakanni Jataka further attests to this aspect, when Siri talks about her qualities that she is happy with those who are righteous, responsible, respectful, munificent, gentle, honest and kind but abandons those who grow proud and conceited after receiving her good grace.‡ Therefore, a person's happiness is their responsibility and they attain whatever is deserved in terms of their conduct. Her association with kingship is also visible in some instances. The Tesakuna Jataka, while mentioning the qualities of a good king, also mentions that the goddess grants greatness and victory to a righteous ruler who is brave, vigorous, non-envious and benevolent towards his people.§ In the Culavamsa, a Sri Lankan Pali text, the term 'Viralakkhi' is used to refer to the goddess/fortune of a successful hero in the battlefield.¶ So, here she is connected with the luck related to military valour or victory in battles. Another text, the Brahmajāla Sutta of Digha Nikaya, prescribes invocation for the worship of Goddess Shri.**

---

* Robert Chalmers, trans., 'Sudhabhojana Jataka', Jataka Tales, 1895, No. 535.

† Siri Jataka, No. 284.

‡ Siri Kalakanni Jataka, No. 382.

§ Tesakuna Jataka, No. 521.

¶ Ghosh, *Concept and Iconography,* p. 108.

** A.K. Coomaraswamy, *Early Indian Iconography*, Vol. 1, No. 3, 1929, p. 177.

In later Buddhist texts, the mention of Lakshmi is prominently seen in Mahayana and Tantric Buddhist traditions. The Suvarnaprabhasa Sutra mentions Shri as the provider of happiness and well-being to the *bhikkhus* (Buddhist monks) by offering them food, garments, medicine, bedding and other necessary articles so that they can expound dharma in the world.[*] According to Mahayana tradition, she is also considered the daughter of Hariti, who was originally a Yakshi, but later was adopted as the goddess/protector of children.[†] *Niṣpaṇṇayogāvalī*, a Tantric Buddhist text, mentions many tantric Mandalas[‡] where the goddess is positioned.[§] Shri is placed along with a series of other deities in one of the Mandalas known as Durgatiparisodhana. Another Mandala referred to as the Bhutadamara Mandala, mentions eight goddesses placed in eight quarters, and Shri is placed in the eighth segment. In Kalachakra Mandala, Shri and Lakshmi are placed on two petals of a lotus Mandala.[¶]

Lakshmi appeared in Buddhist texts until the seventh century, and with the advent of Vajrayana Buddhism, Vasudhara (stream of gems) became the goddess of wealth. After this time period, Lakshmi was visible in Buddhist traditions outside the subcontinent of India. In Tibetan Buddhism, the goddess became

---

[*] Shaw, *Buddhist Goddesses of India*, p. 105.

[†] Coomaraswamy, *Early Indian Iconography*, p. 177.

[‡] A Mandala is an idealized representation of the world/cosmos in a geometric pattern. It is an energy grid that symbolizes the flow of the divine and demonic, human and animal impulses in the universe, as they interact in both constructive and destructive patterns. Often used in religious and ritualistic practices, it is a tool through which an individual mediates between the cosmos and his/her inner self, thus realizing the whole universe as self (microcosm). For further details, see D.G. White, *Tantra in Practice* (Delhi: Motilal Banarsidass, 2001), p. 9.

[§] Ghosh, *Concept and Iconography*, pp. 109–10.

[¶] Ibid., p. 110.

a minor wealth deity. However, in Japanese Buddhist mythology, Lakshmi was adopted as Kichijoten, one of the seven fortune gods.* She is considered the goddess of happiness, fortune and beauty. Similar to Lakshmi, Kichijoten is also shown as standing on a full-bloomed lotus in her iconography.

Lakshmi in Jain Tradition

In Jain tradition, Shri and Lakshmi are present in both texts and temples. The Kalpa Sutra, a Jain text about the lives of Tirthankaras, mentions Shri in the description of the conception dream of Mahavira's mother Trishala. The text states that Trishala dreamt about fourteen auspicious symbols when Mahavira descended into her womb. One of these symbols was the appearance of Goddess Shri with four arms holding lotuses, adorned with various ornaments, two elephants flanking her sides and a golden aura behind her.†

Lakshmi is also found adorning many Jain temple structures. Her icons and sculptures are found at the Jain temple of Sarnath, the cave temples of Udaygiri and Khandagiri, the Parsvanath temple at Khajuraho, the Mahavira temple at Osian and the Vimlavasahi temple (Jain group of temples) at Mount Abu. In Rani Gupha, a group of caves in Udaygiri, the form of *abhisheka* Lakshmi (symbolizing the consecration of the goddess) is sculpted on the *torana* (gateway), where she is depicted as holding a pair of lotus, rising from a lake of lotus and flanked by two elephants consecrating her.‡ The form of Gaja Lakshmi is found in the eastern corridor of the Mahavira temple. In the Vimalavasahi temple, one

---

* Coomaraswamy, *Early Indian Iconography*, p. 177.

† Hermann Jacobi, trans., 'Kalpa Sutra', in *Jain Sutras* (Delhi: Motilal Banarsidass, 1964), p. 232.

‡ Ghosh, *Concept and Iconography*, p. 153.

of the most popular Jain temples, the goddess is depicted as a four-armed Gaja Lakshmi seated in Padmasana (lotus pose) on a pedestal supported by lotus and water vases.* She holds lotuses in her upper two hands and her lower hands are in *dhyana* mudra (meditative hand pose).

Lakshmi is also celebrated in the festivals of Jains. Diwali is among the most important festivals of the Jain tradition. The goddess is worshipped as a family deity in the homes of many Jain traders or business people. However, there is another prominent significance of the festival for them. For the Jains, Diwali is the celebration of the nirvana (enlightenment, emancipation) of Mahavira, the twenty-fourth Tirthankara.† The Kalpasutra, describing the life of Mahavira, states that he died and attained nirvana in Pavapuri on the day of *amavasya* (no moon). The next day after his death, eighteen kings of Kasi and Kosala, nine Mallas and nine Licchhavis fasted and lit lamps in their homes, saying, 'Since the light of intelligence is gone, let us make an illumination of material matter.'‡ The Jain New Year begins on the day following Diwali and people (mostly traders and businessmen) buy new account books for the upcoming year. This day is also commemorated because, in the Jain tradition, non-violence is considered the most important tenet; therefore, most Jain people prefer mercantile trade as an occupation as this does not involve harming any living being in daily life. The practice of burning firecrackers is also not followed by them as it might accidentally harm live creatures in the environment.

---

* Sehdev Kumar, *A Thousand Petalled Lotus: Jain Temples of Rajasthan* (Delhi: Abhinav Publications, 2001), p. 124.

† 'Diwali in Jain Dharma', *Times of India*, 26 October 2011, accessed on 31 May 2023.

‡ Kalpa Sutra, p. 266.

The presence and adaptation of Shri/Lakshmi in traditions beyond Hinduism exhibit the rich cultural and religious diversity of the Indian subcontinent. In Buddhism, she is depicted as the provider of material support for the monks and as a symbol of fortune and well-being. In Jainism, she is venerated as the goddess of wealth and prosperity, associated with auspiciousness and abundance. From the early Buddhist cave temples to the Jain temples, Shri/Lakshmi has found her place in different religious contexts, evolving and taking on new meanings. The portrayal of Shri/Lakshmi in Buddhist and Jain texts and temple structures demonstrates the diverse interpretations and symbolism associated with her.

8

LAKSHMI OF THE MOUNTAINS

SUNITA PANT BANSAL

FOR ME, SINCE childhood, Lakshmi has been embodied in the tiny footprints that my mother, grandmother and aunts made with rice paste and *geru* (red ochre clay) in their respective puja shrines or places of worship. The process of making those little footprints always fascinated me. It was a part of *aipan*, the sacred geometry or ritualistic art of rangoli native to the Kumaon region of Uttarakhand.

Any aipan would always start with a *bindu*, or central point, followed by a grid of dots, which when connected would reveal beautiful patterns. The entire cosmos also began with a single bindu, my grandmother would say. Years later, my grandfather explained to me that the bindu of an aipan is symbolic of the *anuswara* of Oum, the humming sound at the end of it, the cosmic reverberation of existence itself, of the universe. Such a simple, beautiful yet powerful representation of the highest consciousness!

Apart from footprints, my grandmother would also make Lakshmi *yantras* for Diwali. For every festive or religious occasion, from birth to death, there are different, very specific patterns and yantras in the Kumaoni aipan, representative of the particular god or goddess of the occasion.

In the Lakshmi yantra, the central point or bindu represents the goddess herself, the source of all creation. Around the bindu, a grid of thirteen lines of thirteen dots each is made, from where the yantra emerges. The bindu is then connected with crisscrossing lines to single dots on all sides; the nine dots thus connected form a flower, or the seat of Lakshmi. The nine dots represent Nava Durga or the nine forms of the primal goddess Shakti.

This flower or Lakshmi's seat is further enclosed within two opposing triangles merging or overlapping together, forming a six-pointed star. The base of each triangle is made by connecting nine dots. The upward-pointing triangle represents Shiva or consciousness (Purusha) and the downward-pointing triangle represents Shakti or transformative energy (Prakriti).

The remaining dots are connected to form geometric patterns, the last row forming a square. This square is encircled within eight lotuses, making the final yantra.

A lotus itself signifies purity and perfection, and the eight lotuses of the yantra symbolize Lakshmi's eight attributes of wealth, food, patience, knowledge, victory, vitality, majesty and fortune (*dhan, dhanya, dhairya, vidya, jaya, veerya, gaja* and *saubhagya*). Reverence for these attributes translates into reverence for the goddess herself.

The yantra is further decorated all around by geometric patterns, floral designs and rows of dots. Finally, the circular aipan is enclosed within a square and the empty spaces filled up with Lakshmi's footprints. This square represents the earth and four cardinal directions, which may be shown as doorways in the centre of each side.

The Lakshmi yantra is drawn on the floor in front of the altar, where the idol of the goddess is placed right in the forefront. On the day of Lakshmi worship, the other gods step back a little. The same applies to any other god or goddess when their day of worship comes, but one thing remains constant all through, and that is the importance given to the fresco or wall aipan called *jyunti patta.*

The main panel of this elaborate wall painting depicts the triad of Parvati, daughter of the Himalaya *parvat,* the presiding deity of the hills, and wife of Shiva, flanked by Saraswati, wife of Brahma, and Lakshmi, wife of Vishnu. These three mother goddesses together are called Tridevi or Jiva Matrika and have Ganesha as their attendant. The other decorative elements comprise lotuses, leafy creepers, conch shells, birds, trees and geometric patterns involving lines and dots. The tree in an aipan signifies Kalpavriksha, the wish-fulfilling tree, and the dots signify life. In fact, a dot-less aipan is made only on the twelfth day of a person's death. Once the mourning period is over, a fresh aipan with dots is made to indicate the resumption of normal life.

It was only decades later that I realized that our Kumaoni Lakshmi yantra is a simpler version of the Shri Yantra, the latter formed by nine interlocking triangles radiating from the central bindu. I like to believe that the former is the core of the latter.

While all Kumaoni aipans are drawn using only three fingers—the forefinger, middle finger and ring finger of the right hand, with the ring finger being the primary one used for the main drawing and the other two for embellishing it—Lakshmi footprints are made using the outer part of clenched fists as a stamp, topped with little dots for the toes.

So, those little footprints were my first image of the goddess, something I could also draw very easily on my own, giving me a sense of proximity to her.

During Diwali, Lakshmi footprints were made on every doorway of the house, whether coming from outside or leading to other rooms. According to my mother, Lakshmi could enter our house from any doorway, not necessarily the usual front door, and then she had to be directed into all the rooms so that the entire house could be blessed by her. And because she would get to see the entire house, it was imperative that it be neat and clean, as that's what is done to welcome any guest. Just like we did when my grandmother visited us, for instance.

For me as a young girl, Lakshmi was a grandmother-like, benign, indulgent, nurturing, generous presence, always looking out for us, always ready with her blessings. According to one story that my grandmother told me, in the beginning, the cosmic soul, the unmanifest Narayana, desired to create the cosmos but lacked the resources to do so. As he pondered over this, his dormant energy burst forth, manifesting as Lakshmi. She placed the seed of divine desire in the palm of her hand and unleashed the forces of creation, and that is how all forms of life came to be. This undoubtedly was and is my favourite story to date.

My grandfather was more philosophically inclined. According to him, the spirit or consciousness (Purusha) was a lame person and the transformative material aspect (Prakriti) a blind person. Both of them needed each other to walk the path of life. Spirituality needs matter to enrich and evolve the process of creation, and matter needs a spiritual eye to guide its way through the blind alleys of life. Since then, the six-pointed star of the Lakshmi yantra began to represent the indispensability of the material and spiritual aspects of life for me, and unconsciously became the bedrock of my own way of living.

Worship for me has never been ritualistic; it has always been an attitude. For instance, reverence to wealth—one of Lakshmi's attributes—for me would imply that we use it for the good of humanity and not hoard it or cage it in our vaults. Used correctly, material wealth becomes a means for generating selflessness and compassion. If we are able to help even one family or person in their time of need, like in sickness or maybe by paying their college fees, we do not lose much of our wealth but gain a lifetime of blessings.

If used incorrectly, wealth leads to vanity, narrow-mindedness and selfishness. The wealthy have much more material wealth than they can possibly use in their lifetime, yet they continue to hoard. In fact, the more they have, the stingier and more selfish they become. Isn't it disrespectful to cage Lakshmi like this!

Likewise, reverence to food entails not wasting it. Throwing away food is like throwing away Lakshmi, a gross insult. Patience as a virtue needs no explanation, and respect for knowledge has been our staple since childhood.

Respect for victory is important to understand, though. The successes or victories that we attain in life inspire us to do more, to grow more, to attain more, whereas the smallest of failures pulls us down. It stands to reason, then, that we must revere our victories, however minuscule they might seem, as they lead us to the eventual path of prosperity. To revere our achievements we must pause to think who all and what all have made our victory possible. It is important to be grateful. The best way to work this out is to consider every little achievement an award and think of an acceptance speech thanking everyone connected with it.

Vitality, yet another of Lakshmi's attributes, is crucial to achieve anything in life, hence it needs to be respected. After all, very little can be accomplished through a weak and suffering body and mind. Health truly is wealth.

The attribute of majesty refers to our persona, the aura we emanate, the impression we leave on people. We should strive to become useful members of our society so that people respect us and look up to us. That's what they did to their kings or queens in the past. In fact, the ruling power and dominion associated with the office of the king, even the cushion upon which he sat, was referred to as 'Shri' in Vedic literature.

The word 'Shri' basically evokes abundance, affluence, physical health, beauty, grace and authority, the qualities personified by Goddess Lakshmi, Shri Lakshmi. That is why Shri is also used as a prefix to a god's name, or while addressing a teacher or any revered person. In my family, we never used Mr or Mrs, it was always Shri or Shrimati. Simple things like this left a deep impression on me.

The last, the most popular yet least understood attribute of Lakshmi, is fortune, which is an integration of both its forms, perishable and imperishable. Money, property, harmonious relationships, friends, family, power and recognition constitute perishable fortune. They should be respected but not at the cost of ethics. Pursuing such a fortune as an end in itself defeats its very purpose. It results in pain and misery through petty jealousies among family and friends, leading to disagreements and other more serious animosities.

Imperishable fortune comes in the form of divine qualities and good karma. It is characterized by a mind that is progressively more relaxed, uncomplex and profoundly integrated.

If used sensibly, perishable fortune can be utilized for cultivation of spiritual virtues by renouncing all egoistic involvement, and simply pursuing objects because they are needed in our life for our evolution, while maintaining the spirit of surrender. Once we do that, we become truly prosperous, materially and spiritually. I feel blessed to be born in a family where we had such role models in our grandparents and parents who taught us the real meaning of 'surrender'.

In essence, understanding or revering Lakshmi means acknowledging that the wealth that comes to us is not ours; we are simply its caretakers. Money has always been considered a means to buy security and comfort. Even in the scriptures we rarely find a rishi who has given up his worldly duties. After all, how can a man who is unable to face the challenges of meeting his social and economic responsibilities ever achieve his spiritual pursuits!

The classic example is the story of the Mahabharata. It would not have taken place if the sage Vyasa had not begotten children at his mother's request.

The worship of Lakshmi is characterized by a reverent attitude towards these attributes, which collectively, and not individually, govern both the spiritual and material aspects of our lives. The concept of Lakshmi, therefore, is not restricted to material abundance. It actually represents prosperity and richness in spirit, thought and behaviour.

At times it may feel necessary to refine ourselves and shed off all the impurities acquired on this journey of our life, but that does not mean we should abandon all worldly pursuits. We must remember that apart from wealth, Lakshmi also symbolizes patience with knowledge—in other words, wisdom.

Early exposure to scriptural stories made me understand very clearly, at a young age, that we are born in this world for a reason, and with all its imperfections this *is* our *karmabhoomi*. Since god has chosen this for us, who are we to defy his wish and renounce it!

In the Bhagavad Gita, Lord Krishna has advised us neither to live only for material happiness nor to renounce everything, but to follow the middle path. The ideal way is to float like a lotus after having learnt to swim in the pool of life. That is probably why Goddess Lakshmi sits on a lotus, the symbol of transcendence.

Wisdom also means to appreciate the constructive forces in this universe and within our own self, and to recognize the power of manifestation. And what *is* manifestation? It is the idea that we can actualize our desires by using the power of our subconscious beliefs. This was something I learnt from my parents and grandparents much before I read Rhonda Byrne's bestseller *The Secret*.

So, who *is* Lakshmi? A divine energy that transforms dreams into reality. She is the perfect creation, self-sustaining, self-contained nature or Prakriti. She is also the delightful, dreamlike expression of divinity or Maya, and she is the boundless, bountiful energy or Shakti. To realize her is to rejoice in the wonders of life.

The representation of Lakshmi, as for any god or goddess, is the representation of her attributes. I recall being mesmerized by the beauty of Raja Ravi Varma's painting *Gaja Lakshmi*, a print of which hung at my grandparents' house. Wearing a red sari with a golden border—the red symbolizing activity and the gold denoting prosperity—Lakshmi is seen standing on a lotus, indicating that while living in this world and enjoying its wealth, we should not become attached to it. The gaja, or elephant, symbolizes royal splendour and power as well as fecundity.

Lakshmi is shown with four arms representing the four directions, thus symbolizing her omnipresence and omnipotence. The arms at the back carry lotuses while the ones in the front are making gestures of granting boons and protection. One can wax eloquent about the symbols of Lakshmi's eight attributes depicted through her various representations—in the end, it boils down to just metaphors nudging us to imbibe those attributes within ourselves and discover our own power, our own Lakshmi.

My personal favourite allegory of Lakshmi, the complete goddess, remains those tiny white and red footprints on the threshold of my house, prompting me to go within my own self. They are my grandmother's legacy and have been passed on to my daughters as well, seen on the doorways of their flats in Sydney and Montreal, a constant silent reminder to them of their own Lakshmi-energy, which is literally and metaphorically in the palms of their hands. One has to just clench one's fists and see their undersides to recognize and understand Lakshmi's presence in one's life.

SECTION 2

EXPLORING LAKSHMI'S MYSTIQUE: CREATIVE INTERPRETATIONS

'Myth embodies the nearest approach to absolute truth that can be stated in words.'

Ananda K. Coomaraswamy,
Hinduism and Buddhism

9

CHURNING OF THE OCEAN

KORAL DASGUPTA

WALKING BRISKLY THROUGH the deformed caves and curved rocks of Kailasa, Bhargavi slowed near the cliff. Her father, Sage Bhrigu, stopped behind her. 'What happened, daughter?'

Her gaze was locked on the eastern ranges of the valley. A mild hum reverberated from there. Shankar was meditating. The meditative phases multiplied his profound energy, lending life force to every other form of existence.

'Father, why do I feel that Shankar is in danger?'

Sage Bhrigu's eyes glistened. His astrological charts had hinted of a significant cosmic reshuffle long back. Nature was restless. When Bhargavi had showed no interest, the sage was disappointed. He waited to hear her now with his heart pounding loudly.

Bhargavi looked worried. Shankar's meditative thrum exerted an irresistible pull. Melody may not have a meaning but it ferries a feeling. An enormous cycle of energies balanced among his respiration, Shankar was progressing deeper into self-absorption. From the esoteric isolation, she heard him calling out for her!

'Father, I think Shankar needs help,' Bhargavi said anxiously.

The snow-clad peaks of Kailasa cast still reflections on the azure water of the Mansarovar. Her father smiled, with tears in his eyes. 'Daughter, you have started hearing the prophesies of the sacred legends.' He blessed her. 'We have reached the phase when I will have to make the biggest sacrifice for you to experience a colossal transformation.'

Bhargavi was yet to comprehend Bhrigu's words when nervous footsteps raised a symphony from the other side of the valley. Devraj Indra and his administrative troop marched towards Shankar's abode with sullen faces. Bhargavi gasped. The sound of the footsteps bore faint whispers from a time that was yet to come, leading her towards a hidden doorway, a portal to another world where great ambition was conspiring towards a great massacre. She rushed to them without looking behind. Sage Bhrigu did not follow her; he only wiped his misty eyes. It was time for him to let go of Bhargavi.

The angry Sage Durvasa had cursed Devlok. All magic had left the Devas, making them vulnerable to the attacks of the guileful Asuras, who were waiting for an opportune moment to strike. Without their weapons, the Devas could not hold their ground. They were fearing eviction. Brahma had no solution to the problem. Upon Vishnu's advice, the Devas initiated communication with the Asuras. Both parties agreed to join hands for a rare mission: the search for the nectar of immortality! The great ocean would have to be churned. Resources were in place. The goal was clear. The opposition was in agreement. Everything was sorted. 'We're here to seek permission from the Adidev.' Indra folded his hands respectfully before Shankar.

'It won't be simple.' Devi Saraswati stood apart from the gathering. 'If Amrit arrives, halahala would come too. The nectar of immortality would be accompanied by the lethal poison. The law of duality.'

A hush fell upon the bystanders. When the well-laid plan was on the verge of rejection, Shankar raised his calming hand. 'I will consume the halahala.' The voice resounded with the beats of his damaru. The man of few words explained no further. The shaken others were a mesh of uncertainties, clustered into thick chunks of ice—too slippery to walk over and too stubborn to melt. Shankar had not waited to consider the implications of his assurance. He was back to his meditation, his chest rising and falling with divine excitement. Vibhuti, his sacred ash, dispersed, rejoicing in the rhythm, and fell back for resettlement. Everyone left. Bhargavi ran after Saraswati.

'Devi, can halahala overpower Shankar?' She was deeply concerned for the great *tapasvi*, who was an important celestial citizen with critical responsibilities. Shankar's infinite vigour sponsored the divine visions of the creator, Brahma. The energy circulated through intricate pathways engineered by Vishnu to sustain everything in the universe till Shankar came back to destroy and rebuild. Brahma, Vishnu and Shankar were the Trinity.

'Halahala is a dark mystery.' Saraswati was distraught. Her vast array of wisdom had not returned any reference. 'No one knows its blend. So no one would know how to diffuse it.' She lamented, 'Existing knowledge will attempt to predict the consequences, and that is when halahala will make a fool of intelligence. It needs the strength of absolute intuition coupled with selfless passion to win over this destructive potion.'

'What does this entail?' Bhargavi was confused.

Saraswati was patient, as always. 'It means no genius can conquer halahala. Only innocence can.' She took Bhargavi's hand in hers. 'If halahala is not controlled, it could paralyse Shankar and destroy the entire ecological system. Everything will perish.'

Bhargavi's fingers entwined tightly around Saraswati's. 'What if I drink the halahala on his behalf?'

'Risky proposition.' Saraswati declined the noble offer. 'Halahala might flood out of you and affect the world. Shankar is experienced in recycling outworn matter. He is the right choice for imprisoning it.'

'Devi, tell me how I can help.' Bhargavi knelt before the hoarder of divine knowledge. 'I will shield Shankar with everything it takes.'

'Every threat comes with an opportunity,' Saraswati advised. 'If the opportunity is discovered and escalated, Shankar will expense expanded capacities.' Her eyes were shining. 'Magnify the mission of the Trinity. Invoke Brahma to dream more, push Vishnu to sustain further. Shankar will be inspired to augment untrodden networks. The mystery will naturally unravel the healing from halahala.'

Till the edge of Kailasa, Saraswati accompanied her. A curtain of fluffy clouds fluttered in the breeze, mischievously shielding the unknown below.

'Your moment of truth is here, Bhargavi. The Trinity needs you. Now!' Saraswati provoked her. Her heart pounding between anticipation and fear, Bhargavi released her grip from the cliff.

The free fall cutting through space seemed to go on for eternity. The ocean received her within its womb with a series of waves splashing ashore. Salty water entered readily through her mouth and nose. Bhargavi stayed afloat, slowly acclimatizing with the fancies of the ocean. Secrets will be shared only when there is trust.

Below the water surface, life blossomed with colours of its own. Millions of sea creatures fluttered in different shapes and sizes through the underwater hillocks. Bright corals harmonized with anonymous plants. The turbulence propelled her from one end to the other. A prism of light refracted through the transparent waters, birthing a web of luminance. The sea folks flocked in to bathe in the lustre and spurted out gleefully into jubilant patterns of orange, violet, indigo and green. Where were all these forms of life before? Overwhelmed, Bhargavi looked up. The sun god had enhanced his radius. Intrusive beams were streaking down, showing her everything but not conveying much. If Surya could see the fortune here then the churning wouldn't be required. There had to be more layers to the ocean, treasuring its occult secrets where sunlight could not reach.

Filling herself with as much air as she could, Bhargavi stretched her hands wide and whirled around in speed with all the strength she could amass. The water resisted her audacity. But the winds rushed in to assist. A rotary current generated around her, forming a funnel in the middle of the ocean. She took a penetrating plunge. The whirlpool took her below the surface layer into the twilight zone, where sunlight was faint. The octopus and crabs hunted for prey, a swordfish whizzed past. The colourful sea fish were no longer in sight. A few snails, with beautiful conch shells on their backs, volunteered into the labyrinth, swirling their way down with her.

When she descended further towards the end of the funnel, the light was completely gone. The midnight layer of the ocean was visited by starfish and vipers, along with luminescent creatures appearing sporadically with gentle light emerging from their bodies. They did nothing to service her eyesight. The water was freezing. Her body ached with the tremendous aqua pressure. Revulsive creatures sat upon her, chewing weird beetles. Their saliva and skin made boils pop up on her shoulders. Shellfish swam between her arms, leaving red scratches. Solid fibres with a foul smell and itching algae crawled in. They wrapped around her legs like thin snakes. She struggled to be free, dragging herself on the ocean floor, wriggling to carve a way out of the captivating riddle. Negligent of the abysmal plain which sloped and steeped unpredictably, Bhargavi stumbled on a boulder and slid over the tough marine sediments to reach the bottom of a bizarre inverted plateau. She fumbled with her palm. The erosion could be the result of a potent meteor strike on the ocean floor. It still emitted extensive obnoxious gases. Even inside the deep waters, her hands and legs were charred by whatever they touched. The body hurting, nauseated and clueless about the possible options to proceed, she passed away.

She woke up in the middle of the crater, pushing aside a blanket of deposits accumulated over her. Blinded amid the unknown, Bhargavi stretched a foot forward. Something moved there. She withdrew immediately. It inched closer. She bent to touch it with shaking hands. An oval, streamlined structure met her palm. It was lined with scales, somewhat like a shell. There was a slimy protrusion in front and long flippers on the sides. Must be a sea turtle, she deduced. Slight movement below her palm meant the turtle had felt her too. It tamely approached her as if it had found a friend amid the forbidden waters. On her feet it placed its soft flippers, tickling the skin and massaging the ankle. Bhargavi ran the tip of her fingers over its little head. It swayed happily, blushing because of her tapping. Kurma, the turtle.

Not a word exchanged, nothing heard, not even a glimpse of each other in the monstrous darkness, the turtle fathomed that a formal name had been conferred upon it. On her outstretched arm it pressed its mouth warmly, flapping in exhilaration like a devotee rejoicing in the attention of its coveted deity.

Lakshmi, the purposeful!

Bhargavi heard these words out of nowhere, as if Kurma was returning the favour by honouring her with a new moniker. The daughter of Bhrigu had dissolved in the dark waters. A new woman stood up in her place.

The still of the saline was unnerving. No turbulence manoeuvred her way ahead. Indistinct particles descended, stroking her before meandering towards the direction of their choice. Some were long, shapely and blunt. They injured her. A few were sharp and curved. Lakshmi caught one of them just before it hit her eye. She kept her hands in motion to deflect everything that came floating. Whether these were living or non-living, venomous or organic, she couldn't say. Lakshmi crawled up the crater and placed her foot on the bed of the ocean. It was uneven, haphazardly thorned with pointed fossils. When she tried to walk on it anyway, Kurma slipped beneath her foot. The company felt pleasant and empowering. She bent again to lift it up in her hands. What she felt below was not the tiny posterior of a sea turtle. Kurma was growing! The shell expanded from the size of a palm-top to a full hand; the head was as big as the midday sun. The proportions continued to multiply till its flippers were large enough to girdle around Lakshmi and settle her gently on its back.

Kurma navigated through the water without waiting for instructions. The water it pushed back with its flippers was thrashing upon Lakshmi. Dead weeds and decayed leaves strayed in abundance, along with dry branches of plants that could no longer be moisturized. Infrequent water organisms came wafting and parted ways. Creator Brahma seemed generous in producing nasty creatures for deep-water habitation. She escaped the nudge of a notorious few threatening to pull her away from Kurma and choke her by the neck. Kurma swivelled in time, changing direction. Vicious sighs bubbled through the water when the target was missed. Could Kurma see? Or was it armed with amazing reflexes? Something whizzed past its belly. Lakshmi gripped the shoulder of the reptile, caressing its wrinkled chest. It brushed its mouth again on her fingers, encouraging her to overcome fear and embrace the adventure.

Under the ocean, life was active. Whether kind or rowdy, small or big, beautiful or scary—mortal anatomies anchored by the water environment were diverse. Why was the land so barren?

Everything was gibberish till now, nothing concrete. No clue of halahala yet. The ocean safari was getting rudderless. Eventful, yet stagnant. If Amrit and halahala were to emerge from the ocean, then every pleasant and unpleasant element here had the probability of being added on as ingredients. All the wealth and every kind of trash was right here. It needed investigation. Lakshmi stopped fiddling with the few samples she had collected on the way. Kurma noted the change in Lakshmi. It did not stop her. As she pushed with her feet, the sea turtle applied an upward pressure to set her free. Lakshmi landed on the ocean floor, displacing the water around her. A few things floated away with the force, a few others rushed in.

If such a small jump could result in movement, she wondered, the churning of the ocean would cause tremendous recoupling and decoupling of the water's resources! The question was, which elements could come together, producing what? Lakshmi closed her eyes, trying to decipher the mystery. Raining upon her were dead organisms along with the secretions of living ones. The organic matter nourished the enormous ecosystem, influencing ocean chemistry, giving rise to life-generating gases and dissolving inorganic imprints by bacterial decomposition. Couldn't these be assembled for the production of Amrit? The possibility raised hope. Lakshmi stretched out her hand, looking for Kurma. It was nowhere. She slapped around impatiently. Just before she gave up, Kurma returned with a supply of sea minerals, vitamins and acidic fluids trailing behind its tail.

Was Kurma following her thoughts?

The components bubbled, crushed and dissolved by free will. They mingled rapidly, manufacturing rich therapeutic juices. The freezing water turned mellow. Lakshmi dived inwards to the warmth. It cured the bruises all over her body, instantly nullifying the effects of horrific toxins. Revitalized immunity soared through her. Amrit!

Exhausted with the colossal discovery, Lakshmi dropped on to the bed of the ocean. The troubling questions gushed back. The ocean floor produced Amrit. The ocean surface was buzzing with life. What stopped life from flourishing on land? Did Surya radiate harmful elements which wind dispersed but water diffused? Lakshmi clutched her neck with her fingers, her eyes bursting with excitement. Amrit would empower the Devas to release life-boosting properties for the survival of creatures on land! The toxic constituents in the environment above water would be naturally reduced.

The biosphere was calling for prosperity. Lakshmi felt drawn into the mission of unconditional expansion. Nothing felt more liberating than the mountain of challenges before her waiting to be flattened.

The first concern carved ridges on her forehead. She had fainted in the middle of the crater, disabled by poisonous stimulants. Could those be the constituent components of halahala? For Amrit to be unadulterated and impactful, the unhealthy deterrents of the ocean must be removed. Lakshmi bit her lip. Halahala would be the first outcome from the churning of the ocean. Shankar wouldn't get Amrit before consuming halahala. If the scattered toxicants had resulted in her collapse, what would the complete composition do to Shankar? Her insides sank.

Something soft tickled her back. In the dark, Lakshmi felt a masculine touch ascending from the waist and cupping her face. A gentle press on her shoulders allured her towards creative endeavours, unshackling her from the anxieties of distribution. Thrilled, Lakshmi splashed into the water to reach this source. She could confiscate nothing. Only a playful creeper twirled around her wrist, tethering her with a vague lover. A soft bud, like a gift from the loyal, slept at its end. Bedding the bud on one palm, she chased the presence again, following the loops of the creeper. He shifted mischievously, titillating her from all sides, reclining her and flipping her, pulling her legs to straighten her and bending her knees with a slight touch on her spine. Lakshmi circled into the water and took a sudden backflip. Kurma locked again within the fold of her elbow. It lovingly wriggled its head below her chin. With its flipper girdling her neck, Kurma swam again through the infinite waters.

Divine mischief divulged at the base of the ocean. Who was this? Why did the partnership transcending vast uncertainties feel so real? When a wheel of speculations took her nowhere, the sea turtle tapped her palm. The sealed bud exploded with a thousand plates, opening into a gigantic lotus. As she walked into the centre of the countless petals that never stopped unfolding, the secrets of the ocean unravelled before her.

The boundless ocean floor appeared as the holy workstation of the Trinity. The cosmic discipline had readied for disruption.

Life created by Brahma would now be introduced to land. Vishnu would strategize their sustenance with his phenomenal delivery chain. Shankar would control the configurations, enabling transitions from one form of energy to the other. The Trinity was waiting for the goddess now, to overcome stability and steer the universe towards prosperity.

Placid tranquillity crowned over her head. Serene happiness on her face glowed like gold. Tough realizations perched inside her as fertile intelligence.

Creatures on land would evolve into civilizations. Civilizations would long for growth. Growth would multiply needs. Unrestrained needs would make way for greed, jealousy, arrogance and anger. Prosperity would be interpreted by the foolish as mere wealth.

The abundance of the goddess demanded powerful affiliation with impartial detachment. 'Vishnu,' she recalled, her heart fluttering with the swaying petals of the lotus. Prosperity must be routed through Vishnu's recondite tracks, endorsing social inventions and skilful innovations, moving past Karma with future dreams, restricting the insensitive gluttony of individuals. Lightness dawned finally.

'Vishnu, was it you in disguise as Kurma?' Lakshmi wondered. The cryptic companion returned, touching her sensuously, persuading her to trust his mysterious pathways.

A monumental upheaval interfered with the trance. The ocean quivered on the surface, sending turbulence into the dark waters. The sea creatures panicked. Lakshmi turned on her seat. The lotus moved rapidly towards the centre of the ocean. The Devasur had arranged for the mountain of Mandara to churn the ocean. The colossal peak had been dropped into the water. Nagraj Vasuki volunteered to be the rope. The Asuras' eyes shone with greed as they held the head of the serpent, too arrogant to be pulling a silly snake by its rear end. The Devas were committed to assume one or the other form of nature, empowering life on land with the consumption of Amrit. Surya, Varuna, Indra and all others stood holding Vasuki's tail. In spite of the deft planning, Mandara was sinking in the voracious ocean waters. Kurma appeared again and slipped between the ocean floor and the base of Mandara, balancing the mountain on its back. Brahma sat on the peak of the mountain.

Amid roaring cheers, the Devas and the Asuras started pulling Vasuki. Shankar settled on the shores, facing the mouth of the ocean. The Devasur rotated Vasuki with gusto. The king of snakes was nauseated. It threw up potent venom, killing the strongest Asuras and alarming the rest. The ocean floor quaked vigorously, rising into crests and falling into troughs with the revolving Mandara, displacing large volumes of water. A series of seismic tides rose rapidly, launching gigantic waves. Following a bounteous automated system, the waves rushed towards Shankar, entering and filling him with saline water.

The divine had initiated action. Lakshmi smiled in gratitude. It was now her turn to perform. Quickly, she started rolling the inorganic trash and toxins out of the ocean, lining them into the aqua trackway conceived by the seismic tides. All inorganic matter integrated on its way, infusing with the angry curses of sea creatures whose peaceful residence was usurped by the dreadful churning. The furious compound hurled towards Shankar, releasing intense heat ahead and refining the water it left behind. The Devasur watched with bated breath. The devastating halahala raced into the open mouth of Shankar at demonic speed. Overthrowing Surya, the emerging smoke blanketed the sky. Shankar trembled in pain, with the malignant pollutant entering unbarred, horrifying the world with a tumultuous bellow, threatening absolute termination.

The unblended particles of halahala with their high oil concentration were countered by the salty water that filled Shankar till his neck. The oily soot resisted penetration. The neck of Adidev turned blue with the impact of halahala, his body burning with fever. Weary and weak, his breathing slowed. The world blurred before him. Shankar rested himself on the shore for recovery. With the biggest risk off the radar, the Devasur cheered in unison. The mysterious water track receded into the ocean.

Lakshmi joined her hands in relief. Shankar was safe.

The churning resumed with great hopes for magical manifestations. Collective prayers invoked the goddess of prosperity. The first to come out from her samples was a lumpy rock with inconsistent pores collected from the site of the asteroid strike. Her creative ruminations showed a large, round satellite that would grow and shrink in turn, controlling the tides of the ocean in the process. She released the rock. It rolled out, merging with identical substances on its way. Chandra beamed from the eastern horizon, borrowing benevolence from Surya to brighten up the spots when the god of light was turned away. Beginning its first phase of growth, Chandra arched on Shankar's matted hair, sending cold waves to nullify the heat. Shankar sat up from his retreat.

Delighted, Lakshmi pulled out a dead leaf from her collection and let it flow with the current. She imagined beautiful five-petalled flowers with red stalks blooming when Chandra shines and sheds before daylight. Born was the Parijata plant with a lasting fragrance and many medical values amid the congregation of leaves and stalks littered in the ocean.

Organic matter decomposed from marine organisms took shape as Airavata, a majestic white elephant. Mineral components of the ocean bonded to birth Kamadhenu, the cow delivering plenty of milk to nourish the flow of life. Madira, the goddess of intoxicants, stood up in beauty from the serene waters, walking her way out to mesmerize her audience with unlimited dreams. The dead branches compounded into Kalpavriksha, the wish-fulfilling tree. Discarded shells consolidated into the gigantic conch Panchajanya, its music destined to travel through time. A group of Apsaras, celestial dancers, emerged from the waterbed with a vow to express information through art. Fine fibres catapulted into a seven-headed horse, Uchchaihshravah. It galloped its way out, raising a mystic storm. Many gems were thrown ashore with the fertile attention of Lakshmi, passionately indulging in her endless capacity to create.

With all other byproducts processed under her treasure trove, Lakshmi put into effect the creation of Amrit. Every form of impurity gone and sediments recycled, the ocean itself had turned into the nectar of life, brimming with nutrients to vitalize bodies and heal minds.

The Devasur still churned the ocean, waiting for their coveted treasure. Vasuki was drained of all its strength. But the enormous snake didn't cower from its commitment.

Lakshmi charioted her gigantic lotus towards Kurma, positioned at the base of Mandara. Before bidding farewell, she needed one last vehicle from Vishnu. From Kurma's mouth emerged Dhanavantari, the physician, clutching on to the stem of the lotus with a large pot in hand. He knelt before the goddess with his hands on her feet. Lakshmi raised his palms towards her and handed over a jovial herb and a squirming leech—the last of her collections.

Amrit would empower the environment. Life on land would be introduced with the herb and the leech under the surveillance of Dhanavantari.

Above the ocean, the Panchajanya played out melodiously. Vishnu was inviting his consort to surface. Lakshmi blushed. The lotus zoomed upwards, crossing the layers of the ocean, towards sunlight. The Devasur stared in awe, chanting divine hymns to glorify the goddess. Wearing the armour of unlimited potential, bejewelled with an ocean of secrets in her possession, appeared the goddess of prosperity—bestowing beauty, fertility, grace and fortune to the universe. Petals of the lotus showered droplets into the rugged fangs of Vasuki. The wonder serpent raised its hoods with rejuvenated exuberance and disappeared into its own world. When Dhanavantari peeped from the water, the Devasur roared with joy. They rushed ahead to devour the nectar of life from Dhanavantari's pot.

An ocean of nectar was left behind, lashing down with the music of the Panchajanya.

10

ENTICING LAKSHMI

BULBUL SHARMA

'OPEN THE DOORS, open the windows. Lights! Switch on all the lights. Hurry, hurry. Get the lamps ready. We must not let the auspicious hour pass. Look how fast dusk is approaching. Ma Lakshmi will pass us by!' a shrill voice rang out as the evening light faded gently and dusk began to spread its soft, velvety shadows over our house. We ran around, calling out to each other hysterically, opening all the doors and windows of our huge, decrepit house, tripping over each other in our hurry to please the goddess. We hoped and prayed that she would see how eager we were to welcome her into our home; how desperate we were to seek her blessings.

'O Ma Lakshmi, welcome to our humble abode,' we chanted all day long as we carried out age-old rituals to entice the goddess of wealth, prosperity and all things precious, Ma Lakshmi, into our home. The beautiful, forever alluring Shri or Lakshmi was the most precious gift to appear during the churning of the ocean of milk. A shimmering, golden light spread over the universe as the ocean churned and swirled. Fountains of pearl-white foam rose in the air, and then, during a most auspicious hour, emerged Lakshmi in all her splendid glory, carrying a pot of precious nectar. Along with her from the swirling white waters rose Uchchaihshravah, the unique horse; Airavata, the divine elephant; Kalpavriksha, the wish-fulfilling tree; Kamadhenu, the heavenly cow beloved of the gods; the moon, resplendent and bright; the divine physician, Dhanavantari; and finally, the heavenly, scented flower, Parijata.

Not just the entire universe, but the heavens too were mesmerized by the appearance of Shri. How beautiful she was, how gracefully she stood poised, like a true goddess, on the giant lotus blossom. The heavenly musicians began to sing her praises as celestial nymphs danced before her. Ganga, Yamuna and Saraswati and many other sacred rivers followed in her wake. Heavenly elephants appeared and collected the sacred water in golden vessels to pour over the goddess. The ocean of milk rose in waves to present her with a garland of flowers that would never fade. Gods and demons were speechless with wonder as they beheld this stunning vision of beauty and grace.

From time immemorial, Goddess Lakshmi has fascinated us mortal beings too. She is one of the most sought-after goddesses in the Hindu religion and is regularly invoked to bring good fortune. A hymn from the Rig Veda gives a detailed description of her many virtues. She is said to be forever bountiful and bestows upon her worshippers gold, cattle, horses, jewels and an abundance of food.

The puja rituals carry on. Mango leaves, marigold flowers, lotus petals and green coconuts are arranged and then rearranged again, and as I listen to the women of the household chant melodious words in Goddess Lakshmi's praise, an image rises in my mind. The sky is inky black and the beautiful goddess is passing by our house, resplendent in her red-and-gold sari. It seems she has freshly emerged from the ocean of milk to stand by Lord Vishnu's side, to become his gracious and gorgeous consort for all his avatars. A glossy owl sits near her and watches us with round, yellow eyes, and then turns its head around to bow to the goddess as she stands perfectly balanced on a massive lotus with a thousand petals.

I open my eyes and see dusk speedily approaching our house and race to open the doors and windows. Velvety shadows gather around me. 'Come to us, O goddess of plenty. Grace us with your divine presence, even for just a few moments. Cast your golden light on our house, we beseech you,' sing the women softly. A gentle evening breeze, cool and fragrant, brushes past my face, and I hope it is Goddess Lakshmi, forever benevolent and generous, blessing me with just a tiny bit of wealth.

It is believed that a house blessed by Goddess Lakshmi will never want for anything, and that is why girls are very often named after this benevolent goddess. A newlywed bride is often called Lakshmi, and when a girl child is born it is said Goddess Lakshmi herself has graced the house with her presence.

So why should we not welcome her into our homes with much fanfare and joy? Everyone in our large household longed for the gifts that only Goddess Lakshmi could bestow upon them. Some wanted fame, others needed money and someone needed good luck in his new job. Except for victory in battle and horses, we desired practically everything Ma Lakshmi could give us.

Early in the morning, on the day of Lakshmi Puja, the women of the household bathe at dawn and start preparations for the puja by first creating a beautiful *alpana* pattern on the floor with coloured, powdered rice. A curved pattern of a pair of feet, signifying the goddess's graceful lotus feet, is drawn near the doorway. Then a small terracotta vessel, known as a *ghot*, is brought in with much fanfare. As we gather around watching, the most competent woman in the family with a proven track record of painting perfect swastika motifs begins to draw the sacred lines with vermilion powder mixed with mustard oil. No one dares to disturb her, but my younger sister breaks the rule of silence and says, 'My stomach is growling with hunger.'

And then a few others begin to whisper too, and a small rebellious group emerges as the complicated preparations carry on endlessly. 'Why can't they hurry up,' we mutter, but taking care to keep our voices soft in case the goddess hears us and is offended.

The women in charge of the rituals are made of sterner stuff and they ignore us. We can do nothing but sit back and hope Goddess Lakshmi will bring us some food soon. We wait, trying not to think about it. The other women have been fasting too but they do not show any weakness of character like my sister and I or demand a snack.

Now this group of fasting women, their freshly washed hair cascading down their backs, dressed only in simple red or yellow cotton saris, sit down in a circle and start spreading out a row of mango leaves on the floor. Each leaf has been chosen for its vivid green colour and unblemished texture. If a single black mark or moth-eaten hole is sighted by the eldest woman of our clan—our formidable grandmother, who is an authority on every matter of life and death; especially death—then the leaves have to be thrown away at once.

'Have you girls no eyes to see? Just imagine! Bringing dirty, old mango leaves to place before the goddess. She will take one look at them and turn her face away,' the old lady reprimands us as she picks up a slightly damaged leaf. Her greatest fear is that Goddess Lakshmi will pass by our house due to some mistake on our part in this ritual of worship and bestow her blessings on our neighbours' house. Another great worry in our family is that Lakshmi's sister Alakshmi, who is the opposite of her, will step into our house and snatch away our few remaining possessions.

'That will be a terrible calamity to befall us,' cries the old lady. We all tremble with fear as we imagine such a disastrous thing happening to us due to one slightly damaged mango leaf. 'Forgive us, Ma. Do not pass us by,' we pray fervently. The unfortunate leaf is thrown away at once and a fresh green one quickly put in its place.

Once the mango leaves have passed scrutiny, the women place five or seven perfect ones on the ghot. Then a few bananas, a gleaming green coconut and some other fresh fruits available in the house are arranged around the ghot in a circle along with some sweets. A special sweet made with coconut and jaggery called 'naroo' is always offered to the goddess.

As a little girl I once stole not one but three bananas from the ghot and greedily gobbled them up before anybody could catch me. Fortunately, the wrath of the goddess of plenty did not fall upon me, as predicted by the elderly ladies of the clan. I realized then that Goddess Lakshmi does not seem to be too particular about the fruits and flowers offered to her, unlike her erudite sister Goddess Saraswati. The goddess of learning and wisdom demands that a pile of sweet, gleaming, jade-green ber fruit be placed before her on her special puja day. The thing that is never used in a puja offering to Goddess Lakshmi is the tulsi leaf. It is said that Tulsi was Lakshmi's rival for Lord Vishnu's affections in heaven, and that is why she does not like even a single tulsi leaf being offered to her.

In Bengal every religious festival has its own special food, and to celebrate Lakshmi Puja the women of the household cook a delicious, rich khichuri. It is served with a dish made with five vegetables that has an odd, unmusical name—labbdraa—and, of course, deep-fried golden discs of eggplant which are always present at all Bengali feasts. And finally, a delicious, creamy payesh or kheer is placed before you.

My sister and I, with stomachs still grumbling with hunger, watch greedily as the women begin to prepare the delicious prasad offering for the goddess. Sweet, perfectly ripe bananas, creamy milk, fragrant, uncooked rice and sugar are placed before her in brass bowls. Then, after a short period of time, which is considered polite and suitable for her to have partaken of this humble offering, the women remove the bowls. One woman blows the conch and the others make that shrill, trembling sound by rolling their tongues which only Bengali and Arabic women can make to ward off the evil eye.

Then the best part begins. With gold bangles tinkling and much subdued laughter, the women begin to mash the bananas, milk, sugar and uncooked rice with their hands. Deftly and as delicately as dragonfly wings, their hands flutter and dance as the gooey pulp is made ready. In some homes, the gooey mess is offered to the goddess first and then distributed to the rest of the devotees, but my grandmother thinks the goddess prefers the pure, unmashed offering.

Sadly, there is never enough of this prasad to satiate our greed. 'It is Ma Lakshmi's prasad and not a feast to fill your bellies,' scolds one formidable old lady, helping herself to the biggest share. The prasad is doled out. We sit patiently, eyes full of hope that a second helping will be offered to us. Then a rustling sound is heard. A huge wooden box is opened and a bundle of silk cloth unravelled. The sacred book of Lakshmi, called *Panchali*, is now revealed in its somewhat tattered, faded, gold-embellished glory.

'She is Rajya Lakshmi, the consort of virtuous kings; she is Jaya Lakshmi, the goddess of victory; she is Griha Lakshmi, the goddess of domestic prosperity; she is Bhagya Lakshmi, the goddess of good fortune; she is Yasho Lakshmi, the goddess of fame.' As the various names of Lakshmi are invoked and praise is lavished on her divine being by a lady of the house with the most melodious voice, I am transported back to the quiet summer afternoons when an elderly woman who looked after us would tell us stories from mythology.

Her favourite goddess was, of course, Lakshmi, and this is the story we heard over and over again. Ma Lakshmi was sitting in heaven by Lord Vishnu's side when suddenly a handsome man riding a beautiful white horse went past. Goddess Lakshmi was fascinated by the majestic animal and kept staring at it, not realizing that her lord was speaking to her. Infuriated at this, and also feeling a bit jealous of the horse, Lord Vishnu reprimanded his wife, 'How dare you ignore me while I was speaking to you. This is not the way to treat your lord and master.'

'I was only admiring the horse, my lord,' said Lakshmi, immediately begging her husband's forgiveness. Lord Vishnu was still furious and he cursed Lakshmi in rage, 'I order you to go and live on earth as a mare since you seem to admire the animal so much.' Lakshmi was distraught when she heard these cruel words. She stood before Lord Vishnu with her head bowed. 'When will I be reunited with you, my lord?' she asked, crying tears of remorse.

'When you have delivered a son in the very image of me, only then can you return,' said Lord Vishnu. So the goddess came down to earth and roamed around in the form of a white mare. She prayed for a long time, and one day Lord Shiva and Parvati appeared in front of her. When Lakshmi told Lord Shiva of her sorry plight, he immediately sent a message to Vishnu, requesting him to come down to earth in the shape of a horse: 'Grant Lakshmi the son she desires and thus absolve her of your curse.'

Vishnu could not refuse Shiva's request and came down to earth to be with his wife. A beautiful son was born to them and they went back to heaven together to live happily ever after for a million years.

There are numerous stories in Hindu mythology attributed to the goddess of wealth, and since she is Vishnu's consort, each time he is born on earth she is incarnated as his wife. The Vishnu Purana says, 'As Hari descends in the world in various shapes, so does his consort Shri. Thus, when Hari was born as a dwarf, as a son of Aditi, Lakshmi appeared from a lotus as Padma or Kamala. When he was Raghava, she was Sita, and when he was Krishna, she became Rukmini. In other descents of Vishnu, she is his associate. If he takes a celestial form, she appears divine; if mortal, she becomes mortal too, transforming her own person agreeably to whatever character it pleases Vishnu to put on.'

We pray as we look anxiously at twilight approaching. Will she come to us? Will her graceful, *alta*-smeared feet leave a faint crimson mark on the doorstep of our house, or will she pass us by this year? Lamps are lit all over the house, and every window and door is left wide open. 'O Lakshmi, bless us with your divine, graceful presence. Come to us so that we may become rich and prosperous, powerful and famous,' we chant, looking hopefully at the open door as dusk falls and the sky is bedecked with stars.

'She will only grace those households where the women are chaste and obedient. She will come to the homes where lamps are lit and flowers and sweets placed before a ghot. She will only bless those who are kind to their elderly relatives and never envious or unkind to others. O women, be virtuous and kind, pray to her on this auspicious day, and the goddess will bless your house with wealth and prosperity,' we recite the words from *Panchali* in soft voices as our eyes seek her benevolent, divine presence.

11

LAKSHMI'S OWL

PRASANNA K. DASH

ULUKAVAHINI LAKSHMI, THE image of the goddess seated on an owl, is a figure worshipped in Bengal and possibly Assam, but rarely in Odisha and other parts of the country. Lakshmi imagery sometimes shows the goddess riding an owl, or seated on a golden chariot drawn by an owl, or with an owl at her feet. In Bengal, sighting Lokkhi *pencha* (Lakshmi's owl or the white owl: *Tyto alba*) is considered auspicious.

Why is *uluka*, the owl, an inauspicious bird for many Hindus, the vahana or carrier of Lakshmi, the goddess of prosperity, fortune and wealth? There is an interesting folktale about how the owl became Lakshmi's vahana.[1] After the creation of animals and birds, each deity chose one as their vahana according to need and preference. When Lakshmi came down to earth to select one for herself, several animals competed to be chosen, upon which the goddess said: 'I will visit the earth on the new-moon night of Kartika, and whoever meets me first will be my vahana.' On that very dark night when she descended on earth, the owl spotted her first and flew swiftly and in silence to reach her before any other animal could. Lakshmi, pleased with the owl's special ability, chose it for her vahana. The ability to see through darkness is clearly a metaphor for the use of wisdom to cut through worldly delusion. Lakshmi's owl, like other celestial vahanas, is an emblem as well as a symbol. It differentiates and distinguishes Lakshmi from other goddesses. As a symbol, the owl suggests both positive and negative connotations.

The symbolism of the vahanas of Hindu deities is a complex subject. Garuda, Vishnu's vahana, and Nandi, Shiva's vahana, have mythologies of their own. The lion, Durga's carrier, is a carnivore. Garuda feasts upon snakes, and had once resolved to exterminate all snakes owing to which they sought refuge in *patala* or underground. Saraswati's swan is gentle and graceful. Nandi is Shiva's genial doorkeeper who patiently registers all oral petitions made by the devotees of Shiva, but when required becomes a ferocious warrior on the battlefield. Skanda, also known as Kartikeya and Murugan, has a colourful peacock as his vahana, but the bird has limited flying ability and may be a symbol for the narcissistic ego which needs to be kept under control. Ganesha, the god of learning and the remover of obstacles, rides a bandicoot, perhaps owing to its amazing intelligence, tenacity and ability to burrow deep down and carve new paths.

Shashi Tharoor suggests that animals worshipped by tribal communities were incorporated into Hinduism: '. . . many tribes revered animals, but instead of disrespecting them, Hinduism absorbed the animals too, by making them the companions or vehicles (vahanas) of the gods.'[2] Similarly, M.K. Dhavalikar suggests the development of animal worship from the animal totems in tribal cultures with reference to the tribe of Hastikas and other tribes in the north-western region of the Indian subcontinent.[3]

To understand the role of the owl in Lakshmi's imagery, we may briefly consider the representation of the deity in texts and in iconography. The Shri Sukta of the Rig Veda, an ancient prayer to Shri, who is Lakshmi, and the Lakshmi Sahasranama Stotram,[4] taught by the sage Sanatkumara to twelve rishis in the Skanda Purana, make no mention of the uluka as Lakshmi's vahana. In the Shri Sukta, the lotus flower is the dominant symbol for Lakshmi, who is Padmini, Padmavarna, Padmamalini. In the Lakshmi Sahasranama the deity is addressed as Garudarudha, Garudavahini, Khagavahini and Padmasana. Possibly, the inclusion of the owl in Lakshmi's iconography was a much later development.

In visual representation, Lakshmi is traditionally portrayed in Padmasana—seated upon a full-blown lotus, or standing upon one with four (sometimes two) *dik-gaja*s (elephants of the *diga*s or directions) anointing her with holy water. A lotus is in each of her two hands, and *varada* and *abhaya* mudras are shown in the other two hands. Gaja Lakshmi is inscribed in coins found in Kausambi (third century BCE), Ujjayini (second and third century BCE), the Bharhut medallion of the second century BCE, a Sanchi stupa panel of the first century CE and gold coins and medallions issued by the Gupta and Maurya dynasty kings, but no owl is seen in these numismatic artefacts. The earliest available paintings of Lakshmi are from the fourteenth to the fifteenth century CE, but possibly none portray her as Ulukavahini.

Lakshmi imagery ranges from the royal to the rustic, and from the mundane to the mystic. Elephants symbolize royalty and prosperity. The lotus or padma symbolizes pristine purity, the beginning of life from water, and the kundalini or supine serpent power in muladhara chakra. Symbolically, Lakshmi resides in the *bindu* (point) at the centre of Shri Yantra, the tantric geometric pattern.

In older times, Lakshmi was represented by domestic icons: a *purna kalasha* with a lotus placed on top or an earthen measuring pot filled with paddy or rice. In rural agricultural homes, even now prayer alcoves are decorated with woven ears of paddy replicating Lakshmi's crown of gold. For a farmer, Lakshmi resides in stems of paddy; for the hungry she resides in a grain of rice. Even today many people instantly seek forgiveness from Lakshmi if they accidentally step on rice, a coin or a currency note. Calendar portraits of Lakshmi, popular with the trading and business community, show gold coins pouring out of her right hand, the one traditionally featuring the varada mudra, the posture for granting a boon.

When was the owl introduced into Lakshmi's iconography and why?

The Shiva Purana refers to strange occurrences and evil portents which showed up during Tarakasura's penance. This story recalls how Tarakasura sought two boons from Brahma and how these turned into destructive acts through his evil intentions.

Finally, when Tarakasura is born there are unusual phenomena in nature, including 'the hissing and twanging sounds of the hooting and howling of owls and jackals'.[5] For many Hindus, the owl is an inauspicious bird, associated with death and misfortune. Why, then, would a myth-maker incorporate such a bird in the iconography of Lakshmi, the goddess of fortune and prosperity?

Many ingenious speculations explain the owl in depictions of Lakshmi:

- Uluka is not Lakshmi's vahana, but that of Alakshmi (mentioned in the Shri Sukta), the contrarian, inauspicious elder sister, and the harbinger of poverty, hunger, strife and misfortune. The owl, a creature of the night, found commonly in cemeteries and hence associated with death, is an apt carrier for Alakshmi. However, according to some other stories, Alakshmi's vahana is a donkey.

- Lakshmi and Alakshmi, being sisters, are inseparable and they travel together. Hence, Lakshmi's iconography necessarily includes Alakshmi, who, being untidy, ugly and evil, cannot be represented in her actual form. Therefore, the owl represents her.
- Lakshmi is the goddess of wealth. But wealth is a double-edged attribute. Its righteous use earns dharma and moksha; its wrongful use brings harm, misery and misfortune. Upon begetting wealth, one must not succumb to the usual sins of *lobha*, *moha*, *mada*, *matsarya*, but use the wealth for charitable and pious purposes. The owl is a warning to the wealthy to beware of unmerited wealth and its deployment in wrongful causes.
- The owl, an intelligent bird with binocular and night vision and extraordinary hearing faculties, is a symbol of the pious, meditative mind and wisdom, which can see through the *sansara maya* or illusion of reality.
- Lakshmi's vahana is not the reviled *ullu* or *ghugghu* of north India; it is the pencha or white owl (Tyto alba), which in Assam, Bengal and Odisha is deemed highly auspicious, and the harbinger of wealth and good fortune.
- Gaja Lakshmi rides a majestic elephant, and can hardly enter the humble huts or modest dwellings of most of her devotees. Hence, she walks barefoot in the dead of night accompanied by the white owl and quietly enters the premises she chooses. The owl's wings are designed by nature for swift and silent flight. To welcome Lakshmi and guide her to the prayer alcove, the lady of the house draws *jhoti*s in rice paste of miniature Lakshmi *pada*s (feet)—always incoming, never outgoing. The goddess and her vahana are shown the way.
- Lakshmi as Annapurna (plentiful grain and food) and Dharani (mother earth) is the presiding deity of all produce that sustains life. Rodents try to devour a significant portion of

crop produce, and owls keep the rodent population in check. So the owl helps Lakshmi bestow an abundance of food.

Uluka as Lakshmi's vahana portrays only one of her myriad myths and imaginings. Of the many elements in the iconography of Lakshmi—or any other deity for that matter—the vahana signifies an aspect of the multidimensional deity. No single element comprehensively defines the deity. For example, the mouse is a pest for agriculturists, but as Ganesha's vahana it enjoys the same delicacies that are offered as prasad to Ganesha. The owl in isolation may be inauspicious for some since its hooting or screeching at night sounds ominous, but when incorporated in Lakshmi's iconography the bird becomes auspicious.

The one thousand names of Lakshmi include *arupa* (formless), *bahurupa* (myriad forms) and *asankirna* (limitless, unconfined). Lakshmi, Devi or the goddess principle is the prime creative energy in the universe and cannot be fully comprehended even through her thousand names highlighting her tangible and intangible attributes. The goddess, like a god, is *achintya*, beyond the reach of limited human intelligence and imagination. That is why the enabling instruments of text, iconography, myth, mantra and yantra attempt the impossible in representation but stop short.

Texts and iconography indicate that Lakshmi uses not one but several carriers for her travel. In the Shri Sukta she rides a chariot drawn by horses, followed by trumpeting elephants in what is surely a majestic, royal procession. When travelling with Vishnu, her lord and master, she rides on Garuda with him; and when travelling alone she is accompanied by an elephant or an owl. She also rides, in some portrayals, a horse, a lion or a tiger. However, she is traditionally portrayed in Padmasana, sitting on a full-blown lotus, which may be her vahana too. Not infrequently, she walks barefoot to the homes of her devotees. So one cannot determine her favourite vahana. When Lakshmi chooses to visit someone's home, she will reach there in a manner of her own choosing.

Ritual practices endorse the value of Goddess Lakshmi in everyday life. Upon waking up at dawn and before leaving bed, the recitation of the following Prabhata Mantra is recommended:

Karagre vasati Lakshmi karamadhye Saraswati
Karamule tu Govindah prabhate kara darshana
Samudravasane Devi parvata stana mandale
Vishnupatni namastuvyam padasparsham kshymasvame

Translated:

Lakshmi resides at the tip of the hand, Saraswati in the middle, and Govinda (Vishnu) at the base. It is propitious to begin the day by visualizing these deities and offering prayers.

O Lakshmi, the seas are your attire, the mountains your breasts. You are mother earth, O Vishnu's consort, I seek your forgiveness for stepping upon you.

Through this mantra, we remind ourselves of the need for individual enterprise. Shri Lakshmi, Saraswati and Vishnu bless those who leave the bed at dawn, shun idleness and exert themselves to realize *purusharth*, the prime goals of existence. Lakshmi or prosperity in conjunction with the other aspirations promises a wholesome, value-based life.

Notes

1 N.P. Upadhyaya in his article 'Adityavarna: Avadharana Aur Ankan Ke Vich' refers to this folktale.

2 Shashi Tharoor, *The Hindu Way: An Introduction to Hinduism* (New Delhi: Aleph Book Company, 2019).

3 M.K. Dhavalikar, 'Origin of Gaṇeśa', *Annals of the Bhandarkar Oriental Research Institute*, Vol. 71, No. 1/4 (1990), p. 22.
4 Lakshmi Sahasranama Stotram in the Brahma Purana and the Padma Purana are other versions of this stotra.
5 Shiva Purana: 2.3.15, 'The Penance and Reign of Tarakasura', archive.org.

12

LAKSHMI'S AGAMAN: THE ADVENT OF LAKSHMI

BONOPHUL
TRANSLATED BY ARUNAVA SINHA

SUKHENDU TOOK HIS seat again and resumed jiggling his knees. Then he said with a mysterious smile, 'Wondering where to start. Tell me, have you ever seen an owl?'

'I have. In photos . . .'

'Never seen a live one?'

'How would I? Maybe at the zoo . . .'

'How large was it?'

'Can't remember. Not too large.'

'What colour was it?'

I was flustered. I had no idea Sukhendu was going to interrogate me about owls.

'Brownish, so far as I remember.'

'It was a spotted owl that you saw then.'

'Must be . . .'

'But what I saw on that full-moon night of Lakshmi Puja was milk-white. Its body seemed to be covered in white satin. Eyes sparkling like diamonds. Cats' eyes glow in the dark too—you must have seen them—but what I saw was most unusual. The eyes seemed to be smiling, and the glow they emitted was like moonlight, and yet not moonlight either, an extraordinarily bright but soft beam; it gave you hope, not fear. It was the eyes I saw first . . .'

The story was interrupted. Ramdhan appeared.

'You sent for me?'

'Yes. Do you remember which year we bought this house and all this land?'

'Yes, sir, exactly eighteen years ago.'

'Remember the date,' Sukhendu told me.

Turning back to Ramdhan, he said, 'That's what I wanted to know. Come back with your daughter in a bit, you're eating with us tonight.'

'Yes, sir.'

Ramdhan saluted and left. Gazing at his retreating figure in a daze for some time, Sukhendu continued.

'The story of the full-moon night I'm about to tell you took place exactly twenty years ago. When I was nine or ten. You and I hadn't even met. I wasn't promoted to the next class that year. I stayed out of Maama's hair; every time our eyes met he would glare at me and I would have a shiver running down my spine. This was how things were when . . .'

Sukhendu paused and then continued.

'I remember Maami. Such a headstrong woman. I heard her tell Maama: "Look, don't scold Suku. He's already miserable after failing, and then he lives on our charity, don't rub salt into his wounds again." Maama spoke not with his tongue but with his eyes. His glare . . . my god, I'll never forget it.'

Sukhendu looked up at the moonlight and began to jiggle his knees again. Then he chuckled.

'You know, it was that glare of Maama's that has kept me on the right path all my life. It still does. But the glare has softened; I think he has understood by now. At least, he should have after what happened last year. If only Maami was there too; she must have been there somewhere, though I wasn't aware of it. I would have liked to have sensed her presence. She had bullied the girl all her life, but she had realized the truth . . .'

He lapsed into silence again, gazing quietly at the sky. His silence seemed so unique that I remained quiet too. It didn't occur to me to break it with questions, just as no one imagines breaking an expensive crystal vase even if it seems necessary to do it. I was astonished when I followed his gaze. The small cloud, shaped like a boat with a peacock neck that had floated up on the horizon above the dense, dark forest, seemed to have grown larger, the peacock neck much clearer and bigger . . .

It was Sukhendu who finally broke the silence.

'Last year's incident was so strange that it gives me goosepimples to think of it. Here, see for yourself . . .'

Sukhendu drew my hand to his arm. It was true.

'Was it last year's incident then . . .?'

'A household matter, all about money, but very strange . . .'

'How do you mean?'

'You were in England. Like a bolt from the blue there was a court case. It wasn't us who filed the case; our rivals did. The coal mine that we had bought a short while earlier, where Diju works now—it was the Mullicks who had originally wanted to buy it. But I jumped in and bought it instead for these boys; that was a thrilling affair too, I'll tell you that story some other time. Mullick was furious; he produced a document to claim the coal mine was his by rights. Our lawyer Bhajahari Sen is an old hand at litigation. He said we'll win the case, we'll get compensation for our costs too, but you'll have to fight the case first. Which meant having to spend some twenty or twenty-five thousand rupees. I was in trouble. I went to the original owner whom I'd bought the coal mine from. He heard me out smilingly, tapping his head all the while. For two or three minutes he said nothing. Then he spoke. It's not untrue that I've borrowed fifty thousand from Mullick. But it's a lie that I pledged the coal mine as security. But . . . He went back to tapping his head smilingly. Then, smiling some more, he said, why not give it to Mullick, you'll get your money back with interest. Let him take it since he's so keen, or else he'll get me into trouble. Says I gave you fifty thousand expecting to get the coal mine, I don't exactly remember, claims I gave him a letter to that effect, I don't remember though . . . but maybe.'

I lost track of the story eventually. For one thing, I was wondering what the tale of the moonlit night had to do with the coal mine and Mullick and Bhajahari and litigation—but I didn't want to ask, I didn't have the heart to cut him off in full flow. The rapt concentration with which he was speaking made it seem he wasn't so much telling a story as reciting sacred verses. I was feigning attention with nods and smiles and hmmms, but in fact I was distracted and had lost the plot of the story. And yet, funnily enough, I hadn't really, for my subconscious mind seemed to have been following the thread without my own awareness. What had not penetrated the ears had nevertheless made room for itself in my mind. I cannot say why, but the image of another moonlit night was taking form in my head. A most unusual image.

A radiant moonlight had spread across a cloudless sky. I was standing in an enormous field which stretched to the horizon. Even the trees normally visible on such nights in the form of thick as well as slim black lines were not to be seen. The moonlit sky seemed to have pitched headlong on the field. And in the middle of this field stood something like a mound. A temple? How had it appeared here? It seemed to be waxing and waning in size. Like a cloud of suspicion in a joyful life, it shrank, and then grew again. Suddenly, a lamp came on in the dark temple, illuminating the entrance. A rectangle of light appeared, and silhouetted against it was a beautiful young woman . . . Was it Lakshmi . . .?

Something Sukhendu said suddenly pierced my distraction like an arrow and lodged itself in my head.

'So the girl said, don't worry, everything will be fine.'

'What girl?'

'The one I found that night . . .'

'Right, of course.'

I went back to feigning attention. I couldn't possibly tell Sukhendu I hadn't heard him tell me about the foundling he had come across.

Sukhendu continued speaking.

'At first I paid no attention. An invisible hand delivered a resounding slap on my face two hours later when the peon appeared with a letter. I was astonished—who could be writing to me from America? I opened the letter and read it—and although the invisible hand was delivering its slap at that precise moment, I was overcome with joy. A distant cousin of my maternal uncle's had run away to America many years ago. I had no idea he had become a millionaire before his death. His lawyer had written to say he had willed ten lakh rupees in equal proportions to Raju, Biju and Diju . . . I filed the case. We won. Exactly as Bhajahari had said.'

'Cheep, cheep, cheep,' commented the invisible lizard.

Sukhendu returned to resume his story after making all the arrangements for the cooking. He had begun in a disorganized manner, somewhere in the middle. By then I had eaten a couple of cutlets at Mridula's request and was lying back in the camp chair in a corner of the veranda on the east. A moonbeam lit up the floor near my feet. I was trying to doze—that is to say I lay with eyes closed; I felt a little bit drunk but had no desire to analyse what I might be drunk on. A very fine web, not of thread but of light, of light in various shades, seemed to be materializing slowly around me. I was wondering vaguely whether the spider was me or someone else. That was when Sukhendu appeared.

'Are you asleep, Aban?'

'No. Done with the cooking?'

'More or less. The pot can go on the stove as soon as the spices are ready. Shukul will do it. Let me tell you the story, meanwhile. Just as well the boys and girls have gone out. Where was I?'

'You'd just found a little girl in the jungle.'

'Oh, yes. But let me tell you, my credit goes only as far as finding her; I didn't do anything more. Sometimes I wonder whether I should take credit even for that. Perhaps it had already been determined that I would come across her, which was why I couldn't get boar teeth from Raghu, who disposes of dead bodies, and had to go all the way to Shibu in Tejpur. Fortunately, the hour of the rituals was late at night, so Maami was able to put her pot of fruits and sweets on the boar teeth in time. I was rushing back, taking a shortcut through the garden . . . You've seen the garden in our village, haven't you? The one with the kohitur mango tree. I got you those mangoes, don't you remember? How can you forget so easily?'

Sukhendu looked at me and grinned suddenly.

'I remember the mangoes, but what's all this boar teeth business? I don't understand.'

'How will you understand? You've spent all your life in the city. What do you know about the details of Lakshmi Puja rituals? You'd have understood if you knew.'

'You mean boar teeth are needed for Lakshmi Puja . . .'

'Yes, you have to place them in the middle and put a pot of fruits and sweets on them. You know what I think? The history of human civilization, or what they call progress in today's terminology, lurks within these sacred rituals. This whole thing of putting fruits and sweets on boar teeth refers to conquering your foe and establishing the goddess of wealth in your home. It's neither easy nor meaningless. To gain wealth you must defeat the beast, and the boar teeth are symbols of this victory. This is just my theory, of course, whether you accept it or not is up to you. As I was saying, while I was taking the shortcut it was the eyes I saw first. Two tiny full moons, or a pair of cat's-eye gemstones. I can think of many similes now, but at that time they looked like the eyes of a wild cat glowing in the dark. I didn't realize it was a *lokkhi pencha*, Lakshmi's owl, you know, a barn owl. I ran away in fear, but you know me, I won't rest till I get to the bottom of everything. And that was how the whole thing happened. I had no control over it, but Maama and Maami blamed me for everything. According to Maami, things wouldn't have become complicated if I'd kept referring to the foundling as a foundling. She herself used to call the girl Kuruni since she had been found in the jungle. But then it was Maami who complicated matters the most, because although she called the girl Kuruni she knew better. As far as others could see she would scold and even beat the girl, giving her a tongue-lashing constantly, but in her heart Maami was devoted to the girl, she feared her. What I saw for myself one day was so strange, so strange . . .'

Sukhendu stopped suddenly. The web that was growing all around me, around my entire being, also stopped. I felt it had been whispering to me in a mysterious tongue. I found Sukhendu gazing raptly at the horizon. There was no boat-shaped cloud now, only a small white one, drifting by itself. It too seemed to be in search of something wondrous in the grandeur of moonlit outer space. It had been large earlier, but now it was shrinking, becoming smaller by the minute.

'You know what I saw?'

Sukhendu resumed his story unexpectedly.

'There she was, the foundling whom Maami called Kuruni, whom she forced to slave all day, doing the dishes and sweeping and swabbing the floor and washing the clothes, whom she cursed night and day, whom she wished death upon all the time. But in the dead of night, Maami had prostrated herself in front of the girl in devotion. It was an eerie atmosphere, the lamp was winking, the girl was fast asleep, her curls spread over her cheeks and brow, while I stood furtively outside, looking in through the window. Maami was in a pose of genuflection, lowering her head to the floor repeatedly. An odd smile had appeared on the sleeping girl's face, like moonlight on a cloudy night. I watched in silence like an intruder. Strange, so strange. The same woman was a completely different person by day, as though the foundling was a nuisance, as though she would be relieved if the girl left. You know the truth? Maami believed in the evil eye. Do you understand?'

There was an interruption before I could answer. Ramdhan appeared.

Shukul went away. Sukhendu and I glanced at Mridula. I felt the entity standing there, a combination of the moonlight, the mist and an optical illusion that was not Mridula, and it would not return. In the dim light I couldn't tell whether Sukhendu's brow was furrowed, but the look in his eyes was indescribable. Madame Curie must have had a similar look in her eyes when she gazed for the first time at the radium she had discovered. After a few moments he turned to me and shrugged.

'She's up to something. Might as well go on with the story.'

'Yes, do.'

'I felt the foundling wasn't just a foundling and told Maami as much. She was visibly furious with me, and lost no opportunity to declare repeatedly in full daylight that the girl had been foisted on her. But I saw for myself what lay in her heart. As I told you. Maami's display of contempt but secret devotion where the girl was concerned created a difficult situation for Maama. He perceived both her contempt and devotion, which left him uncertain about his own response. If he was kind to the girl his wife scolded him, if he was harsh to her she berated him, if he was indifferent she would say is your heart made of stone. So Maama was angry with me, blaming me as the root cause of all the trouble. And then I had failed in class that year, so his glares grew sharper. Later, of course, he realized the truth; by then he had come to love the girl, and he understood that Lakshmi does not make a loud entry, she appears unobserved, like fruit falling from a tree, and that I was only an instrument.'

13

NAGARLAKSHMI

RABINDRANATH TAGORE
TRANSLATED BY REBA SOM

When famine-ravaged Sravastipura
Woke up to the resounding cry of despair,
Buddha asked of his followers, one by one,
'Who among you will take charge
Of feeding rice to the hungry?'

Hearing which Ratnakar Seth
Sat with head bowed low
With folded hands he said,
'This sprawling metropolis lies hungry,
To meet this starvation
I have no resources, Swami!'

Added Samanta Jaysen,
'I respectfully would accept Prabhu's command
If by tearing my heart asunder
And pouring out my blood any purpose was served.
Today even my home has no rice!'

Panting for breath, Dharmapal gasped,
'What can I say?
Blighted is my luck.
My golden fields have been sucked dry by an unknown devil!
To meet the king's taxes I remain unable,
Reduced as I am to helpless penury!'

All looked at one another
No answer emerged.
In the silent community hall of the blighted city
The Buddha's compassionate eyes
Shone bright as the evening stars.

Then arose with halting steps
With a flushed brow and bowed head
Anathapinda's* daughter, weighed down in pain and with tears,
Taking the dust of the Buddha's feet
In a soft voice she spoke humbly,
'Lowly mendicant am I, Supriya,
Your request will I carry out
Those who cry in hunger
Are my children too.

---

* Anathapinda, or dispenser of victuals to the destitute, was a title earned by Sudatta, a rich merchant of Sravastipura who gave away his wealth in charity. He became a follower of the Buddha and a patron of Buddhism.

To distribute rice to all
I take on today the duty.'

In dismay her words were heard by all.
'Mendicant child! You are but an alms gatherer!
With what overweening pride
Have you taken on your shoulders
This difficult and huge challenge?
What do you have to offer? Tell us today.'

'I am but an impoverished girl
Weakest among all!
Yet I crave your indulgence
That the Master's instructions are rewarded,
My bowl remains replenished in each household
And if you all wish
It can remain forever perennial!
With rice offerings this earth will be saved
Satisfied will be the hunger pangs of famine!'

14

GIVE US MORE, MORE, MORE: POEMS

SANJUKTA DASGUPTA

Binary

After the departure
Of the ten-armed goddess of deliverance
Arrives the soft, submissive angel in the house
The alluring Lakshmi, the goddess of home and hearth
Peace, prosperity, piousness
Radiates as Lakshmi reposes on a blossoming lotus.

But the decks have to be cleared
For the grand arrival of Goddess Lakshmi
An effigy of an ugly rag doll
Is thrashed with sadistic ecstasy
Its severed head, arms and legs
Brutally swept out of the premises
By broom-brandishing males.

'Get out, Alakshmi,
Let not your evil shadow pollute
Our home. Get out of our sight, you
Self-willed, impudent, defiant
Inauspicious, argumentative witch!'

On the full-moon night
The earth was dripping in glowing, golden light
At midnight Lakshmi entered the waiting homes
The priest trembled. He thought he heard Lakshmi say,
'Alakshmi and Lakshmi are immortal Siamese twins, my mortal kin.'

Lakshmi*

Clutching an urn of treasures
The homely goddess
Sits quietly in a room
Like Patience on an altar
Smiling at greed.

Quite unlike her awesome mother
Lakshmi serves as she stands and waits
Dutiful, smiling, beautiful
Accepting pleasure and pain
Like a stoic sage.

Those who kneel and pray
Chant just one tedious anthem
A single phrase reverberates round the walls
Lakshmi smiles as she hears
The deafening decibels.

Give us more, more, more
More than another
Give me more, mother
More than everyone else
We are in love with more.

Lakshmi smiles as she sits in happy homes
Sad homes, poor homes, rich homes
The anthem is the same everywhere

---

* First published in *More Light*, Dasgupta & Co., Kolkata, 2008.

Palaces, huts, apartments, mansions
Bored to death by the same whining song
Sung by the discordant voices
Does Lakshmi regret that she is immortal?

15

LAKSHMI: A POEM

TAMALIKA CHAKRABORTY

She draws the footprints on a scarlet floor*
Left, right, left again
All over the stairs, the lonely corridors
Patient hand at work.
The jingle of red, and white, and gold
Fades out to the heavy heartbeats
That know the truth.
She lights the lamp
That darkens her mind,
Burns the incense
That smells of flesh and blood
Her tired eyes meet the goddess's
To pray, 'not a girl again'.

---

* First published in *Indian Literature*, Sahitya Akademi, Nov–Dec 2021

SECTION 3

WEAVING LAKSHMI'S TAPESTRY: CULTURAL INTERPRETATIONS

'Śrī-Lakṣmī is essentially Aditi, Prakr̥ti, Māyā, Apsaras, Urvaśī, the Waters, all the possibilities of existence substantially and maternally personified. The Lotus is preeminently hers, because she is the Lotus and the Earth, at once the source and support of all existences, Vasudhā or Vasudharā; that is, with respect to their substance, as the Supernal-Sun is with respect to their form. So she is represented either iconically by the Lotus, as Padmā, springing from the brimming vessel (*pūrṇa-ghaṭa*), . . . as Padma-vāsinī, and then typically as receiving a lustral bath of soma-bearing rains down-poured from the skies by the elephants of the Quarters.'

Ananda K. Coomaraswamy,
Elements of Buddhist Iconography

16

BORN OF THE OCEAN[*]

TRANSLATED BY BIBEK DEBROY

THE KING ASKED, 'O Brahmana! How did the illustrious one get the ocean of milk churned? Why was it done? Why did he hold up the mountain and move around in the water? After the gods had obtained the amrita, what else happened? Tell me all this about the illustrious one's supremely wonderful deeds. Hardships have tormented my mind for an extremely long period of time. Therefore, when you describe the glories of the lord of the Satvatas, I am not satisfied.'

Suta said, 'O Brahmanas! Dvaipayana's illustrious son was thus asked. He welcomed this and started to describe Hari's valour.'

Shri-Shuka said, 'In a battle, the gods were attacked by the asuras with sharp weapons and were slaughtered. Large numbers lost their lives and fell down and did not rise up again.

---

* Bhagavata Purana, 8(5)–8(9).

O king! Indra was cursed by Durvasa and the three worlds lost their prosperity.*

'Sacrifices and rites were destroyed. Hearing about this, the great Indra, Varuna and the large number of other gods had a meeting of consultation. But they could not decide what should be done. All of them therefore went to Brahma's assembly hall, on the summit of Meru. Prostrating themselves before Parameshthi, they told him everything. He saw that Indra, Vayu and the others were deprived of their spirits and had lost their radiance. The lord saw that the worlds had lost everything auspicious and that the asuras were thriving. He meditated in his mind and remembered the supreme being. With a pleasant countenance, the supreme and illustrious one spoke to the gods. "I, Bhava, you, asuras and others, humans, inferior species, trees and those born from sweat—all of us have been created from his avataras, lineages and portions. Let all of us go and seek refuge with the one without decay. There is no one who should be killed, no one who should be protected. There is no one to be neglected and no one to be partially shown favours. Nevertheless, for the sake of creation, preservation and destruction, at the right time, he assumes attributes of sattva, rajas and tamas. This is a time for creation and preservation, when he accepts sattva for the sake of the welfare of embodied creatures. Therefore, let us go and seek refuge with the preceptor of the worlds. He loves the gods and will grant us the good fortune." O destroyer of enemies! Having said this, with the gods, Brahma went to the abode of the unvanquished one, which lies beyond the darkness. There, controlling his senses and using divine speech, the lord praised and prayed to the one whom he had never seen, but whom he had heard about from the texts.

---

* Durvasa presented a garland to Indra. Showing disrespect, Indra carelessly flung the garland on his elephant's (Airavata's) head. It fell on the ground from the elephant's head and Airavata trampled it. Therefore, Durvasa cursed Indra.

Chapter 8(6)

Shri-Shuka said, 'The large number of gods prayed to the illustrious lord, Hari, in this way. O king! With the resplendence of one thousand suns rising simultaneously, he manifested himself before them. At this, the eyes of all the gods were suddenly dazzled. They were unable to see the directions, or their own selves, not to speak of the lord. With Sharva,* the illustrious Virinchi beheld his form. It sparkled like a dark emerald.† His eyes were red, like the inside of a lotus. His yellow silken garments were as bright as molten gold. All his limbs were beautiful and pleasant. His face was excellent and his eyebrows were handsome. His diadem had expensive gems and he was adorned with two armlets. His cheeks were illuminated by the dazzle of his earrings and his beautiful face was like a lotus. He was adorned with an ornamented girdle, bracelets, necklace and anklets. He wore the Koustubha gem as an ornament and a garland of wild flowers, and Lakshmi added to the radiance. In their personified forms, Sudarshana and other weapons tended to him. With the large number of immortals and with Sharva, the foremost among the gods‡ prostrated his limbs on the ground and praised the supreme being.

'Brahma said, "O one without birth! Through your own maya, you are born, preserved and destroyed.§ You transcend gunas. You are bliss, in the ocean of nirvana. You are smaller than an anu. Your powers are impossible to calculate. I bow down to you. O one whose glory is great! I bow down to you. O supreme Purusha! This beneficial form of yours is sought after by those who follow the Vedas, the tantras and yoga. You are the one who creates and preserves the three worlds. O one with the universe in your form!

---

* Shiva.

† Or a blue gem or blue sapphire.

‡ Brahma.

§ In different incarnations..

We can perceive ourselves and everything in you. You are your own controller. In the beginning, everything existed in you. In the middle, everything exists in you. In the end, everything will exist in you. You are the beginning, the middle and the end of the universe. You are supreme and beyond everything, like the earth in a pot.* You resorted to your maya and everything emanated from you. You created the universe and also entered it. Those who are learned and knowledgeable are united with you and can perceive you in their minds. You create the transformation of the gunas, but you are not affected by the gunas. Fire can be extracted from kindling, milk from cattle, and food, water and a means of subsistence from the earth. In that way, using yoga, men can perceive you in their intelligence. Wise people know you in the gunas and speak about it. O protector! You have appeared before us in all your glory. O one with a navel like a lotus! This is what we have desired for a very long period of time. Having seen you today, all of us are delighted, like an elephant suffering from a forest conflagration is when it sees the waters of the Ganga. We, and all the guardians of the worlds, have sought refuge at your feet for a reason. Please satisfy us. O one who exists inside and outside! We have come to you. You are a witness to everything. What is there that you need to be informed about? I, Girisha, the gods and Daksha and the others are like sparks from a fire.† O lord! Independent of you, what can we possibly understand? Instruct and counsel us about what is best for the gods and the Brahmanas."'

Shri-Shuka continued, 'Thus, Virinchi and the others worshipped him and he understood what was in their hearts. They stood there, their hands joined in salutation and with all their senses restrained. In a voice that rumbled like the clouds, he spoke to them. The lord of the gods was alone capable of accomplishing the

* A pot is created from the earth, the earth exists in the pot and when the pot is destroyed, it returns to earth.

† Not possessing an existence independent of the fire.

task of the gods. However, he desired the pastime of the churning of the ocean and other allied activities. He spoke to them.

'The illustrious one said, "O Brahma! O Shambhu! O gods! Listen to the words I speak. Listen to how all of you gods can obtain the greatest benefit. The daityas and danavas are favoured by destiny. As long as that lasts and until it turns in your favour, it is recommended that you have an alliance with them. O gods! When a task is important, there should be an alliance even with enemies. For the sake of accomplishing an objective, one should behave like the snake with the mouse.* Without any delay, efforts should be made to extract amrita. After drinking it, a living being becomes immortal, even if he is devoured by death. Fling all the herbs, grass, creepers and plants into the ocean of milk. Using Mandara as a churning rod and Vasuki as the rope, churn it. O gods! With my help, churn it single-mindedly. The daityas will suffer the hardship, while you reap the fruits. O gods! You should accept whatever the asuras desire. No success can be achieved through anger, but everything is achieved through conciliation. The *kalakuta* poison will be generated from the ocean, but do not be scared of it. When objects of desire are produced, you should not be greedy. Nor should you be angry."'†

Shri-Shuka continued, 'O king! Having instructed the gods in this fashion, the illustrious Purushottama, the lord who easily follows his own path, vanished from their sight. Having bowed down to the illustrious one, the grandfather and Bhava returned to their own abodes. The gods went to Bali. The revered king of the daityas saw the enemy. Though his own leaders were agitated

---

* A snake and a mouse were caught and trapped in a basket. If the snake ate the mouse, it would continue to remain trapped. Therefore, it had an alliance with the mouse and the mouse gnawed a hole out of the basket. When both were free, the snake ate the mouse.

† If the demons demand those objects.

and uncontrolled, he restrained them. He knew about the time for alliances and the time for war. Virochana's son was on his seat, protected by the leaders among the asuras. Having conquered everything, he was full of great prosperity. They approached him. The immensely intelligent and great Indra assured him with gentle words. Following everything that Purushottama had instructed, he addressed him. This appealed to the daitya,* the other lords of the asuras, Shambara, Arishtanemi and the residents of Tripura. Thus, the gods and the asuras had a fraternal alliance. O scorcher of enemies! For the sake of the amrita, they made supreme efforts. Those extremely indomitable ones used their energy to uproot Mount Mandara. Roaring loudly, they used their strong arms, which were like clubs, to convey it to the ocean. Because the distance was far and the burden heavy, Shakra, Virochana's son and the others were unable to bear it and, helpless, abandoned it along the path. When it fell down there, the golden mountain crushed many immortals and danavas under its weight. The illustrious one got to know that they were broken-hearted. Their arms, thighs and shoulders were broken. He arrived there, astride Garuda. He saw that the falling mountain had crushed the immortals and danavas. He glanced at them and they regained their lives. They became free of their anxiety and their wounds. As if he was playing, he raised the mountain with one hand and placed it atop Garuda. Ascending, and surrounded by large numbers of gods and asuras, he went to the ocean. Suparna, supreme among birds, took the mountain from his shoulder and placed it at the edge of the water. Hari then gave him leave to depart.'

Chapter 8(7)

Shri-Shuka said, 'Offering a share in the fruits, they invited Vasuki, the king of the nagas. Like a rope, they wound him

---

* Bali.

around the mountain and were delighted. O extender of the Kuru lineage! For the sake of the amrita, the gods started to make efforts. Initially, Hari seized the front and the gods were also there. However, the lord of the daityas did not approve of what the great being sought to do. "We will not grasp the serpent's tail. That limb is inauspicious. We have studied and possess learning. Our birth and deeds are famous." Purushottama saw that the daityas stood silently. Smiling, he let go of the front and with the immortals, seized the tail. Kashyapa's descendants divided it up in this way. For the sake of the amrita, they made great efforts to churn the ocean of milk. O descendant of the Pandu lineage! While the ocean was being churned, the heavy mountain had no support and sank into the water, despite being held by those powerful ones. Their minds were distressed. Their radiant faces faded. Despite their being strong, because of destiny, their manliness was destroyed. The lord saw that the lord of obstacles had created this impediment. However, his valour was indomitable and his intentions could not be countered. Therefore, he assumed the great and wonderful form of a tortoise. He entered the water and raised the mountain up. On seeing that the kulachala had again been raised up, the gods and the asuras resumed the churning. The back of the tortoise extended for one lakh yojanas and was like another giant dvipa. O dear one! Using the strength of their arms, the Indras among the gods and the asuras rotated the mountain on his back. That original and immeasurable tortoise bore this rotation and thought that someone was scratching his limbs. Vishnu entered them in different forms and enhanced their strength and energy—asura traits in asuras, encouragement in the large number of gods, and the divine form of ignorance in the Indra among the nagas.* Like another Indra among mountains, the

* That is, he suffused the asuras with rajas, the gods with sattva and Vasuki with tamas.

thousand-armed one appeared on top of that king of mountains and grasped it with his hand. The gods, with Brahma and Indra at the forefront, praised him and showered down flowers on him. He supported it from above and below, and his supreme atman entered them and enthused them. Proud of their strength, they swiftly churned the ocean with the giant mountain and the large number of crocodiles was agitated.

'The Indra among serpents possessed one thousand hard eyes and mouths. Flames mixed with smoke emerged from his breath and robbed the lustre of asuras like Poulama, Kaleya, Bali, Ilvala and others. They were like sarala trees* burnt down in a forest conflagration. The lustre of the gods was also destroyed from the flames in the breath. Their garments, excellent garlands, jackets and faces were covered with smoke. However, controlled by the illustrious one, the clouds rained down sufficiently on them and the breeze blew fragrantly from the waves of the ocean. In this way, the gods and the asuras did their best to churn the ocean. When amrita was not generated, the illustrious one began to churn himself. He was as dark as a cloud and wore golden garments. The earrings on his ears flashed like lightning. The wavy hair on his head glistened. Wearing garlands, his eyes were red. With triumphant arms that ensure fearlessness to the universe, he seized the dandashuka. Resembling another mountain, holding the mountain from above and below, he churned with the churning rod. Because of the churning, the great ocean was agitated and fish, makaras, snakes, tortoises, whales, sea elephants and *timingilas*† were terrified. An extremely virulent poison known as halahala was initially produced. O dear one! Terrible and intolerable in its force, it couldn't be controlled and spread in all the directions, upwards, downwards, whirling and curling around. Scared and

* A kind of pine.
† Timingila is a fish that devours whales (*timi*).

unable to find protection, the terrified subjects sought refuge with Ishvara Sadashiva. They saw the supreme among the gods seated atop the mountain* with the goddess, performing austerities for the welfare of the three worlds. Desiring liberation, sages were worshipping him.

'They bowed down and prayed to him. The Prajapatis said, "O god of the gods! O Mahadeva! O one who is in the atmans of creatures! O creator of creatures! Save us. We have sought refuge with you. The poison is burning down the three worlds. You alone are the lord of the entire universe, of both bondage and emancipation. Accomplished ones worship you. You are the preceptor who delivers those who seek refuge. O lord! Through your own strength and full of gunas, you undertake creation, preservation and destruction. O lord who is a witness to everything! You assume the forms of Brahma, Vishnu and Shiva. He was compassionate and saw that they were suffering and greatly afflicted. The god who was a well-wisher to all creatures spoke to his beloved Sati. Shiva said, "Alas! O Bhavani! Behold the calamity that confronts subjects. Because of the churning of the ocean of milk, a deadly poison† has arisen. It is recommended that I should grant those who seek to save their lives freedom from fear. This much is the objective of any master who wishes to protect the distressed. Virtuous people regard their own lives as fleeting and give those up to save beings. Confounded by his‡ maya, creatures are bound in this enmity. O fortunate one! If a person is compassionate, Hari is pleased in all his soul. O illustrious lady! If Hari is pleased, I and all mobile and immobile objects, are pleased. Therefore, I must consume this poison. Let me make it safe for the subjects." The illustrious creator of the

* Kailasa.

† Known as kalakuta, in addition to halahala.

‡ Hari's.

universe thus took Bhavani's permission and knowing about his powers, she assented.

'He started to devour the poison. He picked up the halahala poison in his broad palm. Compassionate, the creator of all beings devoured it. The poison that was generated from the water exhibited its own strength. It made his throat blue and this became an ornament for the virtuous one. In general, virtuous people torment themselves by accepting the torments of the worlds. This is regarded as supreme worship of the Purusha who resides in all atmans. Witnessing the deed of Shambhu Midusha,* god of the gods, the subjects, Daksha's daughter,† Brahma and Vaikuntha praised him. As he was drinking it, a little bit of the poison trickled down from his palm. This was accepted by scorpions, poisonous snakes and plants and dandashukas.'

Chapter 8(8)

Shri-Shuka said, 'When the one who is seated on a bull drank up the poison, the immortals and the danavas were delighted. As they swiftly churned the ocean, the source of oblations appeared.‡ O king! The rishis who know about the Brahman and perform agnihotra sacrifices accepted her. They did this to perform sacrifices for deva yana and for oblations and clarified butter. After this, the horse named Ucchaishrava emerged. It was as white as the moon. Since Bali desired it, as he had been instructed by the lord, Indra did not wish for it. Airavata, Indra among elephants, emerged next. With its four tusks, it was more glorious than the white mountain the illustrious Hara resides in.§ O king! After

* Midusha is one of Shiva's names.

† Bhavani.

‡ Meaning Surabhi, the cow which yields all the objects of desire.

§ Kailasa.

this, Airavana and the other eight diggajas were generated.* Two jewels known as Koustubha and Padmaraga were produced from the great ocean, and Hari desired to wear those two jewels on his chest as ornaments. After this, Parijat, the ornament of the world of the gods, emerged. Just as you fulfil all desires on earth, it fulfils every kind of desire. Next, the apsaras came out. They wore golden ornaments and were clad in excellent garments. With their gentle gaits and glances, they delighted all the residents of heaven.

'After this emerged Rama, the embodiment of prosperity and supremely devoted to the illustrious one. She illuminated the directions with her beauty, like a flash of lightning atop Soudamani.† All the gods, asuras and humans desired her. Her beauty, grace, youth, complexion and greatness agitated their minds. The great Indra brought an extremely wonderful seat for her. Assuming embodied forms, the best among the rivers brought golden pots filled with pure water. The earth brought all the herbs required for her consecration. Cows brought the five sacred objects.‡ Spring brought the produce of the months of Chaitra and Vaishakha. Following the prescribed rites, the rishis performed all the rituals for consecration. The gandharvas sang auspicious songs and accomplished dancers danced and sang. The clouds produced the sounds from musical instruments like drums, kettledrums, smaller drums, trumpets, conch shells, flutes and veenas, producing loud notes. The goddess Shri was seated, with a lotus in her hand. To the sound of mantras pronounced by the Brahmanas, the elephants in charge of the directions used full pots

---

* Diggajas are elephants in charge of the directions. The number is sometimes given as four and sometimes as eight. The names are not always uniform. In addition to the eight male elephants, eight female elephants are also sometimes mentioned as companions.

† Soudamani can be translated in different ways, a cloud, a mountain, a city.

‡ Milk, curds, clarified butter, dung and urine.

too bathe her. The ocean brought two yellow silken garments. Varuna brought the Vaijayanti garland, with bees intoxicated with honey buzzing around it. Prajapati Vishvakarma brought wonderful ornaments. Sarasvati gave a necklace. Aja* gave her a lotus. Nagas gave her earrings. While benedictions were being pronounced, she picked up a garland of blue lotuses, with bees buzzing around it, in her hand. Her beautiful face and cheeks were illuminated by the earrings. Her bashful smile enhanced her excellent beauty. Her symmetrical breasts touched each other and were smeared with sandalwood and kunkuma. Her stomach was flat. She started to walk and her movement was like that of a golden creeper, with the sounds of her anklets jingling. She was faultless herself and looked around among the gandharvas, the Siddhas, the asuras, the yakshas, the charanas and the residents of heaven for an abode that permanently possessed all the virtuous qualities. But she couldn't find one. "Indeed there are those with austerities, but they have not conquered their anger.† Some possess knowledge, but they are not devoid of attachment. Some are great, but have not conquered desire. Even a lord depends on someone else as a refuge. There are some with dharma, but they are not fraternal towards beings. Some have renounced, but that is not reason enough for emancipation. There are those with valour, but they have not been able to cast aside the force of time. There are those without attachment to the gunas, but they do not want a second.‡ Some possess long lifespans, but do not possess good and virtuous conduct. For those who have good conduct, their lifespans are not known. There are some with both,§ but they

---

* Brahma.

† Lakshmi thinking to herself. In interpretations, specific examples are given of each rejected type.

‡ They do not want a consort.

§ Good conduct and lifespan.

are not auspicious. Someone who is extremely auspicious does not desire me." Having thought about all the virtuous qualities in this way, Rama accepted Mukunda as her groom, though he was indifferent about desiring her. He possessed all the desired qualities. He was supreme and depended on himself alone. Indeed, he transcended all the desired qualities. She approached him with the garland made out of freshly blooming lotuses, with bees intoxicated with honey buzzing around it, and placed it around his shoulders. Smiling bashfully and with shining eyes, she indicated her place on his bosom. The supreme divinity, the father of the three worlds, made an abode for Shri, the mother of prosperity, on his chest. Stationed there, with her own compassionate glances, Shri increases the welfare of the lords of the three worlds. The followers of the gods,* along with their wives, sang and danced, loudly playing on musical instruments like conch shells, trumpets and drums. Chanting mantras and worshipping the illustrious one, Brahma, Rudra, Angiras and all the lords who were creators of the worlds showered down flowers. Shri glanced at the gods, the Prajapatis and the subjects and they obtained all the qualities and good conduct, becoming greatly content.

'O king! However, the daityas and the danavas were neglected by Lakshmi. Dispirited and greedy, they lost their enterprise and became shameless. The goddess Varuni† appeared in the form of a lotus-eyed maiden. With Hari's permission, the asuras accepted her. After this, Kashyapa's descendants continued to churn the ocean, desiring amrita. O great king! An extremely wonderful being arose. His arms were long and thick. His neck was like a conch shell. His eyes were red. His complexion was dark and he was young. He wore a garland and was adorned with all the ornaments. His garments were yellow and his chest was broad. His earrings were

* The gandharvas.

† The goddess of liquor.

polished and were made out of jewels. His soft hair was curled and was beautiful at the tips. The extremely fortunate one was like a lion in his valour. In hands decorated with bracelets, he held a pot filled with amrita. He was born from a portion of the illustrious Vishnu himself. He was known as Dhanvantari and he is the originator of Ayurveda. He has a share in sacrifices. All the asuras saw that he was holding a pot filled with amrita. Desiring the pot and its contents, they seized it. The asuras took away the pot, filled with amrita. The gods were distressed in their minds and went to Hari for refuge. The illustrious one satisfied the desires of his servants and saw that they were distressed. "Do not unnecessarily be dejected. I will use my maya to accomplish your purpose." O lord! For the sake of the amrita, dissension was created in their minds. "I will be first. You won't be the first. I am first, not you." The gods also sought to obtain their own shares. "In a sacrifice, everyone has an equal share. That is eternal dharma." O king! The daityas were filled with intolerance and tried to prevent their own. The weak ones repeatedly protested to the strong ones, who had seized the pot. Vishnu is the lord who knows about all the different techniques. Meanwhile, he assumed the form of an extremely wonderful woman, impossible to describe. She was dark to behold, like a blue lotus. All her limbs were beautiful. Her symmetrical ears were adorned with earrings. Her cheeks, nose and face were beautiful. She was in the bloom of youth, with heavy and round breasts. Her waist was slender. Her face attracted delighted buzzing bees and her eyes were anxious. Her mass of excellent hair dazzled and a garland of mallika flowers was entwined in it. Her shapely neck had a necklace and her beautiful arms were adorned with armlets. Her hips were like an island and a sparkling garment was spread across them, with a girdle adorning it. As she moved, there was the enchanting sound of anklets. She arched her eyebrows and modestly smiled at the leading daityas, glancing at them repeatedly, igniting desire in them.'

Chapter 8(9)

Shri-Shuka said, 'The asuras had given up all affection towards each other and were trying to seize the vessel, snatching it from others. They had adopted the dharma of bandits. They saw the woman advancing. "Her beauty is wonderful. Her body is wonderful. Her blooming youth is wonderful." Filled with desire, they rushed towards her and started to ask, "You possess eyes like the petals of a lotus. Who are you? Where have you come from? What do you wish for? O one with the beautiful thighs! Whom do you belong to? You are churning our minds. We know that we, immortals, daityas, Siddhas, gandharvas, charanas and lords of the worlds have not touched you, or seen anyone like you, not to speak of men. O one with the excellent eyebrows! It is certain that destiny has sent you for embodied beings. Haven't you been fashioned to take pity and delight our senses and minds? O beautiful one! O one with the excellent waist! Because of this one object,* we are challenging each other and relatives are bound in enmity. You should resolve this. Because we are descended from Kashyapa, we are brothers and have demonstrated our manliness. You should divide it properly, so that there is no dispute." Hari, who had used maya to assume the form of a woman, was thus invited by the daityas. The one with the beautiful limbs smiled. She looked towards them and spoke. The illustrious one said, "How can Kashyapa's descendants be attracted to a pumshchali† like me? A learned person never trusts a woman. O enemies of the gods! It has been said that the friendship of wolves and svairini women‡ is temporary. They are always searching for new friends." Teasing in this way, she assured the minds of the asuras, though her intent

---

* The amrita.

† Wanton or unchaste woman.

‡ Loose woman.

was serious. They laughed and handed over the vessel of amrita to her. Having accepted the vessel of amrita, Hari smiled pleasantly and addressed them in these words. "If you accept whatever I do, good or bad, I will apportion the share of the amrita." The bulls among the asuras heard her words. They did not discern the import and agreed. They fasted, bathed and offered oblations into the fire.* They donated to cows,† Brahmanas and other beings, and Brahmanas pronounced benedictions. As they chose, they attired themselves in excellent garments and adorned themselves with ornaments. All of them seated themselves on kusha grass, with the blades pointing to the east. O Indra among men! The gods and Diti's descendants sat down, facing the east. The hall was fragrant with incense, with garlands and lamps. She entered, holding the pot in her hand. Her thighs were like an elephant's trunk. Because of her heavy hips, covered in a silk garment, her movement was slow. Her eyes were intoxicated. Her golden anklets tinkled. Her breasts were like pitchers. Adorned in beautiful golden earrings, she was like Shri's companion. Her nose, cheeks and face were superior to those of the gods. She glanced at them and smiled repeatedly. The end of the garment slipped, revealing her breasts. The gods and asuras were captivated. Asuras are unruly and violent by nature. Thinking that giving them amrita would be like giving it to snakes, Achyuta did not give them a share. The lord of the universe made the two categories‡ sit in separate rows, each sat down in his respective seat in his respective row. She took the pot and went to the daityas, deceiving them with sweet words. She then fed the amrita, which destroys old age and death, to

* This form of Vishnu is known as Mohini. Mohini instructed them about these preliminaries.

† Cows were fed.

‡ Gods and asuras.

those who were seated further away.[*] O king! The asuras adhered to the pledge they had themselves given. Because of their affection towards her and because they did not want to fight with a woman, they remained quiet. They had developed great love for her and did not wish for that love to be destroyed. They also held her in great respect and did not wish to say anything unpleasant. Disguising himself with the signs of a god, Svarbhanu entered the ranks of the gods and drank the amrita.[†] However, the sun god and the moon god pointed this out. As he was drinking, with his razor-sharp chakra, Hari sliced off his head. Since the torso had not been touched by the amrita, it fell down, dead. The head became immortal and Aja[‡] conferred the status of a planet on him. Because of the enmity, on the days of the new moon and the full moon, he attacks the sun and the moon. When the gods had almost finished drinking the amrita, the illustrious Hari, the creator of the worlds, assumed his own form, while the Indras among the asuras looked on. Thus the time, the place, the reason, the objective, the effort and the intention of the large number of gods and asuras was identical, but the fruits were different. Because they sought refuge with the dust on his lotus feet, the large number of gods obtained the fruit of amrita, but the daityas did not. For the protection of one's own physical body and that of the offspring, men do many things with their wealth, deeds, thoughts and words. However, since these stem from differentiation,[§] these are temporary. That which is done without a sense of differentiation is alone permanent. Like watering the root, everything then becomes successful.'

---

[*] The gods were seated further away. Mohini first went to the asuras.

[†] The word used is soma, meaning amrita.

[‡] Brahma.

[§] Duality.

17

DIVINE RIVALRIES: LAKSHMI, GANGA AND SARASVATI*

TRANSLATED BY SWAMI VIJÑANANANDA

THE SRIMAD DEVI Bhagavatam, also known as Devi Purana, was composed into twelve chapters, containing 18,000 verses by the great Veda Vyasa. Though classified as an Upapurana it is the only Purana Veda Vyasa called Maha Purana, meaning the great Purana.

Chapter VI

On the coming in this world of Laksmî, Gangâ and Sarasvatî

1–10. Nârâyana said: 'O Nârada! Sarasvatî lives always in Vaikuntha close to Nârada. One day a quarrel arose with Gangâ, and by Her curse, Sarasvatî came in parts as a river here in this

* Srimad Devi Bhagavatam, Chapter VI.

Bhârata. She is reckoned in Bhârata as a great sanctifying holy and merit-giving river.

'The good persons serve Her always, residing on Her banks. She is the Tapasyâ and the fruit thereof of the ascetics. She is like the burning fire to the sins of the sinners. Those that die in Bhârata on the Sarasvatî waters with their full consciousness, live forever in Vaikuntha in the council of Hari. Those that bathe in the Sarasvatî waters, after committing sins, become easily freed of them and live for a long, long time in Visnu-Loka. If one bathes even once in the Sarasvatî waters, during Châturmâsya (a vow that lasts four months), in full-moon time, in Aksyayâ or when the day ends, in Vyatîpâta Yoga, in the time of eclipse or on any other holy day or through any other concomitant cause or even without any faith and out of sheer disregard, one is able to go to Vaikuntha and get the nature of Śrî Hari. If one repeats the Sarasvatî Mantra, residing on the banks of the Sarasvatî, for one month, a great illiterate can become a great poet. There is no doubt in this. Once shaving one's head, if one resides on the banks of the Sarasvatî, daily bathes in it, one will not have to meet with the pain of being again born in the womb. O Nârada! Thus I have described a little of the unbounded glories of Bhârata that give happiness and the fruits of all desires.'

11. Sûta said: 'O Saunaka! The Muni Nârada hearing thus, asked again at that very moment to solve his doubts. I am now speaking of that. Hear.'

12–15. Nârada said: 'O Lord! How did the Devî Sarasvatî quarrel with the Devî Gangâ and how did she by Her curse turn out in India, into a holy river in giving virtues. I am becoming more and more eager and impatient to hear about this critical incident. I do not find satiety in drinking your nectar-like words. Who finds satiety in getting his good weal? Why did Gangâ curse Sarasvatî, worshipped everywhere. Gangâ is also full of Sattva Gunas. She always bestows good and virtue to all. Both of them are fiery and it is pleasant to hear the cause of quarrels between those two. These are very rarely found in the Purânas. So you ought to describe that to me.'

16–21. Nârâyana said: 'Hear, O Nârada! I will now describe that incident, the hearing of which removes all the sins. Laksmî, Sarasvatî and Gangâ, the three wives of Hari and all equally loved, remain always close to Hari. One day Gangâ cast sidelong glances frequently towards Nârâyana and was eagerly looking at Him, with a smile on Her lips. Seeing this, the Lord Nârâyana was startled and looked at Gangâ and smiled also. Laksmî saw that, but she did not take any offence. But Sarasvatî became very angry. Padmâ (Laksmî) who was of Sattva Guna, began to console in various ways the wrathful Sarasvatî; but she could not be appeased by any means. Rather Her face became red out of anger; she began to tremble out of her feelings (passion); Her lips quivered; and She began to speak to Her husband.

22–38. 'The husband that is good, religious and well qualified looks on all his wives equally; but it is just the opposite with him who is a cheat. O Gadâdhara! You are partial to Gangâ; and so is the case with Laksmî. I am the only one that is deprived of your love. It is, therefore, that Gangâ and Padmâ are in love with each other; for you love Padmâ. So why shall not Padmâ bear this contrary thing! I am only unfortunate. What use is there in holding my life? Her life is useless, who is deprived of her husband's love. Those that declare you, of Sattva Gunas, ought not to be ever called Pundits. They are quite illiterate; they have not the least knowledge of the Vedas. They are quite impotent to understand the nature of your mind. O Nârada! Hearing Sarasvatî's words and knowing that she had become very angry, Nârâyana thought for a moment and then went away from the Zenana outside. When Nârâyana had thus gone away, Sarasvatî became fearless and began to abuse Gangâ downright out of anger in an abusive language, hard to hear: "O Shameless One! O Passionate One! What pride do you feel for your husband? Do you like to show that your husband loves you much? I will destroy your pride today. I will see today, it will be seen by others also, what your Hari can do for you?" Saying thus Sarasvatî rose up to catch hold of Gangâ by Her hair violently. Padmâ intervened to stop this. Sarasvatî became very violent and cursed Laksmî: "No doubt you will be turned into a tree and into a river. In as much as seeing this undue behaviour of Gangâ, you do not step forward to speak anything in this assembly, as if you are a tree or a river." Padmâ did not become at all angry, even when she heard of the above curse. She became sorry and, holding the hands of Sarasvatî, remained silent. Then Gangâ became very angry; Her lips began to quiver frequently. Seeing the mad fiery nature of the red-eyed Sarasvatî, she told Laksmî: "O Padme! Leave that wicked foul-mouthed woman. What will she do to me? She presides over speech and therefore likes always to remain with quarrels. Let Her shew Her force how far can she quarrel with me. She wants to test the strength of us. So leave Her. Let all know today our strength and prowess."

39–44. 'Thus saying, Gangâ became ready to curse Sarasvatî and, addressing Laksmî, said: "O dear Padme! As that woman has cursed you to become a river, so I too curse her, that she, too, be turned into a river and she would go to the abode of men, the sinners, to the world and take their heaps of sins." Hearing this curse of Gangâ, Sarasvatî gave her curse, "You, too, will have to descend into the Bhurloka (the world) as a river, taking all the sins of the sinners." O Nârada! While this quarrel was going on, the four-armed omniscient Bhagavân Hari came up there accompanied by four attendants of His, all four-armed, and took Sarasvatî in His breast and began to speak all the previous mysteries. Then they came to know the cause of their quarrels and why they cursed one another and all became very sorry. At that time Bhagavân Hari told them one by one:

45–67. '"O Laksmî! Let you be born in parts, without being born in any womb, in the world as the daughter in the house of the King Dharma-dhvaja. You will have to take the form of a tree there, out of this evil turn of fate. There Śankhachûda, the Indra of the asuras, born of my parts will marry you. After that you will come back here and be my wife as now. There is no doubt in this. You will be named Tulasî, the purifier of the three worlds, in Bhârata. O Beautiful One! Now go there quickly and be a river in your parts under the name Padmâvatî. O Gange! You will also have to take incarnation in Bhârata as a river, purifying all the worlds, to destroy the sins of the inhabitants of Bhârata. Bhagiratha will take you there after much entreating and worshipping you; and you will be famous by the name Bhagirathî, the most sanctifying river in the world. There, the Ocean born of my parts, and the King S'ântanu, also born of my parts, will be your husbands. O Bharatî! Let you go also and incarnate in part in Bhârata under the curse of Gangâ. O Good-natured One! Now go in full Amsas to Brahmâ and become His wife. Let Gangâ go also in Her fullness to S'iva. Let Padmâ remain with Me. Padmâ is of a peaceful nature, void of anger, devoted to Me and of a Sâttvika nature.

'"Chaste, good-natured, fortunate and religious women like Padmâ are very rare. Those women that are born of the parts of Padmâ are all very religious and devoted to their husbands. They are peaceful and good-natured and worshipped in every universe. It is forbidden, nay, opposed to the Vedas, to keep three wives, three servants, three friends of different natures, at one place. They never conduce to any welfare. They are the fruitful sources of all jealousies and quarrels. Where, in any family females are powerful like men and males are submissive to females, the birth of the male is useless. At his every step, he meets with difficulties and bitter experiences. He ought to retire to the forest whose wife is foul-mouthed, of bad birth and fond of quarrels. The great forest is better for him than his house. That man does not get in his house any water for washing his feet, or any seat to sit on, or any fruit to eat, nothing whatsoever; but in the forest, all these are not unavailable.

'"Rather to dwell amid rapacious animals or to enter into fire than remain with a bad wife. O Fair One! Rather the pains of the disease or venom are bearable, but the words of a bad wife are hard to bear. Death is far better than that. Those that are under the control of their wives, know that they never get their peace of mind until they are laid on their funeral pyres. They never see the fruits of what they daily do. They have no fame anywhere, neither in this world nor in the next. Ultimately the fruit is this: that they have to go to hell and remain there. His life is verily a heavy burden who is without any name or fame. Never it is for the least good that many co-wives remain at one place. When, by taking one wife only a man does not become happy, then imagine, how painful it becomes to have many wives. O Gange! Go to Śiva. O Sarasvatî! Go to Brahmâ. Let the good-natured Kamalâ, residing on the lotus remain with Me. He gets in this world happiness and Dharma and in the next Mukti whose wife is chaste and obedient. In fact, he is Mukta, pure and happy whose wife is chaste; and he whose wife is foul-natured, is rendered impure unhappy and dead while he is living."'

18

THE CURSE OF THE ELEPHANT-HEAD[*]

TRANSLATED BY G.V. TAGARE

Śrī Garuda said:

1–5. I have a very close friend, a Brāhmaṇa hailing from the family of Bhṛgu. The name of his lotus-eyed daughter is Mādhavī. A husband befitting her could not be found by that noble-souled one. Therefore, he said to me: 'O excellent bird, bring a husband suitable to her, if you consider me worthy of honour.' Then the entire earth was searched by me for a bridegroom befitting her. But no bridegroom endowed with all good qualities could be obtained. Then, O Lotus-Eyed One, you were recollected by me in my mind as a befitting husband for her. You are endowed with all good qualities. Hence, O Lord of

[*] *The Skanda Purana*, Part XVI, chapters 81 and 85.

Suras, accept her. Hold her hand in marriage. She is very beautiful. I pray to you with this appeal of mine.

Śrī Bhagavān said:

6. O excellent bird, bring that lotus-eyed girl here. On seeing her myself, I shall do as spoken by you.

Garuda said:

7. It is on account of our fear from your refulgence that the girl and the father had been kept far away by me. How can I bring her here?

Śrī Lord said:

8. My refulgence will not scorch her and her father here. Hence, O excellent bird, bring her quickly.
9. On being told thus by that powerful Viṣṇu, he brought her and also the Brāhmaṇa, a descendant of the family of Bhṛgu.
10. The Brāhmaṇa bowed down to Madhusūdana and came to the side of Viṣṇu, near Garuda, like Lakṣmī herself.
11. Due to child-like innocence the blameless, beautiful girl sat at the end of the bed to the right of the Enemy of Mura.
12. Thereat, Lakṣmī who had the status of the chief queen became extremely furious thinking her to be her co-wife and cursed the girl:
13. 'Since, verily in my very presence, O sinful girl, you set aside all bashfulness and joyously took your seat on the bed of my husband, you will become a hideous Asvamukhi (horse-faced).'

14. When the curse was thus uttered by Śrī, there was a great hue and cry among all those present there. The Brāhmaṇa became angry.

The Brāhmaṇa said:

15. A thousand persons have been requested on behalf of the girl. Not even a single one among them has accepted her even verbally, let alone grasp her hand. How can she have the status of a wife?
16. As long as she has not been handed over with a prior resolve, in accordance with the injunctions of the Gṛhyasūtras and in the presence of the holy fire, Brāhmaṇas and elders (she has no status of a wife).
17. Hence, she is blemishless. But you regarding her on par with your co-wife have made her horse-faced. O sinful one, you will also be elephant-faced.
18. After saying thus, the leading Brāhmaṇa spoke to Keśava: 'A befitting hospitality has been extended to me by your wife! Hence, I shall go to that place where such a daughter shall be born.'

Śrī Bhagavan said:

19. In this matter, O excellent Brāhmaṇa, do not be so enraged. Never can inauspiciousness befall those who come to my vicinity.
20. Hence, she will not become horse-faced in this birth. Take her and go home. Give her to a desirable person.
21. It is the left side of the bed that has been assigned to wives and the right side to kinsmen who may lie for the nonce.
22. Here, your daughter, O Brāhmaṇa, has occupied the spot reserved for kinsmen. So she will be born as my younger sister in the next birth.

23–24. I will incarnate then on the earth on account of some task of the Devas. Since she has been cursed to become a horse-faced one by my wife, I will perform great penance along with her and transform her into one with a splendid face, O Brāhmaṇa, I will make Lakṣmī too so.

Sūta said:

3. By the curse of that Brāhmaṇa, O Brāhmaṇas, she (Lakṣmī) became instantly an elephant-faced one, causing great wonder.

4–5. She was told by Hari: 'O splendid daughter of the Ocean, stay in this very form for some time till the close of the Dvāpara Yuga. Then I shall incarnate on the earth. By the power of my penance, I shall make you splendid-faced once again.'

6. She ignored those words of the wielder of Śārṅga bow. She joyously performed a very severe penance for the sake of a splendid face.

7. She came to this holy spot and took the holy bath thrice a day. She was active and alert day and night and propitiated Brahmā.

8. Becoming pleased with her at the close of a year, Brahmā said to her: 'O beloved of Keśava, I am pleased with you. Request for a boon.'

Lakṣmī said:

9–10. For some reason, O Lord, I have been transformed into an elephant-faced woman by an extremely furious Brāhmaṇa by uttering a terrible curse. Hence, O Pitāmaha, if you are pleased, change me back again to the old form. I do not choose anything else.

Brahmā said:

11. O fair lady, with my favour, your face will undoubtedly become splendid all the more. So go home.
12. O splendid lady, *Mahattva* (greatness) has been granted to you by me from today. Hence, your name here will be Mahālakṣmī.
13. A man who devoutly worships you as elephant-faced shall become a king on the earth and lord of elephants.
14–15. On the second lunar day, O goddess, one who calls you Mahālakṣmī and devoutly worships you through Śrīsūkta will never become poor during seven successive births.

After saying this, the Four-Faced God ceased (to speak).

16. That goddess joyously went to the place where Keśava was staying.

19

THE GLORY OF LAKSHMITIRTHA*

TRANSLATED BY G.V. TAGARE

Śrī Sūta said:

1. After taking the holy bath in the Tīrtha named Jaṭātīrtha that is destructive of all sins and the means of getting the soul purified, a pilgrim should go to Lakṣmītīrtha.

2. With whatever desire in view a man takes his bath in Lakṣmītīrtha he attains the desired object, O excellent Brāhmaṇas.

3. It destroys great poverty. It bestows plenty of foodgrains. It subdues great miseries, and it increases vast wealth and fortune.

4. Formerly directed by Śrīkṛṣṇa while he was in Indraprastha, Dharmaputra took his holy bath here and attained great prosperity.

* *The Skanda Purana*, Part VIII, Chapter 21.

The sages asked:

5. O great sage, tell us how, by taking his holy plunge in Lakṣmītīrtha at the instance of Kṛṣṇa, Dharmaputra obtained prosperity.

Śrī Sūta replied:

6. Directed by Dhṛtarāṣṭra, O Brāhmaṇas, formerly the five Pāṇḍavas of great strength and valour went to Indraprastha and stayed there.

7–8. Once Kṛṣṇa went to Indraprastha on a visit to them. On seeing him, those Pāṇḍavas eagerly received him with great joy and took him to their abode. Kṛṣṇa stayed in that excellent city for some time.

9. Once Yudhiṣṭhira invited the lotus-eyed Kṛṣṇa, the lord of the universe, the son of Vasudeva, honoured him and then asked him.

Yudhiṣṭhira said:

10. O Kṛṣṇa, O Kṛṣṇa of great intellect, tell me, O highly intelligent one, by what holy rite do men obtain great prosperity. On being inquired thus by Dharmaputra, Kṛṣṇa told Yudhiṣṭhira:

Śrīkṛṣṇa said:

11–15a. O illustrious Dharmaputra, there is a Tīrtha on the Gandhamādana mountain, well known by the name Lakṣmītīrtha. It is the sole cause of prosperity. Do take your holy bath there. You will become prosperous. By taking the holy bath there, riches increase and foodgrains flourish in plenty. All enemies perish. The valour of the (devotees) increases.

Formerly Devas took their holy bath in the meritorious Tīrtha named Lakṣmītīrtha. By the merit thereof, O Dharmaputra, they obtained all prosperity.

15b–18. Men who regularly take their holy bath in that Tīrtha, will get before long, earth, wealth and virtue. Do not have any doubt in this regard. O son of Pāṇḍu, by taking the holy plunge in Lakṣmītīrtha wealth is obtained in the same manner as (it is got) through austerities, sacrifices, charitable gifts and blessings. All sins perish and all obstacles disappear always. By resorting to Lakṣmītīrtha, all ailments are cured completely and abundant welfare is obtained in the world. There is no doubt about this.

19. O Dharmaputra, merely by taking his holy bath in this Tīrtha of Lakṣmī, King Avadha obtained Rambhā, the most excellent one among the celestial women.

20. By taking his holy bath in this meritorious Tīrtha, Kubera Naravāhana became owner of the Treasures (*Nidhis*), the chief of which is Mahāpadma.

21–22. Hence, O prominent king, you too, in the company of your younger brothers, the chief of whom is Bhīma, take your holy bath in Lakṣmītīrtha that bestows auspiciousness and welfare. You will (thereby) acquire great fortune and conquer enemies. No doubt need be entertained in this matter, O my father's sister's son, O Dharmaputra.

23. On being told thus by Kṛṣṇa, Dharmaputra of a wonderful appearance, immediately went to the Gandhamādana mountain along with his younger brothers.

24. Then he went to Lakṣmītīrtha, the cause of great prosperity. There, along with his younger brothers, Yudhiṣṭhira observed all the requisite rites and took his holy bath.

25. Along with his younger brothers and strictly adhering to all holy observances, he took his baths for the period of a month in the waters of Lakṣmītīrtha destructive of all sins.

26. He gave plenty of cows, plots of lands, gingelly seeds, gold and other things to Brāhmaṇas. Thereafter Dharmaputra returned to Indraprastha along with his younger brothers.

27–33. Then Yudhiṣṭhira wished to perform Rājasūya sacrifice. Dharmaputra who was desirous of performing the sacrifice invited Kṛṣṇa.

On being invited through a messenger of Dharmaputra, Kṛṣṇa hurriedly came to Indraprastha accompanied by Satyabhāmā riding in a swift chariot yoked with four horses.

On seeing him arrived, Dharmaputra joyously mentioned to Kṛṣṇa about his preparations for Rājasūya. Kṛṣṇa permitted him by saying, 'Let it be done so.'

He then spoke to Dharmaputra these words with cogent arguments: 'O virtuous nephew of my father, listen to my beneficial words. This Rājasūya sacrifice cannot be easily performed by all kings. Only a king who has many hundreds of foot-soldiers, chariots, elephants and horses deserves to perform this Yajña. No one else. At the outset all the ten quarters should be conquered by you with your own might.

34. 'Excellent tribute must be levied (and collected) from the defeated enemies. This excellent sacrifice should be performed by means of that collection of gold.

35. 'I am encouraging you. I am not frightening or warning you because I know cogent reasons. Hence before beginning the sacrifice, begin the conquest of the quarters.'

36. On hearing the wholesome advice of Kṛṣṇa, Dharmaputra praised the son of Devakī and called his younger brothers.

37–40. After calling all his four brothers, Dharmaputra spoke to them making them glad: 'O Bhīma, O mighty one, O Dhanañjaya of great heroism, O twin brothers of tender limbs always ready to destroy the enemies, I wish to perform the great Yajña called Rājasūya. That (sacrifice) should be performed after conquering all the kings in battle. Hence all the four of you along with your vast armies do go to the four quarters to conquer the kings. All of you are valorous and heroic. I shall perform the great sacrifice with the riches brought by you all.'

41–48. On being told thus with great enthusiasm the younger brothers of Dharmaputra, the chief among whom was Bhīma, became delighted. In order to conquer the kings, Pāṇḍavas started from the city and went in all directions.

All of them conquered those kings present in all the four directions. The sons of Pāṇḍu brought those kings under their control. They took with them vast wealth of various sorts given by them (i.e. kings) and hurriedly reached their city where they had Kṛṣṇa to support them.

Bhīma of great strength and valour came there to the excellent city with gold weighing a hundred Bhāras. Then Arjuna of great strength and power came to Indraprastha, taking with him a thousand Bhāras of gold. Similarly, Nakula of great refulgence came to the excellent city of Indraprastha, taking with him a hundred Bhāras of gold.

Taking with him fourteen golden palmyra trees given by Vibhīṣaṇa as well as the vast collection of wealth of the Southern kings, Sahadeva immediately came to his own city.

49. Kṛṣṇa, (the leader) of the Yādavas, gave Dharmaputra hundreds and thousands and hundred thousands of gold pieces.

50–51. With the unlimited wealth brought by his younger brothers and the innumerable riches (gold pieces) given by Kṛṣṇa, Yudhiṣṭhira who had the support of Kṛṣṇa, O Brāhmaṇas, performed the Rājasūya sacrifice. The son of Pāṇḍu gave monetary gifts to Brāhmanas as much as they wished.

52. Yudhiṣṭhira gave foodstuffs to the Brāhmaṇas. Similarly, he gave them clothes, cows, plots of land as well as ornaments.

53. Dharmaputra gave the suppliants the quantity of gold, etc., twice as much again as they would be ordinarily contented with.

54. Even crores of Brahmās could not keep an account of the unlimited wealth thus distributed and could not say that this much of gold and wealth of diverse kinds had been given to the seekers of wealth.

55. On seeing the riches being given to the seekers, the people said that everything he possessed was given away by the king.

56–60. On seeing the inexhaustible treasures with infinite number of jewels and gold pieces, the people said that only a little fraction had been given to the suppliants.

After performing the Rājasūya sacrifice thus, Dharmaputra and his younger brothers rejoiced in that excellent city with flourishing wealth.

It was due to the power of Lakṣmītīrtha that Yudhiṣṭhira, the son of Dharma, got everything, O Brāhmaṇas.

Oh, what a glory of the Tīrtha! This Tīrtha is of great merit. It suppresses great poverty. It yields wealth and foodgrains to men. It destroys great sins. It dispels (the fear of) the great Narakas. It causes great miseries to recede.

61–64. It yields salvation and heavenly pleasures perpetually. It grants excellent wives and good sons to men. It relieves men of their indebtedness. A Tīrtha on a par with this has never existed before, nor will it ever exist.

Thus, O Brāhmaṇas, the glory of Lakṣmītīrtha has been described to you. It destroys bad dreams. It is meritorious. It achieves all that the devotees desire.

He who reads this chapter or listens to this with devotion shall be prosperous with wealth and plenty of foodgrains. There is no doubt at all. After enjoying all pleasures here, he shall attain salvation after death.

20

JATAKA TALE: SIRIKALAKANNI

TRANSLATED BY ROBERT CHALMERS

[257] *'Who is this,' etc.*—The Master told this tale in Jetavana concerning Anāthapiṇḍika. From the time when he was established in the fruition of the First Path he kept all the five first commandments unbroken; so also did his wife, his sons and daughters, his hired servants and his workpeople. One day in the Hall of Truth they began to discuss whether Anāthapiṇḍika was pure in his walk and his household also. The Master came and was told their subject: so he said, 'Brethren, the wise men of old had pure households,' and told an old tale.

ONCE UPON A time when Brahmadatta was king in Benares, the Bodhisatta was a merchant, giving gifts, keeping the commands, and performing the fast-day duties: and so his wife kept the five commands, and so also did his sons, his daughters and his servants and workpeople. So he was called the merchant Suciparivāra (pure household). He thought, 'If one of purer morals than I should come, it would not be proper to give him my couch to sit on or my bed to lie on, but to give him one pure and unused': so he had an unused couch and bed prepared on one side in his presence-chamber. At that time in the Heaven of the Four Kings[1] Kālakaṇṇī, daughter of Virūpakkha, and Sirī, daughter of Dhataraṭṭha, both together took many perfumes and garlands and went on the Lake Anotatta to play there. Now on that lake there are many bathing places.

The Buddhas bathe at their own place, the paccekabuddhas at theirs, [258] the Brethren at theirs, the ascetics at theirs, the gods of the six Kāma-heavens[2] at theirs and the goddesses at theirs. These two came thither and began to quarrel as to which of them should bathe first. Kālakaṇṇī said, 'I rule the world: it is proper that I bathe first.' Sirī said, 'I preside over the course of conduct that gives lordship to mankind: it is proper that I bathe first.' Then both said, 'The Four Kings will know which of us ought to bathe first': so they went to them and asked which of the two was worthy to bathe first in Anotatta. Dhataraṭṭha and Virūpakkha said, 'We cannot decide,' and laid the duty on Virūḷha and Vessavaṇa. They too said, 'We cannot decide, we will send it to our Lord's feet': so they sent it to Sakka. He heard their tale and thought, 'Those two are the daughters of my vassals; I cannot decide this case': so he said to them, 'There is in Benares a merchant called Suciparivāra; in his house are prepared an unused couch and bed: she who can first sit or lie there is the proper one to bathe first.' Kālakaṇṇī hearing this on the instant put on blue[3] raiment and used blue ointment and decked herself with blue jewels: she descended from the heaven as on a stone from a catapult, and just after the mid-watch of night she stood in the air, diffusing a blue light, not far from the merchant who was lying on a couch in the presence-chamber of his mansion. The merchant [259] looked and saw her: but to his eyes she was ungracious and unlovely. Talking to her he spoke the first stanza:

Who is this so dark of hue,
So unlovely to the view?
Who are you, whose daughter, say,
How are we to know you, pray?

Hearing him, Kālakaṇṇī spoke the second stanza:

The great king Virūpakkha is my sire:
I am Misfortune, Kālakaṇṇī dire:
Give me the house-room near you I desire.

Then the Bodhisatta spoke the third stanza:

What the conduct, what the ways,
    Of the men with whom you dwell?
This is what my question prays;
    We will mark the answer well.

Then she, explaining her own qualities, spoke the fourth stanza:

The hypocrite, the wanton, the morose,
    The man of envy, greed and treachery:
Such are the friends I love: and I dispose
    Their gains that they may perish utterly.

[260] She spoke also the fifth, sixth and seventh stanzas:

And dearer still are ire and hate to me,
Slander and strife, libel and cruelty.
The shiftless wight who knows not his own good,
Resenting counsel, to his betters rude:
The man whom folly drives, whom friends despise,
He is my friend, in him my pleasure lies.

[261] Then the Great Being, blaming her, spoke the eighth stanza:

Kāli, depart: there's naught to please you here: To other lands and cities disappear.

Kālakaṇṇī, hearing him, was sorrowful and spoke another stanza:

I know you well: there's naught to please me here.
Others are luckless, who amass much gear;
My brother-god and I will make it disappear.

When she had gone, Sirī the goddess, coming with raiment and ointment of golden hue and ornament of golden brightness to the door of the presence-chamber, diffusing yellow light, rested with even feet on level ground and stood respectful. The Bodhisatta seeing her repeated the first stanza:

Who is this, divine of hue,
On the ground so firm and true?
Who are you, whose daughter, say,
How are we to know you, pray?

[262] Sirī, hearing him, spoke the second stanza:

The great king Dhataraṭṭha is my sire:
Fortune and Luck am I, and Wisdom men admire:
Grant me the house-room with you I desire.

Then

What the conduct, what the ways
Of the men with whom you dwell?
This is what my question prays;
We will mark your answer well.

He who in cold and heat, in wind and sun,
Mid thirst and hunger, snake and poison-fly,
His present duty night and day hath done;
With him I dwell and love him faithfully.
Gentle and friendly, righteous, liberal,
Guileless and honest, upright, winning, bland,
Meek in high place: I tinge his fortunes all,
Like waves their hue through ocean that expand.[4]

To friend or unfriend, better, like or worse,
Helper or foe, by dark or open day,
Whoso is kind, [263] without harsh word or curse,
I am his friend, living or dead, alway.

But if a fool has won some love from me,
And waxes proud and vain,
His froward path of wantonness I flee,
Like filthy stain.

Each man's fortune and misfortune are his own work, not another's:
Neither fortune nor misfortune can a man make for his brothers.

Such was Sirī's answer when questioned by the merchant.

[264] The Bodhisatta rejoiced at Sirī's words and said, 'Here is the pure seat and bed, proper for you; sit and lie down there.' She stayed there and in the morning departed to the Heaven of the Four Great Kings and bathed first in Lake Anotatta. The bed used by Sirī was called Sirisaya: hence is the origin of Sirisayana, and for this reason it is so called to this day.

After the lesson the Master identified the Birth: 'At that time the goddess Sirī was Uppalavaṇṇā, the merchant Suciparivāra was myself.'

NOTES:

[1]: These are Dhataraṭṭha, King of the North, Virūḷha of the South, Virūpakkha of the West and Vessavaṇa of the East.
[2] : Of which the Heaven of the Four Kings is the first.
[3] : Blue is the unlucky colour.
[4] : Perhaps vaṇṇam is really for the Sanskrit vṛṃhan, increasing.

21

JATAKA TALE: KHADIRANGARA

TRANSLATED BY ROBERT CHALMERS

'Far rather will I headlong plunge.' This story was told by the Master while at Jetavana, about Anātha-pindika.

FOR ANĀTHA-PINDIKA, WHO had lavished fifty-four crore on the Faith of the Buddha over the Monastery alone, and who valued naught else save only the Three Gems, used to go every day while the Master was at Jetavana to attend the Great Services—once at daybreak, once after breakfast and once in the evening. There were intermediate services too; but he never went empty-handed, for fear the Novices and lads should look to see what he had brought with him. When he went in the early morning [227], he used to have rice-gruel taken up; after breakfast, ghee, butter, honey, molasses and the like; and in the evening, he brought perfumes, garlands and cloths. So much did he expend day after day, that his expense knew no bounds. Moreover, many traders borrowed money from him on their bonds—to the amount of eighteen crore; and the great merchant never called the money in. Furthermore, another eighteen crore of the family property, which were buried in the river-bank, were washed out to sea, when the bank was swept away by a storm; and down rolled the brazen pots, with fastenings and seals unbroken, to the bottom of the ocean. In his house, too, there was always rice standing ready for 500 Brethren—so that the merchant's house was to the Brotherhood like a pool dug where four roads meet, yea, like mother and father was he to them. Therefore, even the All-Enlightened Buddha used to go to his house, and the Eighty Chief Elders too; and the number of other Brethren passing in and out was beyond measure.

Now his house was seven stories high and had seven portals; and over the fourth gateway dwelt a fairy who was a heretic. When the All-Enlightened Buddha came into the house, she could not stay in her abode on high, but came down with her children to the ground-floor; and she had to do the like whenever the Eighty Chief Elders or the other Elders came in and out. Thought she, 'So long as the ascetic Gotama and his disciples keep coming into this house I can have no peace here; I can't be eternally coming downstairs to the ground floor. I must contrive to stop them from coming any more to this house.' So one day, when the business manager had retired to rest, she appeared before him in visible shape.

'Who is that?' said he.

'It is I,' was the reply; 'the fairy who lives over the fourth gateway.' 'What brings you here?' 'You don't see what the merchant is doing. Heedless of his own future, he is drawing upon his resources, only to enrich the ascetic Gotama. He engages in no traffic; he undertakes no business. Advise the merchant to attend to his business, and arrange that the ascetic Gotama with his disciples shall come no more into the house.'

Then said he, 'Foolish Fairy, if the merchant does spend his money, he spends it on the Faith of the Buddha, which leads to

Salvation. Even if he were to seize me by the hair and sell me for a slave, I will say nothing. Begone!'

Another day, she went to the merchant's eldest son and gave him the same advice. And he flouted her in just the same manner. But to the merchant himself she did not so much as dare to speak on the matter.

Now by dint of unending munificence [228] and of doing no business, the merchant's incomings diminished and his estate grew less and less; so that he sank by degrees into poverty, and his table, his dress, and his bed and food were no longer what they had been. Yet, in spite of his altered circumstances, be continued to entertain the Brotherhood, though he was no longer able to feast them. So one day when he had made his bow and taken his seat, the Master said to him, 'Householder, are gifts being given at your house?' 'Yes, sir,' said he, 'but there's only a little sour husk-porridge, left over from yesterday.' 'Be not distressed, householder, at the thought that you can only offer what is unpalatable. If the heart be good, the food given to Buddhas, Pacceka Buddhas[1] and their disciples, cannot but be good too. And why? Because of the greatness of the fruit thereof. For he who can make his heart acceptable cannot give an unacceptable gift—as is to be testified by the following passage:

> For, if the heart have faith, no gift is small To Buddhas or to their disciples true.

'Tis said no service can be reckoned small that's paid to Buddhas, lords of great renown. Mark well what fruit rewarded that poor gift of pottage—dried-up, sour and lacking salt.'[2]

Also, he said this further thing, 'Householder, in giving this unpalatable gift, you are giving it to those who have entered on the Noble Eightfold Path. Whereas I, when in Velāma's time I stirred up all India by giving the seven things of price, and in my largesse poured then forth as though I had made into one mighty stream the five great rivers—I yet found none who had reached the Three Refuges or kept the Five Commandments: for rare are those who are worthy of offerings. Therefore, let not your heart be troubled by the thought that your gift is unpalatable.' And so saying, he repeated the Velāmaka Sutta.[3]

Now that fairy who had not dared to speak to the merchant in the days of his magnificence, thought that now he was poor he would hearken to her, and so, entering his chamber at dead of night she appeared before him in visible shape, standing in mid-air. 'Who's that?' said the merchant, when he became aware of her presence. 'I am the fairy, great merchant, who dwells over the fourth gateway.' 'What brings you here?' 'To give you counsel.' 'Proceed, then.' 'Great merchant, you take no thought for your own future or for your own children. You have expended vast sums on the Faith of the ascetic Gotama; in fact, by long-continued [229] expenditure and by not undertaking new business you have been brought by the ascetic Gotama to poverty. But even in your poverty you do not shake off the ascetic Gotama! The ascetics are in and out of your house this very day just the same! What they have had of you cannot be recovered. That may be taken for certain. But henceforth don't you go yourself to the ascetic Gotama and don't let his disciples set foot inside your house. Do not even turn to look at the ascetic Gotama but attend to your trade and traffic in order to restore the family estate.'

Then he said to her, 'Was this the counsel you wanted to give me?'

'Yes, it was.'

Said the merchant, 'The mighty Lord of Wisdom has made me proof against a hundred, a thousand, yea, against a hundred thousand fairies such as you are! My faith is strong and steadfast as Mount Sineru! My substance has been expended on the Faith that leads to Salvation. Wicked are your words; it is a blow aimed at the Faith of the Buddhas by you, you wicked and impudent witch. I cannot live under the same roof with you; be off at once from my house and seek shelter elsewhere!' Hearing these words of that converted man and elect disciple, she could not stay, but repairing to her dwelling, took her children by the hand and went forth. But though she went, she was minded, if she could not find herself a lodging elsewhere, to appease the merchant and return to dwell in his house; and in this mind she repaired to the tutelary deity of the city and with due salutation stood before him. Being asked what had brought her thither, she said, 'My lord, I have been speaking imprudently to Anāthapiṇḍika, and he in his anger has turned me out of my home. Take me to him and make it up between us, so that he may let me live there again.' 'But what was it you said to the merchant?' 'I told him for the future not to support the Buddha and the Order, and not to let the ascetic Gotama set foot again in his house. This is what I said, my lord.' 'Wicked were your words; it was a blow aimed at the Faith. I cannot take you with me to the merchant.' Meeting with no support from him, she went to the Four Great Regents of the world. And being repulsed by them in the same manner, she went on to Sakka, king of Devas, and told him her story, beseeching him still more earnestly, as follows, 'Deva, finding no shelter, I wander about homeless, leading my children by the hand. Grant me of your majesty some place wherein to dwell.'

And he too said to her, 'You have done wickedly; it was a blow aimed at the Conqueror's Faith. I cannot speak to the merchant on your behalf. But I can tell you one way [230] whereby the merchant may be led to pardon you.' 'Pray tell me, deva.' 'Men have had eighteen crore of the merchant on bonds. Take the semblance of his agent, and without telling anybody repair to their houses with the bonds, in the company of some young goblins. Stand in the middle of their houses with the bond in one hand and a receipt in the other, and terrify them with your goblin power, saying, 'Here's your acknowledgment of the debt. Our merchant did not move in the matter while he was affluent; but now he is poor, and you must pay up the money you owe.' By your goblin power obtain all those eighteen crore of gold and fill the merchant's empty treasuries. He had another treasure buried in the banks of the River Aciravatī, but when the bank was washed away, the treasure was swept into the sea. Get that back also by your supernatural power and store it in his treasuries. Further, there is another sum of eighteen crores lying unowned in such and such a place. Bring that too and pour the money into his empty treasuries. When you have atoned by the recovery of these fifty-four crore, ask the merchant to forgive you.' 'Very good, deva,' said she. And she set to work obediently, and did just as she had been bidden. When she had recovered all the money, she went into the merchant's chamber at dead of night and appeared before him in visible shape standing in the air.

The merchant asking who was there, she replied, 'It is I, great merchant, the blind and foolish fairy who lived over your fourth gateway. In the greatness of my infatuate folly I knew not the virtues of a Buddha, and so came to say what I said to you some days ago. Pardon me my fault! At the insistence of Sakka, king of Devas, I have made atonement by recovering the eighteen crore owed to you, the eighteen crore which had been washed down into the sea, and another eighteen crore which were lying unowned in such and such a place, making fifty-four crore in all, which I have poured into your empty treasure-chambers. The sum you expended on the Monastery at Jetavana is now made up again. Whilst I have nowhere to dwell, I am in misery. Bear not in mind what I did in my ignorant folly, great merchant, but pardon me.'

Anātha-piṇḍika, hearing what she said, thought to himself, 'She is a fairy, and she says she has atoned, and confesses her fault.

The Master shall consider this and make his virtues known to her. I will take her before the All-Enlightened Buddha.' So he said, 'My good fairy, if you want me to pardon you, ask me in the presence of the master.' 'Very good,' said she, 'I will. Take me along with you to the Master.' 'Certainly,' said he. And early in the morning, when night was just passing away, he took her with him to the Master and told the Blessed One all that she had done.

Hearing this, the Master said, 'You see, householder, how the sinful man regards sin [231] as excellent before it ripens to its fruit. But when it has ripened, then he sees sin to be sin. Likewise the good man looks on his goodness as sin before it ripens to its fruit; but when it ripens, he sees it to be goodness.' And so saying, he repeated these two stanzas from the Dhammapada:—

> The sinner thinks his sinful deed is good,
> So long as sin has ripened not to fruit.
> But when his sin at last to ripeness grows,
> The sinner surely sees ''twas sin I wrought.'
> The good man thinks his goodness is but sin,
> So long as it has ripened not to fruit.
> But when his goodness unto ripeness grows,
> The good man surely sees ''twas good I wrought.'[4]

At the close of these stanzas that fairy was established in the Fruit of the First Path. She fell at the Wheel-marked feet of the Master, crying, 'Stained as I was with passion, depraved by sin, misled by delusion and blinded by ignorance, I spoke wickedly because I knew not your virtues. Pardon me!' Then she received pardon from the Master and from the great merchant.

At this time Anātha-piṇḍika sang his own praises in the Master's presence, saying, 'Sir, though this fairy did her best to stop me from giving support to the Buddha and his following, she could not succeed; and though she tried to stop me from giving gifts, yet I gave them still! Was not this goodness on my part?'

Said the Master, 'You, householder, are a converted man and an elect disciple; your faith is firm and your vision is purified. No marvel then that you were not stopped by this impotent fairy. The marvel was that the wise and good of a bygone day, when a Buddha had not appeared, and when knowledge had not ripened to its full fruit, should from the heart of a lotus-flower have given gifts, although Māra, lord of the Realm of Lusts, appeared in mid-heaven, shouting, 'If you give gifts, you shall be roasted in this hell and showing them therewithal a pit eighty cubits deep, filled with red-hot embers.' And so saying, at the request of Anātha-piṇḍika, he told this story of the past.

Once on a time when Brahmadatta was reigning in Benares, the Bodhisatta came to life in the family of the Lord High Treasurer of Benares, and was brought up in the lap of all luxury like a royal prince. By the time he was come to years of discretion, being barely sixteen years old, he had made himself perfect in all accomplishments. At his father's death he filled the office of Lord High Treasurer and built six almonries one at each of the four gates of the city, one in the centre of the city, and one at the gate of his own mansion. Very bountiful was he [232], and he kept the commandments and observed the fast-day duties.

Now one day at breakfast-time when dainty fare of exquisite taste and variety was being brought in for the Bodhisatta, a Pacceka Buddha rising from a seven days' trance of mystic ecstasy, and noticing that it was time to go his rounds, bethought him that it would be well to visit the Treasurer of Benares that morning. So he cleaned his teeth with a tooth-stick made from the betel-vine, washed his mouth with water from Lake Anotatta, put on his under-cloth as he stood on the tableland of Manosilā, fastened on his girdle, donned his outer-cloth, and, equipped with a bowl which he called into being for the purpose, he passed through the air and arrived at the gate of the mansion just as the Bodhisatta's breakfast was taken in.

As soon as the Bodhisatta became aware of his presence there, he rose at once from his seat and looked at the attendant, indicating that a service was required. 'What am I to do, my lord?' 'Bring his reverence's bowl,' said the Bodhisatta.

At that very instant Māra the Wicked rose up in a state of great excitement, saying, 'It is seven days since the Pacceka Buddha had food given him; if he gets none today, he will perish. I will destroy him and stop the Treasurer too from giving.' And that very instant he went and called into being within the mansion a pit of red-hot embers, eighty cubits deep, filled with Acacia-charcoal, all ablaze and aflame like the great hell of Avīci. When he had created this pit, Māra himself took his stand in mid-air.

When the man who was on his way to fetch the bowl became aware of this, he was terrified and started back. 'What makes you start back, my man?' asked the Bodhisatta. 'My lord,' was the answer, 'there's a great pit of red-hot embers blazing and flaming in the middle of the house.' And as man after man got to the spot, they all were panic-stricken, and ran away as fast as their legs would carry them.

Thought the Bodhisatta to himself, 'Māra, the Enthraller, must have been exerting himself today to stop me from alms-giving. I have yet to learn, however, that I am to be shaken by a hundred, or by a thousand, Maras. We will see this day whose strength is the stronger, whose might is the mightier, mine or Māra's.' So taking in his own hand the bowl which stood ready, he passed out from the house and, standing on the brink of the fiery pit, looked up to the heavens.

Seeing Māra, he said, 'Who are you?' 'I am Mara,' was the answer.

'Did you call into being this pit of red-hot embers?' 'Yes, I did.' [233] 'Why?' 'To stop you from alms-giving and to destroy the life of that Pacceka Buddha.' 'I will not permit you either to stop me from my alms-giving or to destroy the life of the Pacceka Buddha. I am going to see today whether your strength or mine is the greater.' And still standing on the brink of that fiery pit, he cried, 'Reverend Pacceka Buddha, even though I be in act to fall headlong into this pit of red-hot embers, I will not turn back. Only vouchsafe to take the food I bring.' And so saying he repeated this stanza:

> Far rather will I headlong plunge amain Full in this gulf of hell, than stoop to shame! Vouchsafe, sir, at my hands to take this alms!

With these words the Bodhisatta, grasping the bowl of food, strode on with undaunted resolution right on to the surface of the pit of fire. But even as he did so, there rose up to the surface through all the eighty cubits of the pit's depth a large and peerless lotus-flower, which received the feet of the Bodhisatta! And from it there came a measure of pollen which fell on the head of the Great Being, so that his whole body was as it were sprinkled from head to foot with dust of gold! Standing right in the heart of the lotus, he poured the dainty food into the bowl of the Pacceka Buddha.

And when the latter had taken the food and returned thanks, he flung his bowl aloft into the heavens, and right in the sight of all the people he himself rose bodily into the air likewise, and passed away to the Himalayas again, seeming to tread a track formed of clouds fantastically shaped.

And Māra, too, defeated and dejected, passed away back to his own abode.

But the Bodhisatta, still standing in the lotus, preached [234] the Truth to the people, extolling alms-giving and the commandments; after which, girt round by the escorting multitude, he passed into his own mansion once more. And all his life long he shewed charity and did other good works, till in the end he passed away to fare according to his deserts.

Said the Master, 'It was no marvel, layman, that you, with your discernment of the truth, were not overcome now by the fairy; the real marvel was what the wise and good did in bygone days.' His lesson ended, the Master shewed the connexion and identified the Birth by saying, 'The Pacceka Buddha of those days passed away, never to be born again. I was myself the Treasurer of Benares who, defeating Mara, and standing in the heart of the lotus, placed alms in the bowl of the Pacceka Buddha.'

NOTES

[1]: All Buddhas have attained to complete illumination; but a Pacceka Buddha keeps his knowledge to himself and, unlike a 'Perfect Buddha', does not preach the saving truth to his fellow men.
[2]: The first two lines are from the Vimāna-vatthu, page 44.
[3]: This Sutta is referred to on page 234 of the Sumaṅgala-Vilāsinī, but is otherwise unknown as yet to European scholars.
[4]: The verses are nos 119 and 120 in the Dhammapada.

22

GAJALAKSHMI

NIHARIKA K. SANKRITYAYAN

Introduction

LAKSHMI OR SHRI Lakshmi is the goddess of fortune, abundance and agricultural prosperity. She is worshipped in every Hindu house for the prosperity and welfare of the whole family. It appears that in the earliest literature, Lakshmi and Shri were different goddesses. In the Shri Sukta hymn, which is part of a later *khila* or supplement of the Rig Veda, they are mentioned separately.* The Vajasaneyi Samhita mentions these two goddesses as the wives of Aditya, the solar deity. In the Buddhist Jatakas, Lakshmi is known as Lakkhi, the daughter of Shakra and as the goddess of *parivara sampati* (family property) and *panna* (wisdom). The word Shri is used in the Rig Veda in the sense of plenitude and not as a deity. The term Shri is mentioned as benefit,

* J. Gonda, *Aspects of Early Vishnuism*, Utrecht, 1954, p. 176.

advantage, prosperity and well-being. These qualities ascribed to Shri eventually relate her to the later goddess Shri Lakshmi. Shri also suggests capability, and power along with beauty, lustre and high rank. The term is particularly used in later Vedic literature to address royal power and dominion of the king.*

The Shri Sukta hymn provides the primary conceptualization of the goddess Lakshmi:

Om Hiraṇyavarṇām Hariṇīm
Suvarṇarajatasrajām
Candrām Hiraṇmayīm Lakṣmim Jātavedo Ma
Ā Vaha (SS, verse 1)

The verses mean: the one who knows the Vedas, Agni, is prayed to bring Lakshmi—who is described as being golden in colour, dressed in golden-coloured garments, adorned with glittering gold and silver ornaments, and shining with the lustre of the moon—to the worshipper. This in a way establishes the association of Lakshmi with beauty and effulgence.

An important feature of Shri in the Shri Sukta hymn is her association with fertility, a feature that was not necessarily emphasized in earlier usages of the term Shri in Vedic literature.† In the Shri Sukta she is described as moist, perceptible through odour, abundant in harvest and dwelling in cow dung, which is essentially manure. Her son is said to be Kardama, which means mud.‡ Shri is thus clearly associated with growth and the fecundity of moist, rich soil. From the hymns, it also appears that

* David Kinsley, *Hindu Goddesses Visions of the Divine Feminine in the Hindu Religious Tradition*, Motilal Banarsidass, Delhi, 1987, p.18.

† S.K. Gupta, *Elephants in Indian Art and Mythology,* Abhinav Publications, New Delhi, 1983, p. 19.

‡ David Kinsley, *Hindu Goddesses Visions of the Divine Feminine in the Hindu Religious Tradition*, p. 20.

Shri was the tutelary goddess of a primarily agrarian people. A late Sanskrit text, the Nilamata Purana, prescribes the worship of Shri in the form of cow dung cakes. In the references made to Shri, particularly in the Shri Sukta, cattle is mentioned as wealth.

In the Atharva Veda we come across the use of the term Shri differently. The proclamation of victory in war through the beating of drums distributes Shri:

Śreyo Vanvāno*

Shri is connected with *bhuti* which means growth, thriving and material prosperity. Mother earth is invoked to make the sacrifice well established in Shri and bhuti.† In the Brahmanas, the concept of Shri has wider meanings. Shri is identified with different concepts like *prajā* (offspring), *anna* (food), *kṣatra* (ruling power, etc.).‡ In the Buddhist Jataka stories, there is mention of Siri Devi in association with the god Shakra. This is significant as Shakra is none other than Indra, the lord of the heavens. Shri according to other Buddhist mythology is also described as Naga king's daughter who is Sagara, the sea.

The earliest myth concerning to Lakshmi relates her to the churning of the primordial waters (Fig. 1). It is mentioned in the *Udyoga Parva* of the Mahabharata (verse 5, 102) that the gods united with the asuras to churn the waters of the cosmic ocean. In this endeavour, they used the Mandara mountain as their pole and the serpent Vasuki as their rope. As a result of the churning, they obtained the wine called Varuni, the goddess Lakshmi, nectar or amrita, the prince of steeds called Uchchaihshravah and the prince of gems, Kaustubha. The products that came out of the churning symbolize all that is essential for the perpetuation of life,

* Artharva Veda (5, 20, 9).

† AV (12, 1, 6, 3).

‡ Upendra Nath Dhal, *Goddess Lakshmi: Origin and Development*, Oriental Publishers and Distributors, New Delhi, 1978, pp. 23–4.

irrespective of whether they are categorized as 'good' or 'bad'. The development of Lakshmi in the sense of prosperity and well-being can be connected with *lakshma*, meaning symbol. The signs that bring fortune are designated as *punya Lakshmi*; but the signs that bring misfortune and misery are designated as *papi Lakshmi*.

Courtesy: Author

Figure 1: Churning of the ocean (Samudramanthan), temple pillar, Mallikarjuna temple, Pattadakal.

Symbols

The hymn to Shri also mentions two objects that come to be consistently associated with Shri. These are the lotus and the elephant. She is seated on a lotus, is of the colour of a lotus, appears like a lotus, is covered with lotuses and wears a garland of lotuses. Throughout her narration, Shri-Lakshmi is often called Padma and Kamala, 'lotus'. The popularity of the lotus in Indian art and iconography, both Buddhist and Brahmanical, suggests a complex and multivalent meaning associated with the lotus.

One of the most popular and standard depictions of Shri-Lakshmi shows her flanked by two elephants in the so-called Gaja-Lakshmi images (Fig. 2). In this particular image of Lakshmi, where she is flanked by elephants who pour pots of water on her, is an act of performing *abhisheka*. This act is vital to constituting and reaffirming regal power. Significantly, the goddesses' association with royal power is emphasized by her abhisheka and it is the beneficent king who brings plenty and opulence, thus highlighting the association between kingship and fertility.*

It is interesting to note that of all living animals, elephants were selected to be portrayed with Goddess Lakshmi in this fashion. Elephants are the largest of all animals and are found in Africa and parts of South and South-East Asia. Their association with power can be attributed to their gigantic size. In the Ramayana, the celestial elephant Airavata is described as *chaturdanta* with four tusks:

Chaturdantam mahāgajam āruḍhas śailasaṅkāśam

Figure 2: Gaja-Lakshmi, temple pillar, Lad Khan temple, Aihole.

* R. Mahalakshmi, *The Book of Lakshmi*, Penguin, New Delhi, 2009, p. 88.

The elephants exhibit two related meanings. According to Sanskrit tradition, the first elephants had wings and flew about the sky. It is also suggested that these were clouds and showered the earth with rain.[*] The association of elephants with clouds and rain paved the ground for the development of a cult around Airavata.[†] On an occasion these elephants were cursed by a sage when they landed on a tree under which he was meditating and broke his concentration. As a result, the elephants were cursed to remain on land and were stripped of their wings. Elephant's association with rain is an important factor in an agrarian economy. Along with this, the elephants in images of Shri-Lakshmi reinforce her association with the fertility of crops and the sap of existence.[‡]

In mythology, elephants are celebrated as a symbol of royal authority and the lord of the heavens Indra is seated on the white elephant Airavata. The bull and elephant being symbolic of *srestha* or the best of any kind, were often associated with royalty.[§] The elephant represents the cloud that bathes the goddess of prosperity, Shri.

Elephants also suggest royal authority as kings in ancient India kept a stable of elephants, which formed their heavy artillery in military campaigns. Kings often travelled on elephants in ceremonial processions associated with regal power. Kings in ancient India were also believed to be responsible for rain and the fertility of crops.[¶] Jan Gonda culls out information from texts like the Mahabharata and the Jatakas and suggests that where there is

---

[*] Pratapaditya Pal, *Elephants and Ivories in South Asia*, Los Angeles County Museum of Art, California, 1981, p. 25.

[†] S.K. Gupta, *Elephants in Indian Art and Mythology*, p. 11.

[‡] David Kinsley, *Hindu Goddesses Visions of the Divine Feminine in the Hindu Religious Tradition*, p. 22.

[§] C. Sivaramamurti, *Shri Lakshmi in Indian Art and Thought*, Kanak Publications, New Delhi, 1982, pp. 66–7.

[¶] Jan Gonda, *Ancient Indian Kingship from the Religious Point of View*, E.J. Brill, Leiden, 1969, pp. 7–8.

no king rain will not descend. Even if the king transgresses from dharma in any respect whether ritual or moral, or if his *purohita* makes a mistake, rain can simply cease.* It became important for the kings to maintain several elephants as a sign of their power, strength and ability to bring fertilizing rains in their territory. The association of elephants with Shri is stated in the Mahabharata that she lives in '*kumaris*', sacrifices, rain clouds, lakes filled with lotus flowers, royal thrones and also in elephants.† This association with Shri has made the elephant a symbol of life and generative force as well as of prosperity and abundance.

On the other hand, if we look at the Jataka stories, they reproduce some commonly held enriching insights about the elephant. In one Jataka tale, a noble elephant offers his son to some carpenters who removed a splinter from his foot. His son was later bought by the king of Benares, who uses him in a battle against a neighbouring king. The king dies in the battle but his infant heir is protected by the elephant. What is striking about the tale is all those who are touched by the lives of the elephant duo are blessed with enormous wealth and happiness and the animal's nobility attracts the king to him.‡

It has been suggested by scholars that Gaja-Lakshmi was a favourite deity of the merchant community.§ A possible reason could be to save their boats from sinking in the sea and to avoid natural calamities. As in most of the representations of the goddess, she is either shown standing or seated on a lotus. There is also a vessel, *pūrṇa-ghaṭa*, a symbol of prosperity and abundance. It appears that these elephants, pūrṇa-ghaṭa and water indicate clouds and rain.¶

---

* Ibid.

† S.K. Gupta, *Elephants in Indian Art and Mythology,* p. 20.

‡ Mahalakskmi, *The Book of Lakshmi,* p. 89.

§ Niranjan Ghosh, *Concept and Iconography of the Goddess of Abundance and Fortune in Three Religions of India,* The University of Burdwan, Burdwan, 1979, p. 75.

¶ Ibid., p. 76.

Iconography of Gajalakshmi

Elephants are crucial to the Brahmanical pantheon in many ways. Elephants have always been popular and auspicious motifs in the arts of South Asia (Fig. 3).* Some of the finest elephant images surviving from antiquity were rendered in terracotta. Many were votive objects and perhaps were offered to a village deity. In both Sri Lanka and India, elephants are often depicted in a row along the plinth of the temple. Thus, apart from demonstrating the strength and magnificence of the temples, they also symbolize the cosmic character of the shrine since elephants are symbols of the four directions.

Courtesy: Author

Figure 3: Elephants on the basement moulding of Virupaksha temple, Pattadakal.

Images of Lakshmi, mostly accompanied by elephants on either side, are often found on the lintels of temples, doors and gateways across the subcontinent; for example, on the railing of the Bharhut stupa and on the Sanchi gateways. The four images of Shri at

---

* Patapaditya Pal, *Elephants and Ivories in South Asia,* p. 29.

Bharhut are referred to as Sirima Devata. A railing pillar image shows the standing figure of the goddess in the centre of a circle, flanked by an elephant on either side.

The goddess Gaja-Lakshmi is also represented on the Gupta seals from Basrah, Bhita and Rajghat. In many temples of Odisha, the motif of Gaja-Lakshmi is carved in the centre of the architrave over the doorway of the main structure irrespective of the cult affiliation of the shrines. Gaja-Lakshmi is depicted seated on a lotus and is being bathed by the elephants in the Kailasa temple, Ellora. The most important characteristics of the relief are the two Nagas below the lotus seat of the goddess. A spectacular image of the goddess being anointed by elephants is seen in the Mahabalipuram temples built by the Pallavas.

The religious monuments of the Chalukyas in the western Deccan are of outstanding interest for their transition from cutting into rock to free-standing construction, as well as for their range of distinctive architectural styles. One of the significant aspects of the religious history of early medieval south India is the emergence of the temples dedicated to the two Agamic deities, Śiva and Viṣṇu.* The image of Shri as Gaja-Lakshmi is uniquely carved on the lintels of the temples built by the Chalukyas. Along with the images of Shri-Lakshmi and Gaja-Lakshmi, images of Vishnu and Indra are carved. Shri-Lakshmi is depicted in both structural and cave temples. Cave three at Badami is occupied with a majestic Vaikuntha Narayana relief. Vishnu is seated in 'royal ease' on the coils of the cosmic serpent, Ananta, whose hood of five cobra heads protects him. A *nagini* stands on either side, while Garuda is seated. Goddess Shri-Lakshmi is seated to his left (Fig. 4). Vishnu's royal nature is significantly associated with Shri. By the early medieval period, Vishnu is considered the divine king, dwelling in a heavenly

* Kesavan Veluthat, *The Early Medieval in South India*, OUP, New Delhi, 2009, p. 62.

court, Vaikuntha. Vishnu is present wherever righteous kings rule and maintain order. [*] In the representation of Shri as Vishnu's consort, she is shown standing or sitting, to his right, with her left hand holding a lotus and the right hand in the boon-giving posture or *varada-mudra.*[†] Upon righteous rulers she bestows power, prosperity and fertility. This perhaps is the reason for the portrayal of Shri-Lakshmi with Vishnu in Chalukya temples. The main task of the Chalukya rulers was to reflect the existing social order and recreate a parallel world of authority in the realm of religion that would help them in legitimizing the authority. The Bhogāsana form of Vishnu in Badami cave three can be seen as a reinforcement of the image of the Chalukya king and his consorts.

Courtesy: Author

Figure 4: Vishnu with Goddess Lakshmi seated to his left, cave 3, Badami.

---

[*] J. Gonda, *Aspects of Early Vishnuism,* pp. 164–67.

[†] R. Mahalakshmi, *The Book of Lakshmi*, p. 100.

To the south of Aihole, close to the Malaprabha River in the Ramalinga temple group, is a small temple (Fig. 5) dedicated to the goddess Shri in the form of a lotus flower. The lotus is 31 square inches and originally may have been raised on a *pitha* or pedestal in the sanctum, which is now empty. The proximity to the river is significant to the lotus goddess and the temple is unusually oriented to the west in order to face the water.

Courtesy: Author

Figure 5: The Ramalinga temple group, Aihole.

Another temple called Gauda at Aihole has yielded an inscription referring to Goddess Bhagavati. On a crossbeam is an inscription that records the gift of land by the Five Hundred Mahajanas of Aryapura (Aihole), eight Nagaras and one hundred Uralis to Goddess Durga Bhagavati.* It is significant to note that the Five Hundred Mahajanas, which may have been a guild or a governing

* *SII,* Vol. 15, No. 463, p. 342.

group or both, also inscribed the Lad Khan temple.* Durga is the mother goddess and Bhagavati is the feminine form of Bhagavat, or Vishnu, so that the temple dedication and the gift of land were made to Shri, who was beloved of the Chalukya kings. The garbhagriha or sanctum is extraordinary. At the top centre of the doorway above Garuda is Gaja-Lakshmi, or Shri, the dedication of the temple being to the goddess. She holds two lotuses and is seated on a large lotus. Two elephants bathe her from *lotas* or pots held in their trunks. Although the sanctum is now empty, it has been suggested by scholars that a rectangular shape was best for the sanctum of a goddess temple.†

In the Suryanarayana temple at Aihole, only two fragments of ceiling panels from the mandapa survive, one with a central lotus with a rosette border, the other with a diagonal banding. An unusual image of Shiva is carved on the west quadrant, to the right of which is an image of an elephant Similarly in the Lad Khan temple at Aihole, the image of Gaja-Lakshmi is found in one of twelve porch pillars.

A group of four temples at Aihole is called the Konti. Of the four temples, Sarangi matha is on the southeast of the quadrant and is not aligned with the others. An inscribed slab was uncovered at the north-western temple (Fig. 6). It is carved with Gaja-Lakshmi on top and four clear lines of inscriptions below, and another inscription lower down.‡ The style of the Gaja-Lakshmi, is unique to Sarangi matha. The inscription records grants, coins, taxes and fines on festivals, given by the Mahajanas of Aihole. This is the same group that dedicated the Durga Bhagavati (Gauda) temple

---

* Meera Abraham, *Two Medieval Merchant Guilds of South India*, Motilal Banarsidas, Delhi, 1988, pp. 41–68.

† J.C. Harle, 'Three Types of Walls in Early Western Chalukya Temples', *Oriental Art*, Vol. 17, No. 1, 1971, p. 54, note 7.

‡ S.R. Rao, 'A Note on the Chronology of the Early Western Chalukya Temple', *Lalit Kala*, Vol. 15, 1972, p. 15.

and inscribed the Lad Khan east wall. It is suggestive of their active participation in temple patronage around the late seventh and early eighth centuries.

Courtesy: Author

Figure 6: Inscribed slab with Gaja-Lakshmi on top, Sarangi matha, Aihole.

Images of Gaja-Lakshmi appear in temples situated on the outskirts of Badami (Fig. 7). These images are strategically carved on the door lintel. It is interesting that the temples that have yielded the images of Gaja-Lakshmi have also yielded images of Lajja-Gauri and Saptamatrikas, which are predominantly fertility goddesses.

Courtesy: Author

Figure 7: Gaja-Lakshmi on the door, Badami-Mahakuta Road.

Siddhanakolla is an isolated site situated south of Aihole, famous for its association with the fertility cult and houses Lakulisha temple and two sub-shrines. One is structural and houses the Saptamatrikas and the other is a natural Aditi/Lajja Gauri shrine. The image of Gaja-Lakshmi is carved on the door lintel (Fig. 8). The images found at Siddhanakolla revolve around the symbolism of procreation represented by Lakulisha, Lajja-Gauri, Daksha and the Saptamatrikas.

Courtesy: Author

Figure 8: Gaja-Lakshmi on the door of Shiva temple, Siddhanakolla.

It thus appears that the goddess cults occupied a very significant place in the sacred geography of the Malaprabha valley from ancient times. From the medieval period, small shrines were dedicated to the goddess, especially Lajja Gauri, Saptamatrikas and Shri-Lakshmi.* The majority of the temples of the goddess were located outside the major sites of Badami, Aihole and Mahakuta. A significant aspect of the iconography of Shri in the Chalukya landscape is the presence of Shri-Lakshmi with Vishnu in the temples. As kings cannot rule without the authority that is bestowed by Shri, her presence makes the royal authority stronger and her absence makes it weak and ineffective. The association of Shri with Vishnu, the supreme divine king as her husband, is therefore appropriate. Her presence as Gaja-Lakshmi in the sculptures is unique to Aihole of all the Chalukya sites and nearby fertility shrines.

Bibliography

Abraham, Meera, *Two Medieval Merchant Guilds of South India*, Motilal Banarsidass, Delhi, 1988.

Buitenen, J.A.B. van, *The Mahabharata,* The University of Chicago Press, Chicago, 1980.

Dhal, Upendra Nath, *Goddess Lakshmi: Origin and Development,* Oriental Publishers and Distributors, New Delhi, 1978.

Ghosh, Niranjan, *Concept and Iconography of the Goddess of Abundance and Fortune in Three Religions of India,* The University of Burdwan, Burdwan, 1979.

---

* For a detailed study on Lajja Gauri, Yellamma and Saptamatrikas, see Niharika K. Sankrityayan, *Structures of Patronage, Social Transactions and Sacred Landscape: Brahmanical Iconography in the Western Deccan c. 550–750 CE,* unpublished Phd thesis, Centre for Historical Studies, Jawaharlal Nehru University, New Delhi, 2014.

Gonda, Jon, *Ancient Indian Kingship from the Religious Point of View*, E.J. Brill, Leiden, 1969.

Gonda, Jon, *Aspects of Early Vishnuism*, Utrecht, 1954.

Gupta, S.K., *Elephants in Indian Art and Mythology,* Abhinav Publications, New Delhi, 1983.

Harle, J.C., 'Three Types of Walls in Early Western Chalukya Temples', *Oriental Art*, Vol. 17, No. 1, 1971.

Kinsley, David, *Hindu Goddesses Visions of the Divine Feminine in the Hindu Religious Tradition*, Motilal Banarsidass, Delhi, 1987.

Mahalakshmi, R., *The Book of Lakshmi*, Penguin, New Delhi, 2009.

Pal, Pratapaditya, *Elephants and Ivories in South Asia*, Los Angeles County Museum of Art, California, 1981.

Rao, S.R., 'A Note on the Chronology of the Early Western Chalukya Temple', *Lalit Kala*, Vol. 15, 1972.

Sankrityayan, Niharika K., *Structures of Patronage, Social Transactions and Sacred Landscape: Brahmanical Iconography in the Western Deccan c. 550–750 CE,* unpublished PhD thesis, Centre for Historical Studies, Jawaharlal Nehru University, New Delhi, 2014.

SII, Vol. 15, No. 463.

Sivaramamurti, C., *Shri-Lakshmi in Indian Art and Thought,* Kanak Publications, New Delhi, 1982.

Sontakke, N.S., Kasikar, C.G. and others ed., *Rg Veda Samhita with the Commentary of Sayanacarya,* 5 volumes, Vaidika Samsodhana Mandal, Poona, 1933–51.

Veluthat, Kesavan, *The Early Medieval in South India*, OUP, New Delhi, 2009.

Whitney, W.D. and Lanman, C.R., *Artharva Veda Samhita,* 2 volumes, Harvard Oriental Series 7–8, Cam-Mass, 1905.

23

THE FORM OF GODDESS LAKSHMI[*]

TRANSLATED BY ALKA TYAGI

Vajra said:

O promoter of the Bhṛgu race! Speak to me of the form of Lakṣmi, the mother of the entire universe and consort of the great Lord Viṣhṇu. (1)

Mārkaṇḍeya said:

O king! Near Hari, Lakṣmi should be depicted in her divine form with two arms carrying lotuses in hands and embellished with all the ornaments. (2)

The golden-hued goddess should be clad in white garments with a beauty unrivalled on earth. Separately, the goddess should be presented with four arms, sitting on an auspicious throne. (3)

[*] *Vishnudharmottara Purana*, Chapter 82.

O fortunate one! Her throne should be a lotus with beautiful pericarp surrounded with eight-fold petals. (4)

O strong armed one, the goddess should be seated like Vinayaka and the stalk of her auspicious lotus should be made long. (5)

Her right hand should be near the armlet and the left hand, O king, should carry a beautiful pot of nectar. (6)

The other two hands, O king, should carry conch and the holy fruit bilva. Behind her, a pair of elephants should be shown pouring contents from two pots. (7)

Make a gorgeous lotus over the head of the goddess. Know it to be good fortune and the conch prosperity. (8)

Bilva is the sign of universe and nectar is the essence of water. O the best of the twice born, know the lotus in Lakṣmi's hand as magnificence. (9)

Consider the two elephants as reservoirs of treasures of conch and lotus. Or represent her standing tall holding conch and lotus in her hands. (10)

Gloriously standing on a lotus, the graceful one (goddess) should be shown shining like the inner glory of a lotus. With two arms and charming limbs, she is adorned with all jewels and ornaments. (11)

Make two bright Vidyādharas flying over her head adorned by the crown. (12)

Their right hands should touch the head. Holding swords in other hands, they should be eagerly looking at the goddess. (13)

Rājaśri, Svargalakṣmī, Brāhmīlakṣmī and Jayalakṣmī should be made near the goddess. (14) All the Lakṣmis should be of beautiful forms and well adorned. (15)

The lotus on which Lakṣmi stands, know it to be Keśava, O noble king, as without making the Madhusudana with her, she, the mother of the universe, doesn't stay even for a moment. (16)

Thus, the chapter named as 'Lakṣmī-rūpa-nirmāṇa' (Making the Image of Lakṣmi) in the *Vajra- Mārkaṇḍeya* dialogue in the *Viṣṇudharmottara-Puraṇa* is completed.

24

LAKSHMI: THE BRAND RHETORIC

MALASHRI LAL

NEXT TIME YOU encounter a Lakmé shop selling 'absolute perfect radiance skin-brightening crème' and other such products, remember Goddess Lakshmi as the inspiration behind the first indigenous cosmetic brand name in independent India. Lakshmi and Lakmé are inseparable. After Independence in 1947, when Indian industry was struggling to establish a stable economy, the prime minister and his cabinet realized that Indian women were spending precious foreign exchange on buying expensive, imported beauty-care items. Pandit Jawaharlal Nehru approached industrialist Jehangir Ratanji Dadabhoy Tata for a solution.* The seeds were sown for an Indian brand of cosmetics that could woo women away from 'foreign goods' by promising the same results and at a much lower price.

* Sukriti Vats, 'From Lakshmi to Lakmé—Story of India's First Cosmetic Brand, Envisioned by PM Nehru', Print, 12 June 2022.

While the oils and potions were being developed in association with a French team, the quest for a name began. The initial suggestion of 'Lakshmi Beauty Products' wasn't sassy enough—and French collaborators Robert Piguet and Renoir came up brilliantly with 'Lakmé' which was a French version of the goddess's name. The French link endured steadily as Simone Tata, the wife of Naval H. Tata, joined Lakmé as its managing director in 1961 and rose to become the chairperson in 1982.

Today, Lakmé products are exported to more than seventy countries worldwide, and Goddess Lakshmi must surely be amused because the colonialist vision of India has been replaced with admiration for Indian modernity. The name 'Lakmé' to Indian women in the 1950s denoted a conjoining of East and West—exotic yet local, seductive yet modest. When the cosmetic brand Lakmé launched in India in 1952, its tagline was: 'If colour be to beauty what music is to mood, play on.' Shyamoli Verma, India's first supermodel, endorsed the brand by displaying traditional Indian clothes and classical instruments with a gorgeous makeover of Indian skin, lips and eyes. Goddess Lakshmi must have smiled with indulgence as her French protégée Lakmé continued on a steady run of commercial success.

Linking Lakshmi to Lakmé was no arbitrary spin. According to historical sources, '*Lakmé* was an opera written by Léo Delibes, a French Romantic composer, set to a French libretto by Edmond Gondinet and Philippe Gille, and was first performed in 1883 at the Opéra-Comique in Paris.'* In the story, Lakmé is the daughter of a Brahmin priest who falls in love with Gerald, an officer in the British Army in India. While he wishes to rescue her from the authoritarianism of her father, he is also committed to his own country and career. The opera, which was popular then, and surprisingly continues to be performed occasionally—

* https://mapacademy.io

such as in 2012 in Australia—is replete with mysterious rituals and stage artefacts, and the singers are dressed in excessive jewels and elaborate headdresses. Clearly, the storyline and the staging details demonstrate allegiance to the popular orientalism of the 1880s where the 'gaze' was trained ambiguously at the marvels of the East. It suggests 'the White man's burden' on one hand and gestures towards an attractive nativism on the other.

Much has changed with the evolution of independent India but the brand value of Goddess Lakshmi has endured. The Government of India's welfare schemes for the girl child have often used the lure of Lakshmi's name to convince parents from deprived backgrounds to register for the benefits. Largely a consequence of census figures that repeatedly showed an adverse sex ratio, indicating that girls were subjected to foeticide and possibly infanticide in many parts of the country, these schemes started appearing in 2008 and have continued till now in some form or other.

The Dhanalakshmi Scheme, launched on 3 March 2008 by the Ministry of Women and Child Development, was a 'conditional cash transfer' for the girl child. The aim of the scheme was to value the life of a girl child and not treat her as a liability. It attempted to stop child marriage, encourage education and cover medical expenses. Parents were offered an attractive insurance for keeping their daughters safe.* In terms of popular understanding, Lakshmi is the goddess of wealth. By linking the birth of a girl child to this aspiration for prosperity, the public rhetoric hoped to convince parents that the child brought material assets with her to ensure her nurture, and that her well-being would help the family too. The basis was monetary as the cash transfers were linked to signposts such as birth registration, immunization, school enrolment and attaining the age of eighteen. A substantial insurance of Rs 1 lakh

---

* https://vikaspedia.in

would be granted at that point.* Since monitoring such a scheme was an astounding task, reports showed a large number of roadblocks mentioned by implementing agencies as well as potential beneficiaries.

The original Dhanalakshmi Scheme is no longer available and has been recast in new programmes such as Beti Bachao Beti Padhao, started on 22 January 2015. From the point of view of mythological interpretation, one is glad to see the shift away from monetary incentives in the name of Lakshmi to a more holistic view of empowering the girl child through education. Moreover, the patriarchal norm of marriage as the ultimate goal by which to judge the survival and wellness of a girl child ought to be cast away.

I read of a success story from the village of Badasahara in Odisha. Thirteen-year-old Mamina (name changed) wanted to continue her studies in school but her destitute parents, surviving on a family income of Rs 3000 a month, wanted her to marry a man aged forty. Somehow, word reached a child protection officer, who took the case to the appropriate authorities. The entire village was called to gather and Mamina declared her determination to study to everyone. The father had no choice but to make a public commitment to allow her education to continue.†

Lakshmi is a goddess who has deep cultural connotations. In Bengal, the words 'Lokkhi' (Lakshmi) and 'Alokkhi' are commonly used for 'good girl' and 'unruly girl'. In August 2021, the Lakshmir Bhandar scheme was started by the government of West Bengal to ensure monthly, basic income support to the

---

* https://india.unfpa.org/sites/default/files/pub-pdf/UNFPA_PolicyBrief_07-04-20166pm.pdf

† 'Success Stories and Progress Report: Beti Bachao Beti Padhao', Nayagarh, Odisha, https://wcd.odisha.gov.in/sites/default/files/202106/doc20170729_130918%20%281%29.pdf

women heads of 1.6 crore households. The following year, the scheme won the SKOCH award in the category of 'women and child development'. Under this programme, the government provides Rs 500 per month to general category families and Rs 1000 to SC/ST families, but it is specific to women-headed households, thereby showing that financial control gives dignity to women and works better than doles for the girl child.

A lovely story doing the rounds is of Dipali Santra, who used the Lakshmir Bhandar money to start a florist's shop in Patulia, School Para, Khardah. Her husband is a helper while their son buys flowers from the wholesale market. Dipali strings garlands and deftly arranges bouquets. Hibiscus and marigold are in high demand as offerings to deities. Goddess Lakshmi has indeed smiled upon Dipali and lifted the family out of poverty.*

Far away from Bengal, the Bhagyalaxmi Scheme was created in Karnataka in 2006. It is said that the prime goal of the Karnataka government was to promote the birth of girl children in below-poverty-line (BPL) households and to raise the status of the girl child in the family in particular and society in general. Financial assistance is provided to the girl child through her mother, father or natural guardian subject to the fulfilment of certain conditions.† According to an evaluation report in 2016, 85.5 per cent respondents believed that there was a changed attitude towards girls and they were no longer considered a burden.‡

In yet another part of India, the Ladli Laxmi Yojana was introduced by the Government of Madhya Pradesh in 2007. According to a news report in the *Pioneer* on 8 February 2023,

---

* *Get Bengal*, 14 July 2022.

† Bhagyalaxmi Scheme of Karnataka, Vikaspedia.

‡ 'Evaluation of the Performance of Bhagyalakshmi Scheme in Karnataka State in the Period 2010–11 to 2015–16', Karnataka Evaluation Authority, Government of Karnataka, April 2019.

the chief minister said that the Ladli Laxmi Yojana had proved to be a scheme that changed the lives of the daughters of the state. It was proclaimed, 'With the implementation of the scheme, not only did the girls get scholarship amounts, but a new era of their empowerment has started. With the expansion of the scheme, now the government will also do the work of depositing fees for higher education in Ladli Laxmi 2.0.' A programme held in Bhopal on 7 February 2023 invited a large number of the beneficiaries to the stage and some talked of their journey from destitution to sustainability. The *Bharat Express* cites Sulochana Sahu narrating how she worked in a sewing factory in adverse circumstances and raised two daughters. Both girls have now received the benefits of the Ladli Lakshmi Yojana. Sulochana mentioned the family's story of calamity in highly charged terms, standing as an epitome for what welfare schemes can achieve in bringing about desirable social change.

Finally, one may ask why the name of Goddess Lakshmi is so resonant in each of these stories. The answer lies in the adaptability of Indian mythology to the circumstances in which it is placed. A positive development is that the goddess is no longer on a pedestal but walking freely among the populace of contemporary India. We live in a stratified society, no doubt—yet Lakshmi finds her way through opera performances and high-end cosmetic stores to the bylanes of marginal villages. She is equally sought after by brand-conscious socialites as well as women eking out a living. Our research about the goddess shows this to cohere with her characteristics. She is a wandering or *chanchal* goddess, with a core determination to find her true devotee—the *sevak* or *sevika* with a pure heart. Hence, over time, Lakshmi has not aged in the imagination of India's people. Forever pertinent, forever bountiful, she finds her way to those deserving her attention. Attach her name to a product or a scheme and see her blessings flow!

25

KAMALATMIKA

MENKA RAI

KAMALA OR KAMALATMIKA is the tenth deity among the Dasha Mahavidyas, the Tantric representations of various essences of the Supreme feminine or Prakriti. Kamala is the Tantric aspect of Lakshmi, adopted in the Shakta-Tantric tradition to complete the circle of the ten Mahavidyas. Her imagery is similar to Gaja Lakshmi, flanked and bathed by elephants on both sides. The Beej Mantra for Kamala is '*shri*', which is another epithet of Lakshmi.* According to mythology, the consort/Bhairava of Kamala is Sadashiva, another aspect of Narayana. The goddess is worshipped in many temples situated in different parts of the Indian subcontinent, sometimes in a grouping of ten and sometimes individually. Kamala is worshipped as the deity of affluence, wealth as well as children and family well-being. The

* Sarbeswar Satpathy, *Dasa Mahavidya, and Tantra Sastra* (Calcutta: Punthi Pustak, 1992), p. x.

goddess is invoked by worshippers through various rituals, mantras and meditative practices to attain material and spiritual wealth.

To understand the essence of Kamala or the Tantric Lakshmi, it is important to delve into the context of the Mahavidya tradition. The ten Mahavidyas, literally translated as 'great knowledge', is one of the popular categories of Shakta-Tantric deities worshipped on the Indian subcontinent. In theology, goddesses have often been associated with knowledge. In Vedic tradition, Vac or Saraswati is the goddess of knowledge; in Puranic tradition, Devi (Durga/Mahamaya) is termed as Vidya/Mahavidya, knowledge personified, and gradually in Shakta-Tantric tradition as the Mahavidya, personification of 'great knowledge or revelations'. These goddesses are associated with the process of creation and involution of the cosmos, each Mahavidya representing a different stage of creation and sustenance of *jiva* (life).*

The origin of the Dasha Mahavidyas is narrated in the Mahabhagavata Purana.† When Sati's father Daksha organized a *yajna* (sacrifice), he invited all the gods and sages except Shiva because of his dislike for his son-in-law. However, when Sati heard of the sacrifice, she was furious and wanted to attend despite not being invited by her father. She asked Shiva for his permission, but he forbade her to go to the sacrifice without an invitation. She tried to convince him to reconsider his decision, but Shiva forbade her repeatedly. This enraged Sati even more, and she started manifesting in her different *raudra rupa*s (terrible forms). Seeing her terrible manifestations, Shiva got scared and tried to run away from her from different directions. Seeing him scared like a common human, the goddess then manifested in her *saumya* rupas (gentle forms) as well.

---

* Satpathy, *Dasa Mahavidya*, p. vii.

† Pushpender Kumar, ed., *Mahābhāgavata Purāṇa* (Eastern Book Linkers, 1983), 8.45–60.

Thus, Shiva was circled by ten different forms of the goddess from ten directions. Afraid of the different manifestations, Shiva asked about the identity of the goddesses and what had happened to his wife, Sati. At this, the goddess in her terrible form as Kali laughed and replied that she was his Sati and there was no need for him to be afraid. She identified the different forms as Kali, Tara, Tripura-Sundari, Bhuvaneshvari, Bhairavi, Chinnamasta, Dhumavati, Bagalamukhi, Matangi and Kamala. The spectrum of divinity among the Mahavidyas ranges from horrific goddesses to beautiful and peaceful goddesses. Among all the Mahavidyas the qualities of three goddesses—Tripura-Sundari, Bhuvaneshvari and Kamala—are auspiciousness, benevolence and purity.*

David Kinsley equates the Mahavidyas with different feminine aspects of society as well as the different stages of women's lives by studying the physical attributes of the goddesses symbolically. He also tries to explain the historical evolution of these goddesses by suggesting that the evolution of the Dasha Mahavidyas is in response to the origin of the myth of the Dashavatara of Vishnu and the roles and forms of the goddesses as a counterpart of the Dashavatara in the Puranic tradition.†

On similar lines, the formulators of Mahavidya Tantric tradition have personified the different aspects of the Supreme goddess in ten forms. In the myth, the goddess also recounts the method of worshipping all her ten forms using mantras, *yantras*, puja, *homa* (sacrifice), hymns, *kavaca* (hymns for protection) and *vratas* (vows).‡ The Tantric affinity of the Mahavidyas is indicated by the method of worship mentioned in the narrative.

---

* Jae Eun Shin, *Change, Continuity and Complexity: The Mahāvidyās in East Indian Śākta Traditions* (New York: Routledge, 2018), p. 18.

† David Kinsley, *Tantric Visions of Divine Feminine: The Ten Mahāvidyās* (New Delhi: Motilal Banarsidass, 1998), p. 20.

‡ Mahābhāgavata Purāṇa, 8.83.

According to Puranic and Tantric traditions, the Mahavidyas are mostly worshipped either in the form of images or as yantras, with specific Beej Mantras for different goddesses. The Mahavidyas are also conceived to be in the mantra form of the different aspect of the Supreme goddess, as in Tantra, *shabda/vak* is considered to be endowed with power, indicative through terms such as *shabdabrahma/paravak*.*

According to Sarbeswar Satpathy, the Mahavidyas represent the various stages of the evolution of the universe and subsequent involution—that is, the descent of the soul or consciousness into the universe. The first stage is represented by Kali, the personification of time, and the last stage by Kamala or Kamalatmika, the one with the soul of the lotus. The cycle of creation begins with Kali, who symbolizes ultimate knowledge and supreme desire, and ends with Kamala, who is associated with material wealth and beauty.† She represents the unfolding of the material creation, without which no creation can sustain. Similarly, David Kinsley suggests that Kamala represents realities distant or opposite from Kali.

---

* Satpathy, *Dasa Mahavidya*, p. x.

† Satpathy suggests that all the Mahavidyas are representations of different stages of creation. Kali represents the supreme desire which started the process of creation. Tara represents the action of creation as she is the presiding deity of all actions and functions of the world and the bestower of fruits. Ṣodashi represents the power of consciousness imbibed within creation. Bhuvaneshvari represents the process of maintenance and protection of the world. Bhairavi represents knowledge and the warning that if proper knowledge is not acquired it might lead to destruction. Chinnamasta symbolizes a detached life, that the world should be enjoyed without attachment. Dhumavati represents the ugly side of creation and the smoke surrounding her symbolizes the transition between ignorance and knowledge. Bagalamukhi represents the spirit of confrontation and enmity. Matangi represents worldly power and Kamala symbolizes all sorts of embellishment and affluence. Ibid., pp. vii–x.

She represents a state of consciousness preoccupied with material well-being and security which is the starting point in the process of spirituality, whereas Kali's consciousness represents ultimate knowledge, which is the goal of spirituality.*

David Frawley, analysing from the point of view of Tantric philosophy, suggests that Kamala governs the outer form of beauty and therefore she is able to unfold the divine nature in the process of creation. She is the one who creates forms in the outer world.† Therefore, she is also associated with the earth, Bhudevi (another consort of Vishnu, also considered another form of Lakshmi), symbolizing the tangible form of creation. As she has power over the material unfolding of the inner consciousness in the realm of creation, she also eliminates material as well as spiritual poverty.‡ Therefore, Kamala is worshipped for conceiving children and family well-being as the goddess of fertility and childbirth. Her association with the lotus also indicates her association with all kinds of creation. There are several symbolisms of the lotus in theology and philosophy, such as life and fertility, cosmic order, vigour, beauty, creation, spiritual purity, power and authority.§ Therefore, Kamala also bestows sovereignty and fertility on the worshipper.

The imagery of Kamalatmika is the same as Gaja Lakshmi. Therefore, Mahavidya Kamala is also referred to as the Tantric Lakshmi. Kinsley suggests that the formulators of Mahavidya Tantric tradition altered the character of Lakshmi to fit her in the category. The goddess is described in the Kamala Tantra as having a golden complexion, flanked by four white elephants on

---

* Kinsley, *Tantric Visions of Divine Feminine*, p. 232.

† David Frawley, *Tantric Yoga and the Wisdom Goddesses* (USA: Lotus Press, 1994).

‡ H. Rodrigues, *Kamala*, 2017, https://www.mahavidya.ca/2017/12/22/kamala, accessed on 2 November 2023.

§ Kinsley, *Tantric Visions of Divine Feminine*, p. 225.

both sides pouring water/ambrosia on her from a golden vessel (*kalasha*) held by their trunks. The goddess is four-handed, posing her upper hands in the *varada* (symbolizing granting of boons) and *abhaya* mudras (symbolizing protection) and holding lotuses in the lower hands. She is wearing silken garments and ornaments decorating her body, with a *mukuṭa* (diadem) on her head.*

Though both deities are the same, the difference between Lakshmi and Kamalatmika lies in the nature of the two forms. In her representation as Kamala, she is removed from marital and domestic contexts because Vishnu is absent when she is a Mahavidya.† As a Mahavidya, the goddess is an independent deity. The role of her husband Vishnu is minimal in the mythologies of Kamala. She is not the gentle, ideal wife of Vishnu, rather she is a demon-slayer in her terrible form. The Mahavidyas are often depicted as helping the goddess or Shiva in slaying different Asuras. The Mahavidyas are powerful, independent goddesses as their authority is not derived from association with any male deities. Their power, in turn, sustains the gods and enables them to perform cosmic functions. Male deities are mostly shown in supporting roles. The Todala Tantra mentions the consort of the Mahavidyas, and the consort of Kamala is Sadashiva (another form of Vishnu).‡ But the consorts are referred to as Bhairavas, who in Tantric traditions are the male companions of the goddess in the process of creation. Therefore, the dominant role is mostly associated with the Mahavidyas rather than the Bhairavas.

Another difference between Lakshmi and Kamala is that as a Mahavidya she is mostly associated with Shakta Tantrism and Shaivism. According to Puranic mythology, the Mahavidyas are different forms of Sati, therefore Kamala is an aspect of Shiva's

* Satpathy, *Dasa Mahavidya*, p. 72.
† Kinsley, *Tantric Visions of Divine Feminine*, p. 229.
‡ Eun Shin, *Change, Continuity and Complexity*, p. 219.

wife. In the Shakta Pramoda, among the 1000 names she is referred to as Shiva, Gauri, Raudri, etc.* She is mostly associated with fierce qualities as suggested by epithets such as Kalaratri, Kapali, Ghora, Tamasi, etc., which are also used to refer to other fierce goddesses such as Kali and Durga. She is also placed in the role of demon-slayer, as she is called the slayer of Madhu, Kaitabha, Shumbha, Nishumbha and Durg.† These demons were killed by Durga, therefore Kamala is another aspect of the goddess.

In essence, Kamala is another aspect of Goddess Lakshmi, representing the metaphysical and creative forces of the Supreme feminine. However, the goddess is not just a physical deity but rather as a Mahavidya representing an abstract understanding of the dynamic feminine forces. Kamala exemplifies the manifold nature of the divine feminine and plays a crucial role in driving seekers on their spiritual and substantive journeys. Her symbolism, rituals and associations within the Dasha Mahavidyas enrich the spiritual landscape of the Indian subcontinent, offering devotees a profound connection to the divine feminine in all her aspects.

---

* Kinsley, *Tantric Visions of Divine Feminine*, p. 230.

† Ibid.

26

INVOKING LAKSHMI

CONSTANTINA RHODES

THE TANTRIC PERSONALITY of Lakṣmī continues to express itself as the lovely, sweetly smiling lady of the lotus, bestower of all auspiciousness, bounty and prosperity in the world. However, this same Lakṣmī also dons the accoutrements of the fierce goddesses. She may bear a lotus, discus and conch, and also a sword and a necklace of severed heads. She may be attended not only by smiling, sweet-natured, plump young elephants who shower her with life-giving rains but also by poisonous cobras whose hoods sway menacingly as they stand poised by her side. So too we shall see that, from some perspectives, the goddess pervades one's consciousness and indeed all that exists, even beyond the time–space continuum. In this regard, we shall see that the Tantric Lakṣmī expresses herself as Kuṇḍalinī Śakti—the divine power that exists within our own bodies . . .

Every form of Lakṣmī—whether Vedic, Puranic or Tantric—is worshiped for abundance and prosperity in the world. We have already considered an epithet of Mahā Lakṣmi extolled in the Purāṇa: She is the 'bestower of worldly success and spiritual liberation' *(bhukti-mukti-pradāyinī)*. In this, we recognize attention to the material world and the freedom to disengage from it. In the Puranic consciousness, spiritual liberation is a goal that may remain distinct from that of pleasure-wealth-virtue. The Tantric Lakṣmī, however, instead of focusing directly on liberation, applies her awesome powers to destroy whatever stands in the way of a successful, fulfilling existence on earth, right here, right now. Instead of *mukti* (spiritual liberation), she grants *siddhi* (spiritual power). The 'Song for the Lakṣmī of Spiritual Power' ('Siddha Lakṣmi Stotram') reiterates this in its closing verses:

> This song was composed by the gods
> For the benefit of all living beings . . .
> For Laksmi is the destroyer of every affliction
> And the bestower of every success.

Lakṣmī as Kuṇḍalinī

As we further appreciate the complexities of Lakṣmī's identity, we are reminded of her ever-present manifestation as the lotus goddess. In the Vedic materials, we find the first literary expressions to laud the primordial goddess of beauty and fecundity, embodied in the lotus. The Puranic materials develop the symbolism of the exquisite flower whose roots in the mud and blossom in the air remind the worshipper that even when entangled in the mire of worldly existence, one may transcend to the pristine realms of the liberation of the spirit. In the Tantric imagery of the lotus, we encounter the fulfilment of Tantric wisdom. The Tantric perspective allows us to stand back and view the entire situation holistically, beholding the roots, the stalk and the flower as the integral organism that it is. The roots stretch deep into the mysterious, subterranean realms that are the essential foundation of all life in this world. Often, it is the very darkness, turbulence and messiness of life that fuels the most successful of Tantric spiritual endeavours. The Tantric practitioner does not attempt to transcend or to escape the earthly situation but to engage with the energy of life in the fullness of its expression—to ride *with* that energy as it moves through the entirety of our beings. Success in this endeavour constitutes its own kind of liberation from the shackles of the world.

In the symbolism of the lotus lies the image of the human born into the earthly realm of *saṃsāra*; the ocean of existence is the venue for an individual's karmic struggles and triumphs. The Tantric understanding of the lotus goddess as the goddess of supreme wisdom may be seen again in this imagery. Of significance, however, is not so much that one ascends from the lower or baser or 'muddier' centres upwards to attain the highest space in the rarefied element of air or the ethers, but rather, Lakṣmī's message in the Tantras is one of integration. One attains siddhi—spiritual or magical success, attainment, accomplishment, perfection or power—*while remaining consciously and intentionally rooted* in the moist, life-engendering soil of the earth. One need not relinquish materiality for spirituality, sexuality for asceticism. Instead of a separation of categories, there is a marriage of complementary segments, a conscious integration of what only appear to be disparate elements to create a harmonious, differentially patterned, vibrant whole. Again, we are reminded that the root of the term *tantra* is 'to weave'. The Tantrika does not seek to relinquish the 'base' station in exchange for the 'transcendent' but rather to enliven and integrate all aspects of being.

Just as the lotus epitomizes the essence and form of Lakṣmī's nature, encompassing the myriad dimensions of 'spirituality' and 'materiality', so too does the subtle body of a human contain the form of a lotus within itself. Yogis and intuitives from many esoteric traditions have witnessed in meditation the internal structure of these subtle bodies, in which the central stalk or channel, like the lotus stalk, reaches down to the energies of the earth and upwards towards the etheric realms. This central channel is called the *suṣumnā nādī*, and it is located along the physical spinal column. Along this stalk are seven centres of energy, envisioned as round spinning vortexes, variously labelled as *cakras* (wheels) or *padmās* (lotuses), each with specific numbers of petals in specific positions and of specific hue. Along the vertical axis, the first cakra, called the 'root support' (*mulādhāra*), is located at the base of the torso, roughly at the spot of the perineum, and is connected energetically with the earth. Here is where the Kuṇḍalinī Śakti resides, envisioned as a coiled snake, lying dormant until her arousal. Kuṇḍalinī Śakti, the great serpentine power of transformation, is recognized as a manifestation of Lakṣmī herself.

Each subsequent cakra, moving higher up the axis, resonates with aspects of an individual's consciousness; the highest is the 'thousand-petalled' *(sahasrāra)* lotus on the crown of the head, abode of Lord Siva. When the awakened goddess rises to the crown cakra, she merges there with Śiva, and the bliss of their union creates the full opening of the thousand-petalled lotus, experienced as both the exquisite collapsing of limited consciousness and the blissful expansiveness of divine consciousness. The fullness of this experience resonates outwards around the crown, relaxing back downwards like a waterfall over the body, towards the earth, and cycling back up again into the first—the earth-based—root cakra, the place from where the cycle may continue again. Without that full circuit and effulgence, the wisdom of integrative consciousness may become lost in the 'transcendent', and the practitioner may remain literally ungrounded, unsettled and unfulfilled (as well as feeling 'spacy'). The experience is not complete unless it is integrated throughout the entire being, for it is with integration that authentic spiritual transformation occurs.

It is the goddess herself who initiates the process of transformation, for her energy in the form of Kuṇḍalinī moves throughout the centres, causing each of the lotuses to open, allowing the divine transformative energy to activate that centre, purify it of blockages and move farther upwards, enlivening the consciousness. *The Secret Heart of Lakṣmī (Śrī Mahā Lakṣmi Hṛdayam)* speaks of the holistic transformation that occurs in this process; it reminds us that the awakening is not only at the crown of the head, but in one's entire being as it scintillates with the integrative consciousness that results from that awakening and merging. One may experience something like 'heaven on earth', with the focus on both the heavenly and the earthly. More specifically, the poet of this text speaks of experiencing one's body as Vaikuṇṭha, the heavenly realm where Lakṣmī dwells with Lord Viṣṇu. So too are all of the faculties of an individual's perception transmuted into the magnificent awareness enjoyed by the gods:

At the moment of awakening,
Let my body become Vaikuṇṭha,
From the seat to the forehead and in the crown of my
head.
Grant that my eyes become the abode of Śrī.
Grant that my speech becomes anchored in the Realm of
Truth.
O Lakṣmī, grant that by experiencing
A mere portion of your essence within me,
I may inhabit that glorious White Island
Illumined by its own splendour.

The Power of Tantric Songs: *Waking Up the Goddess*

Alchemy of the Goddess: The Magic of Transformation

According to the Tantric traditions, the way to achieve true prosperity is by focusing not so much on its forms as on its essence, going behind the specific expressions to the source from which they spring. In this way, the worshipper participates with the goddess in the manifestation of prosperity. Because their verses constitute the body and the essence of the goddess, recitation of the Tantric songs is believed to unite the worshipper with the source of all life, all abundance, all prosperity.

The Secret Heart of Lakṣmī and the Goddess's Marvellous Elixir

Just as Tantra recognizes an interior map of the body, so does Indian alchemy (*rasāyana)* consider such changes as eminently tangible within the physical and subtle bodies. This aspect of goddess worship is still relatively unexplored, and its texts and traditions remain obscure. The lengthiest, most passionate and in many ways most intriguing song in our collection is *The Secret Heart of Lakṣmī* (*Śrī Mahālakṣmi Hṛdayam*). It consists of 108 verses plus another dozen or so introductory verses that guide the worshiper in the process of applying the text in its ritual and experiential context, moving from pure devotional lyricism to the urgent evocation of the goddess's energy to arise within the worshipper. Its verses seek to awaken the goddess and generate her mysterious elixir that effects an alchemical transformation within the body and the consciousness of the devotee.

This text comes to us without written commentary. Its colophon, that is, its scriptural signature, states only that it is contained within the *Atharvana Rahasya* (Secrets of the Atharva Veda). This designation refers in name, at least, to the lineage of the Atharva Veda, that limb of the ancient Veda containing some of the earliest recorded expressions of magical religiosity. Sometimes called the 'fifth Veda', the Atharva Veda is a compendium of sacred formulas concerned with inner knowledge as well as spiritual communication with and influences upon the physical and material worlds, addressing such concerns as the appeasement of illnesses, rivalries or debilitating conditions of nature and the elements. The Atharva Veda also contains more goddess worship than any of the other Vedas combined. The 'secret' *(*rahasya*)* traditions of the Atharva Veda developed independently of the Vedas and in a much later time period, although they were consciously aligned with the spirit of the original sacred songs and mantras specifically focusing on mystic knowledge, personal transformation and worship of the goddess.

The Secret Heart of Lakṣmī (Śrī Mahālakṣmi Hṛdayam) describes an alchemical process of transformation with the 'magical elixir' of the goddess operating as the philosopher's stone, that is, the agent of change:

> O Śrī, in addition to the Wish-fulfilling Jewel
> And the Tree of Paradise,
> There exists a delightful, magic elixir
> Formed from just a portion of you.
> As this nectar moves through me,
> Touching all of my parts from head to toe, *Hak!*
> It transmutes them into a body of gold.

This golden, invincible body is the one that may be attained by the Tantric worshipper who is devoted to Lakṣmī and has received even the smallest amount of her favour. The recitation enlivens the verses, and the 'nectar' is an etheric manifestation of the goddess's essence. Just as the goddess takes form as the Kuṇḍalinī Śakti, or energy within the subtle body, so too does she manifest as the exquisite nectar tasted by yogis who have achieved a certain level of spiritual mastery.

The poets of the esoteric songs acknowledge that a mere glance from the goddess is enough to set the transformative process into motion. In fact, a mere glance initiates spiritual perfection (siddhi); however, it is a matter of the mind's catching up with the bestowal of grace that slows down the realization of that perfection. The poet thus asks for continuity in the flow of blessings so that the alchemical process of transmutation—or spiritual transformation—may become realized completely:

O Indirā, lady of the blue lotus,
Just a glance from you—
And my desires
Are satisfied here in this world,
For you are the Wish-fulfilling Jewel,
The celestial tree of the gods,
And the nine eternal treasures.
And yet, a marvellous elixir there is,
Distilled from the nectar of your compassion.
Secreted from just a portion of you,
It fulfills desires beyond imagination.
May this your nectar flow with steady ease.
O Kamalā, lady of the lotus,
Just as the touch of magic elixir
Transmutes iron into gold,
So, O Mother, does the touch of your gracious glance
Transform even the most inauspicious
Into a blessing of splendid good fortune.

While beholding this amazing journey into the interior realms of alchemical transformation, it is important to remember that these practices are intended to enhance the lives of the goddess's devotees—here in this world. An esoteric text specifically for householders, *The Secret Heart of Lakṣmī* therefore eloquently concludes:

> O Goddess, it is you who protect
> This most secret of teachings,
> A scripture brought into existence
> For the benefit of householders.
> Let its power flourish within me.
> Let me ever abide in your bounteous grace.

The Potency of a Woman's Recitations

As in the epic and Puranic materials, the Tantric songs acknowledge women as living embodiments of the goddess. Because women are 'extensions' (*kalā*) of the goddess's essence, they are closer to the full identification with the goddess that the Tantric songs generate. Just as the goddess is visualized carrying the round, golden urn filled with the seed-syllables that engender all life, so are women envisioned as nourishing the potent mantras within their bodies and giving birth to the fruits of their recitation. One of the *phala* ('results') verses of *The Secret Heart of Lakṣmī* offers the image of a woman literally pregnant with its verses:

> A woman impregnated
> With this scripture's sacred mantras
> Gives birth to prosperity for her family,
> And her husband becomes equal
> To the lord of Śrī.

Misfortune never destroys
The lineage of a man
Whose woman immerses herself
In the sacred mantras of *The Secret Heart of Lakṣmī*.

A woman's recitation of the mantras, then, is particularly efficacious. Women by nature contain and nourish the *ova* of creation and new life. As we considered earlier, the belly-round urn containing the goddess's seed-mantras is yet another form of the female body. The most fertile environment for the seed-mantras of the goddess is the womb-essence of a woman. As she nourishes them within her own body and with the power of her recitations and intention, a woman, by virtue of her own feminine power, then may give birth to prosperity, a blessing enjoyed by the entire family and lineage.

The feature of a woman's magical nourishment of seed-syllables, and subsequently her magical power over mantras and indeed of all speech, appears throughout the rich textual traditions of the Tantric goddess. In her brilliant study of Nīlasarasvati (Blue Goddess of Speech), Loriliai Biernacki brings to light textual elucidations of such principles. In one passage that she translates from the *Bṛhannīla Tantra,* for example, we learn: 'The restrictions which men contend with [in the practice of] mantras are not all there for women. Anything whatsoever, by whichever [means], and moreover in all ways [is attained], for women magical attainment [siddhi] occurs, without any doubt . . . for a woman, by merely contemplating [on the mantra] she in this way becomes a giver of boons. Therefore, one should make every effort to initiate a woman in one's own family.'

If we read the Tantric texts in our collection closely, we find very clear indications that some of these texts are intended specifically for women to recite. Let us consider, for example, the *Song-Amulet of the Lotus Goddess (Kamalātmikā Kavacam*), a text whose mantras are literally applied to the body of the practitioner so as to create a mantle of power and protection, and further, to homologize the worshipper with the energies of the goddess. As with other song-amulets, the worshipper begins by systematically blessing each part of the body with the ritual placement of mantras on each of its parts. Here, the worshipper is clearly female, for the prayers call for the placement of the mantras 'on my two breasts' *(stanadvandve)*, 'on my feminine private parts' *(guhye,* literally 'secret' or 'private'), and, reaching the head, 'on the parting of my hair (*sīmante*). The latter is a 'body part' that is specifically feminine and that signifies the shared essence of a woman, the goddess Lakṣmī and auspiciousness itself. It is in the parting of the hair that married women place red powder to signify their auspicious state of marriage.

27

ALAKSHMI: SYMMETRY AND ASYMMETRY

TANASHREE REDIJ AND P.P. JOGLEKAR

LAKṢMĪ, THE GODDESS of beauty, wealth and prosperity, is the most prominent Goddess of the Indian mythology. Due to her beneficial characteristics, she is beloved to everyone. However, the same mythology gives the evidence of another goddess, Alakṣmī, who is extremely opposite to Lakṣmī. Goddess Alakṣmī is malevolent in nature whereas Goddess Lakṣmī is benevolent. Alakṣmī is closely connected with Śaiva cult (Dhere 2007: 35–36) and Lakṣmī with Vaiṣṇava cult. In nature both of them are opponent to each other which is suggested by their name. As Lakṣmī is the goddess of wealth and prosperity, Alakṣmī is the goddess of poverty, ruin and misfortune. She is a malignant deity and people were terribly afraid of her. All the misfortune, ill luck, ruin or destruction in one's life is generally thought to be due to the influence of Alakṣmī. On the other hand prosperity or happiness in one's life is considered due to the favour of Lakṣmī.

This dual concept 'Alakṣmī and Lakṣmī' is reflected in literature, iconography and folk religion as well. This article provides a brief account of Goddess Alakṣmī and to an extent of Goddess Lakṣmī in order to trace their origin and development. Also, an attempt is made to look at how much of this concept is reflected in actual practice or in modern rituals.

Modern Rituals of Alakṣmī

Today generally no one follows the original rituals given in the ancient texts, neither the Vedic sacrifices nor the Vrata. But still some people worship Alakṣmī in their own way which sometimes reminds us of the old rituals. The custom of driving out Alakṣmī through the courtyard of houses by making the noise of the winnowing baskets and drums during Diwali as told in Padma Purāṇa is still in practice. Upendra Nath Dhal (1978: 153) has done an ethnographic study of the reflection of ancient Alakṣmī worship rituals in modern times. In Punjab, on the next morning of Diwali, the eldest woman in the house takes a corn sieve or a winnowing basket and broom, and beats them in every corner of the house saying, 'God abide and poverty depart.' The sieve is then thrown out of the village towards the north or east. It is believed that the object takes away the poverty and disaster with it.

In Gujarat, this custom takes place on the first day of Kärttika, which is their New Year's Day (Dhal, 1978: 153). In some parts of Gujarat, on Dhanaterasa, first day of Diwali, before doing Lakṣmī Pujana women worship the threshold of the door to the entrance of Lakṣmī and the existence of Alakṣmī. Then they recite whole Śri-Sukta in the honour of both the goddesses. Then on the next evening, they take the vadās of black grams from the house and throw them out. This leads to 'the chasing Alakṣmī out' (Rawal, personal communication, 2009).

The Hindus of Monghyr in Bihar observe this custom on the Bhutacaturdasi day, on the fourteenth day of the dark fortnight of Kärttika. But their practising method is somewhat different. They make an image of Alakṣmī in cow dung and drag her and humiliate her saying 'Lachmi ghar, dariddar bahar' (Dhal 1978: 153). In several districts of Bengal, J.N. Banerjee refers to another form of this ritual in a different style. There a Kṣanika (temporary) image of Alakṣmī is made of cow dung and is worshipped on the new-moon night of Diwali, then this crude image is taken outside the house with the beating of winnowing fan and discarded (Dhal 1978: 153). The same custom of making temporary image of Alakṣmī in cow dung is also prevalent in Gomantaka (Goa) region (Joshi 1967). This tradition is originally mentioned in Krtyacandrika.

This tradition of making sounds and driving out the evil spirit is common. Harsh sound irritates everyone. For that Purāṇakarās (authors of Purāṇās) have ordered to use harsh, irregular objects, like winnowing baskets and drums. But in daily worship, the ringing of bell and Sankha is thought to be as auspicious.

In some houses of Maharashtra, this Alakṣmī Puja is performed on the Dussehra, the tenth day of the first half of the Aśvina month. Previous nine days are known as Navaratri. In these days people worship various imprints of Sakti in the form of Kalasa. During these days they collect dust and dry dirt of the house. On Dussehra after immersion of the Śakti, in afternoon people worship that dust and dirt and offer the Nevedya to it in the corner of the house. Then in the evening they immerse Alakṣmī in the form of dirt with offerings in public dustbin. Worshipping dust and dirt and throwing them into dustbin is nothing but the worship of Alakṣmī and chasing her out.

To chase Alakṣmī normally one lamp is lighted at the back door of the house. Then that lamp is brought at the front door of the house. On its way to the front door, it is taken to each and every corner of the house and then thrown out of the house. And again, another lamp is lighted at the front door and taken inside the house. This is a common ritual in rural Maharashtra. It suggests giving a way to Alakṣmī to go out and Lakṣmī to come inside. Generally people believe that the Alakṣmī, being unlucky, stays at back door and Lakṣmī stays at front door.

On the dark night of Śravana month, women in Maharashtra perform a small vrata. In the evening, they light lamps in the house for the expulsion of Alakṣmī. The story of this vrata refers to both the goddesses without names. The woman in the story asks both of her brothers-in-law to stand at both the front door and back door. She tells them, 'Both of you keep watch on the doors. Take a promise of not returning again from a lady who will go out from the back door. And the one who will try to enter house from the front door, take a commitment from her to stay forever in the house.' This vrata is locally known as 'Diwyachi Awasa'.

Iconographic Depiction of Alakṣmī

Alakṣmī is inauspicious goddess who causes poverty, ruin, destruction, etc., hence her images are made up of perishable things like cow dung, as well as her worship is temporary. Therefore, we do not find many images of Jyeśthā–Alakṣmī as those of Lakṣmī.

Purāṇa give her description as कालास्या (black face), रक्तलोचना and रक्तनयनां (red eyes), रुक्षपिङ्गलकेशा and रुक्षपिङ्गशिरोरुहाम (having rough and tawny hair on head), जरन्ती बिभ्रति तनुम् and जरठां बिभ्रति तनुम् (having aged looks), स्थूलास्यां and विततां (fat), शुभान्वित् and शुभे (one who has skin pigmentation).

She is goddess with two arms. She holds Nilotpala flower in her right hand and her left hand rests upon the seat or vice versa. Sometimes she is shown holding a skull in her left hand. (Kriyādhikaraṇa: 5.198) She sits on Bhadrasana by hanging her legs down. She wears Mukuṭa on her head and tilaka on forehead.

Her hair is well braided, ornamented and in a particular style, namely vāsīkābandha. She wears black or red silken garments and a fine necklace. Her face covers two large eyes with big cheeks, thick raised nose and hanging lower lip. She also has large pendulous breasts descending till navel with a big belly. Mostly a crow is shown on her banner. Sometimes a bull-faced boy is shown at her right back. Normally the temple of Alakṣmī is built outside the village, in a forest or near a water tank or on the bank of river or beyond the agricultural field. Though taxes were exempted on the temples of Jyeśthā–Alakṣmī during the rule of Chola emperors, they were neglected (Joshi 1967: 490).

References

Apte, Chintamani Mahadev 1894. Padma Purana (Part 2–4). Pune. Anandashram.

Apte, H.N. 1898. Krsna Yajurvediya Taittiriya Brahmana. (Vols 1–3). Pune: Anandashram Sanskrit Series.

Apte Vaman. 1890. Sanskrit-English Dictionary. Pune. Shiralkar & Co.

Arya, Raviprakash and K.L. Joshi 1997. Ṛg-Veda Samhitā. (4th volume). Delhi: Parimal Publications. Bhagvat, Durga 1991. Siddhartha Jātaka. (Vol. 3). Pune: Varada books.

Bhatta, Shrilakshidhar 1953. *Kṛtyakalptaru.* Baroda. Gaekwad's Oriental Series.

Bhatta G.H., Jhala G.C. & others 1969. The Valmiki Rāmāyana. (Vols 1–5). Baroda: Oriental Institute.

Bhattacharya, Jivananda Vidyasagar 1888. Brahmavaivarta Purāna. Calcutta: Saraswatiyantra.

Bhattacharya, Jivananda Vidyasagar. 1885. Linga Purana. Calcutta: Saraswatiyantra.

Bhattacharya, Taranatha 1873. Vachaspata. Calcutta: Kavyaprakasha Press.

Chand, Devi 1982. Atharvaveda. New Delhi: Munshiram Manoharlal.

Dange, Sadashiv 1986. Encyclopedia of *Purāṇic* Beliefs and Practices. Vol. 1 New Delhi: Navrang.

Dhal, Upendra Nath 1978. *Goddess Lakṣmī: Origin and Development*. New Delhi: Oriental Publishers and Distributors.

Dhere, R.C. 2007. *Lokdaivatānche Viswa*. Pune: Padmagandha Prakashan.

Eliade, Mircea. 1987. *Encyclopedia of Religion*. Vols 4th & 6th. New York: Macmillan Publishing Company.

Hastings, James. 1982. *Encyclopedia of Religion and Ethics*. Vol. 6th. New York: Charles Scribner's Sons.

Hemadri 1985. *Caturvargya Cintāmaṇi*. Varanasi. Chaukhamba Sanskrit Sansthan.

Joshi, K.L. 2002. Atharvaveda. Delhi: Parimal Publications.

Joshi, Mahadevshastri 1967. *Bharatiya Sanskrutikosh*. Pune: Bharatiya Sanskrutikosh Mandal.

Kumar, Pushpendra 1998. Taittirīya Brāhmaṇa. (Part 1–2). Delhi: Nag Prakashana.

Maxmuller 1966. Ṛg-Veda Samhita. Varanasi: Chaukhamba Sanskrit Series Office.

Nilakantha Sastri 1937. Colas. (Vol. 2). Madras: University of Madras.

Panashikar, Vasudeva 1915. Amarakoṣa. Delhi: Chaukhamba Sanskrit Pratithana.

Pandya, Ramashish 1998. Etymology & Acārya *Yāska*. Bihar: Pravogha Sanskrit Prakashana.

Prabhudesai, P.K. 1968. Adishaktiche Vishwarup. Vols. 1 to 4. Pune: Tilak Maharashtra University.

Sharma, Shriram 1970. Vāmana Purāṇa. Bareli: Sanskriti Sansthan.

Sharma, Vidyadhar 1990. *Female Deities in Vedic and Epic Literature*. Delhi: Nag Publishers.

Shastri, Bhimsen 1920. *Laghusid- dhāntakaumudi.* (4th part). Delhi: Bhaimi Prakashana.

Shastri, Srikant 2000. Atharvaveda Samhitā. (Part 1&2). Delhi: Mahadeva Pustakalay.

Shyam Kishore Lal 1980. *Female Divinities in Hindu Mythology and Ritual.* Pune: University of Pune.

Shrisukhanandanatha 1921. Shab-darthachinta-mani. Banaras: Motilal Banarsidass.

Vishvabandhu 1965. Ṛg-Veda. (Vols. 7). Hoshiarpur: Vishveshvarananda Vedic Research Institute.

Weber, A. 1964. Śrimad Vājasaneyi Mādhyandina Sathapatha Brāhmaṇa. Varanasi.

Whithey, W.D. 1987. Atharvaveda Samhita. (Vol 1). Delhi: Nag Publishers.

SECTION 4

UNRAVELLING LAKSHMI'S NARRATIVES: FOLK INTERPRETATIONS

'The Sanskrit words for "lotus", *kamala* and *padma,* when provided with the long *ā* of the feminine ending, denote the goddess who dwells in the lotus: Kamalā, Padmā. Identical with Śrī Laksmī, the wife of Visnu, who is the creator and maintainer of the world, she is luck, prosperity, and good fortune incarnate. She presides over the fertility and moisture of the soil and over the jewels and precious metals in the womb of the earth, and is represented standing on the lotus, as the other gods on their animals or vehicles. For just as the bull Nandi is the animal symbol of Śiva's divine nature and the wild gander that of Brahmā, so is the lotus the vegetable symbol of the goddess Śrī Laksmī.'

Heinrich Zimmer,
The Art of Indian Asia

28

BALI'S SACRIFICE

SUKUMARI BHATTACHARJI

THE DEMON VIROCHANA'S son Prahlada was a truly good king, so Lakshmi remained his constant companion. Soon, however, Indra requested Lakshmi to leave Prahlada, because the Gods felt rebuked by her action. As Indra was the king of heaven, Lakshmi had to oblige him. She abandoned Prahlada, who was quiet and meek and generally an unenterprising king. As soon as she forsook him, Prahlada was sapped of his royal might.

Now, Prahlada's son Bali, was equally virtuous, but unlike his father, he was bold and valorous. He told his father that Lakshmi favoured only those who were brave and enterprising. So, when Bali inherited his father's throne, he fought against all his enemies and won victory after victory. Gradually, he defeated even the Gods and reigned in heaven.

Attracted by his prowess, victories and piety, Lakshmi now decided to dwell with him as was her wont. The Gods were alarmed at the prospect because if Lakshmi left them for Bali, who was after all a demon, they would soon be vanquished by evil powers. So, they took recourse to tricks and stratagems, as they often did in such predicaments.

They heard that Bali was celebrating a recent victory with a sacrifice and had vowed that he would not turn anyone away, without fulfilling their desires. So, Vishnu assumed the shape of a dwarf and asked Bali to grant him as much land as a dwarf could cover in three steps. Bali agreed and Vishnu placed the first step on Bali's head. The dwarf-incarnate kept pressing his foot harder and harder until Bali was pushed down to Patala, the nether region. The pious demon now began to rule there.

For some strange reason, Lakshmi did not accompany Bali to the netherworld even after he had passed this supreme test of piety and remained with the Gods who had tricked the demon king so nefariously. And because Lakshmi remained with them, the Gods regained their former prosperity and glory.

29

TULSI: THE SYLVAN FORM OF DEVI

NILIMA CHITGOPEKAR

'No plant in the world commands such . . . respect, adoration, and worship . . . as does *tulsi.*'—K.D. Upadhyaya, *Indian Botanical Folklore* (1964)

Blossoming in the centre of the *angana*, or courtyard, of many Indian households, Tulsi, a species of basil, is an important sacred plant in Hinduism. Worshipped as a goddess in her own right, one could say that Tulsi is a plant embodiment of Devi.

Origins

The rise of Tulsi from a mere plant to one representing sacrality can be traced to the period between 200 BCE to 300 CE. During this time, Brahmanism was assimilating an assortment of popular and widespread cults. In the process, animals, trees, mountains and rivers came to acquire deific connotations.

Tulsi was one such natural entity that became a part of the religious matrix. American cultural geographer Frederick J. Simoons notes, 'Hindus sometimes call the tulsi plant *tulsi-mata* ("mother tulsi"), which is in accord with the way they address the sacred cow as *go-mata* ("mother cow") and the sacred Ganges River as *Ganga-mata* ("mother Ganges").'

Part of the Vaishnava Pantheon

The process of deification often draws its legitimacy by inserting the deity in the wider mythological framework. So Tulsi became a part of the Vaishnava myths. Sometimes considered a manifestation of Lakshmi, she is often referred to as Shri Tulsi, Shri being another name for Lakshmi, and Lakshmi Priya, which means Lakshmi's beloved. To further embed Tulsi firmly in the Vaishnava system, she is also connected to Vishnu, the preserver, and his avatars. Scholars draw attention to how she is Vaishnavi, or one who belongs to Vishnu, Vishnu Vallabha, or Vishnu's beloved, and when seen as Rama or Krishna's wife, Rama Tulsi and Krishna Tulsi, respectively.

Tulsi may also have associations with other deities, including Shiva, the destroyer. Some scholars have pointed out that sometimes Shiva's image is created from the soil that nurtures the Tulsi plant. Select communities in Odisha and Kerala link her with their local deities and supernatural beings. Even so, as Indian anthropologist R.S. Khare writes, she is the 'central sectarian symbol' of Vaishnavism.

Auspicious Nature

The Padma Purana says that every part of the Tulsi plant has purifying powers. If Tulsi wood is used to cremate the dead, they are freed from all sins and go to heaven. Bathing with the clay in which Tulsi grows is equal to bathing in a holy place. An important part of many Vaishnava rituals is the offering of garlands made of Tulsi leaves or Tulsi-infused holy water to deities. They also use the wood of the plant stem to make beads for the string used to do *japa*, or meditative mantra repetition.

IN TODAY'S TIMES

Revering Tulsi

The common practice is to plant Tulsi on an auspicious day, particularly on Sankranti, or a day when the Sun transmigrates from one constellation to the next, or during the Hindu month of Shravana (July–August). Traditional Hindu homes usually have the plant in the courtyard of their homes. Women mostly worship the Tulsi plant early in the morning after their bath and then in the evening.

The Wedding of Tulsi

During the Hindu month of Kartik (October–November), many homes and temples across India play host to a celestial wedding. Called Tulsi Vivah, or Tulsi's wedding, it is the union of Vishnu, the preserver, and his beloved Tulsi.

In Hindu traditions, *kanyadaan,* or giving away a daughter, is believed to be the biggest offering one can ever make to the divine. It has the power to free one of all sins, no matter how extreme. So every year, many daughterless couples perform Tulsi Vivah where they marry the Tulsi plant, as their daughter, to Vishnu.

Imitation of a Hindu Wedding

In terms of its scale, the Tulsi Vivah can range from a close-knit homely affair to a grand celebration, but in its essence, it resembles a traditional Hindu wedding. The setting includes a *mandap* or a marriage pavilion, with *agni* or sacred fire at its centre. The Tulsi plant, believed to embody the goddess, is wrapped with a traditional red sari and embellished with jewellery to look like a bride.

Sometimes, a paper face with a nose ring, earrings and a bindi is placed on it to give anthropomorphic connotations. The groom Vishnu, or his avatar Krishna, appears as a brass statue, a picture or a shaligram stone. Dressed in dhoti, he is offered sandalwood paste and the *janeu,* or sacred thread.

A Brahman priest is called upon to recite the mantras and conduct the rituals. The bride and the groom are connected through a *mala* or cotton thread, in a re-enactment of the ritual of *gathbandhan*, or alliance. The bride is offered a *mangalsutra,* or auspicious necklace, to confer marital status upon her. Throughout the ceremony, and especially in the end, the participants shower puffed rice, mixed with turmeric and *kumkum,* or vermilion, on the couple to celebrate their union.

Decorating Her Home

Tulsi Vrindavan and its surrounding area is often decorated with traditional motifs.

Mythological Context

The antecedents of this ritual can be traced to mythology. There are several stories of Vishnu's union with Tulsi. American cultural geographer Frederick J. Simoons recounts the most popular version. In it, Vishnu was once drawn to the beautiful and faithful Vrinda. Owing to the intensity of her fidelity, her husband, Jalandhara, an ordinary, low-caste man, mutated into an invincible Asura. Meanwhile, Vishnu tried to seduce Vrinda who evaded his advances and disregarded him in favour of her husband. Not being able to get Vrinda this way, the god disguised himself as Jalandhara and managed to trick her. Vrinda fell into the trap.

No longer shielded by the fervour of her fidelity, Jalandhara died. Vrindra, shocked at Vishnu's misdemeanour and heartbroken at her husband's death, cursed the god so he would turn into a stone. Vishnu retaliated and turned her into a plant. Over time, she became Vishnu's beloved.

In another version, Vrinda threw herself on the pyre of her husband, but Vishnu could not let go of her and transformed her into the Tulsi plant. In the Devi Bhagavata Purana, the goddess performs a difficult penance to be reunited with her husband Vishnu.

'Krishna's marriage to Tulsi . . . reflects the world of values and conventions that shape and inform human conjugal relations.'*

Modern-Day Rationale

There are also practical implications of this ritual. It is believed that on Shayani Ekadashi, or the eleventh day of the bright fortnight of the Hindu month of Ashada (June–July), Vishnu retires to sleep in his abode in Ksheersagar, the ocean of milk. His slumber lasts for four months, a period traditionally known as Chaturmas. Since Vishnu's consciousness is practically absent in the universe during this period, Hindus are prescribed to stay away from auspicious ceremonies, such as weddings. When Vishnu rises from his long and deep slumber on Prabodhini Ekadashi, the eleventh day of the bright fortnight of Kartik, it signals the commencement of the marriage season in India. Tulsi Vivah is celebrated to commemorate this.

---

* Tracy Pintchman, 'The Month of Kartik and Women's Ritual Devotions to Krishna in Benares' (2003).

30

MANABASA LAKSHMI PURANA: THE REDEEMER OF THE POOR

BALARAM DAS

TRANSLATED BY LIPIPUSPA NAYAK*

THE MOTHER, WHO is also the mother of creation, slipped into the guise of an old Brahmin woman. She covered a long path, stopping at each home and every household, but nowhere did she find the sacrosanct environ she was looking for. In one house, a young maiden lay on a bed in a deep slumber. Another maiden was so overwhelmed by sleep that her robes had fallen off, exposing her body. Elsewhere a woman's tresses had splayed on the floor while she was asleep. Thus Maha Lakshmi took account of the spectacle and left for the lane where the *chandaals*—the poor who performed menial duties—lived.

* Translated from the Odia, 2021, Black Eagle Books.

Shriya, a woman in that lane of chandaals, lived outside Puri, the premises of the kingdom of Lord Jagannath. And lo! Her greatness as a devotee was not known to the gods. She swept clean the streets of the kingdom of Lord Jagannath every day with rapturous devotion for the Lord.

On that day, Shriya had left her bed when the night was still in its third quarter and fetched the dung of a single-coloured cow from the streets. With the dung and water she swabbed the floor of her house and veranda in meticulous swathes. She also sprinkled a few drops of the urine she had collected from a calf, and consecrated her house further. Then she drew murals on the floor of her house with raw rice paste. She drew an intricate lotus motif with sixteen petals. She lighted a wicker lamp filled with ghee that had ten mouths to bear ten wicks, placing it at the centre of the mural. On this mural, she spread out fruits and tubers of ten colours. She kept a thread of ten hanks on this. She became restive and fetched raw rice and ten stems of *duba*, the creeper grass. She also offered incense, burning wicks dipped in ghee, sacred food, flowers and aromatic oil on the patterns she had drawn. Then she invoked the gods:

> I worship you, O Lakshmi and Jagannath!
> Glory be to You, Mother, the homemaker of Hari, Hari is the Emperor of the Universe.
> I am ignorant in the matters of religious rituals as I am from a low servile caste, and on top of that,
> I live in the lane of the chandaals, and I am a chandaal woman.
> O Lotus-Faced Mother, please deign to accept my veneration.

Lakshmi, Vishnu's Maharani, was passing by along the main street. She could not ignore the pleadings of the chandaal woman and was moved with her piety. The lotus motif in the house too tempted Lakshmi. So she entered the house of the chandaal woman and materialized on the lotus motif. The entire household of the poor woman glittered to an unusual radiance in the presence of Lakshmi, and when the Goddess had graced the house, how can I even think of a metaphor to narrate the splendour of the spectacle?

'Now, dear Shriya,' said Lakshmi, 'ask and carry for yourself a boon, since I've been pleased with you. I promise you, I'll wipe out your woes.'

The poor woman tells, her hand placed on her head:

> What can I ask for? I do not know how to ask for a boon.
> Well, give me a billion auspicious cows.
> Give me riches, Mother, which should measure up only to Kubera's, provide a son to my lap, give enough gold bangles and armlets to cover both my hands, and make me immortal through the four eons of Satya, Dwapara, Treta and Kali, the eon of sin.

Lakshmi heard her and said: 'You have lost your head. I can give you all you have asked for except that I have no power to bestow on you immortality. How could you ask for this boon? You will wallow in immeasurable wealth as long as you live. After your life on this earth expires, you will reach at the abode of Vishnu. Keep this penance for me every day; let your being lie at the feet of Lakshmi–Narayana.'

Out there Lord Jagannath and Lord Balaram had been to the woods for a hunt. The episode of Lakshmi and the poor woman Shriya was revealed to Balaram when he sat in meditation.

Lord Balaram called out his younger brother Lord Jagannath and said: 'Look at the ways of your wife, Hari, she has visited the house of a chandaal woman. She goes around the houses of people from lower castes. Thereafter she enters our Grand Temple without taking a bath.

'And she does this every day, and makes us, the brothers, outcasts of society. Since she carries the title *the-redeemer-of-the-poor*, she cannot bear the poor to suffer. She has graced the house of the woman chandaal as the low-caste woman has been worshipping at her feet on the day of Sudasha Vrata, the propitiatory penance in her honour. My dear Krishna, if you so need your wife, hurry up and erect a palace in the lane of the chandaals. Or else listen to our words and chase her away. If you pamper a spouse like Lakshmi, we will run into destitution and eternal deprivation.'

Hari listened to his brother's palaver and said: 'You suggest that we chase her out of the Grand Temple. But how and where will we ever get another homemaker like her after that? If she has erred, let me offer a suggestion for her atonement: let us invite respectfully the gods from the heaven. Let's spend five hundred thousand rupees to hold the ritual of absolution and re-induct Lakshmi to our society. And yet, if we find her flouting the principles and rituals of the Temple again, we will drive her out from there—this is my pledge before you, Elder Brother; after all the Princess of the Ocean has made a mistake without her knowledge; wouldn't you forgive her for once, Brother?'

Balaram said: 'Listen to me, Govinda, you are also called Bhavagrahi, the one who understands emotions. If your Lakshmi stays in the Temple, I will not. If you are obsessed with your wife, O Krishna, construct a royal mansion in the chandaals' lane. Don't come to my Grand Temple again, keep off its borders along with your woman.'

Jagannath, the lord of the universe, could no longer stand the upbraiding of his elder brother. 'I shall leave her,' he said, and his lips became scarlet. He retired to the Temple, paused at the entrance, the Lion Gate, and breathed out deeply looking upwards.

Shriya had been worshipping at the painting of the feet of Lakshmi. The Goddess was pleased with the devotion of Shriya and bestowed boons on her. Shriya used to live in a hut which resembled a wasp's burrow and with the blessings of Lakshmi it turned into a palace of sandalwood. Her house, which never had food grains for the next meal, was now stacked with pure gold at every corner. The woman in whose house a son never played now bore five sons with the blessings of the Goddess. 'Possess more prosperity and many more sons,' the Goddess blessed Shriya and proceeded on her divine sojourn.

The chandaal woman came to luck because of Lakshmi. Now, Narada, you must track attentively the strings of this remarkable tale.

Lakshmi, the spinner of great miracles, appeared at the Lion Gate of the Temple. She saw the two brothers Lord Jagannath and Lord Balaram covering the entrance. 'Let me get in,' she said, 'as I have to cook the special meal of the day, and today is the holy tenth day of the lunar month.'

'Have you lost your head?' asked Jagannath, her husband. 'Why did you visit the street of the chandaals? I did not see this, but Elder Brother has seen you there. Had it been I, I would have covered up your misdeed. Lakshmi! You may go away now; we have no further business with you. Brother has upbraided me enough because of what you have done.

'Therefore, Soulmate! Listen to my words. Everyone in the three worlds calls you the strange goddess. In spite of being the goddess of my household, you roam like a strange woman. You unite a thousand homes to make one; you break one home to a thousand ones. Such are your divine dispensations and miracles. Now go away, Lakshmi, don't live in my Abode. Elder Brother is infuriated with you.'

She walked out of the Temple and walked along alone. The maids who waited on her in the palace followed her.

Then the goddess mulled over her options. She remembered Vishwakarma, the architect of the universe. At that moment Vishwakarma happened to be in Baikuntha, the abode of Vishnu in Heaven. Vishwakarma made himself available at her command instantly and prayed: 'Do assign me a duty, O the goddess of great miracles!'

The goddess looked at Vishwakarma and proclaimed: 'The Lord has called me a lowly woman and has thrown me out of the palace. Will you build a humble hut for me?'

Vishwakarma rushed as soon as he received orders from the goddess and erected a mansion of length and breadth each six miles. He built the walls of each room of the mansion with gold and studded every wall with diamonds, jades and rubies. Pearls glistened from the joints of the beams and rafters, which were supported by pillars of corals. Lakshmi the lotus-faced expressed her immense satisfaction and praise to Vishwakarma for his work and the architect then headed back for Baikuntha, in heaven.

There Lord Jagannath and Lord Balaram had a very comfortable sleep and woke up from the deep slumber four hours after daybreak. 'Aye Jagannath,' said Balaram, 'I don't hear a noise around, not even the voice of Mudi Ratha, our chief servitor and custodian of the sanctum sanctorum. Where have the chambermaids gone? Where are the Temple clerks and the servants? There is no water even to wash our face. What do we do, tell me, Jagannath.'

Lord Jagannath replied: 'Great Brother! Such things happen when one is deserted by Goddess Lakshmi.'

'Listen, younger brother! Must you talk like that about your silly wife?' asserted Balaram. 'When someone's wife sulks and makes herself scarce, doesn't her house-master himself cook food?'

Then the brothers went into the storeroom. The room was absolutely empty. 'What has happened?' yelled Balaram. 'What happened to the fifty-two billion treasures of the palace? Even when millions of people are provided with food from this store, the stock never runs out. And who could have emptied the store house in such a short span of time?'

As they rummaged through the room, Balaram found a gold ring and secured it in the end of his cloth, carefully tying the end with seven knots. 'Did you get something, Great Brother?' asked Jagannath.

Balaram said: 'I have got riches, that is a gold ring.'

Jagannath said: 'Brother, why are you preserving a worthless lump of brass?'

Balaram replied: 'What a turn of events! The gold ring that I had found turned to low-quality brass! The ornament that had been carved out of pure gold did not measure up to a damaged cowrie, that is our twisted fate!'

The brothers walked out of the storeroom and went to the Divine Kitchen. Balaram stood at the door and Jagannath went inside. Black soot of the kitchen smeared his face and body. The face of the Lord, that had always been dark, shone more with the coating of soot.

Then the Brothers went and inspected the Divine Granary. The granary that stored millions of tonnes of rice did not have even an empty husk. The Brothers, desolate and downcast, arrived at the banks of Indradyumna, the Temple Pond, and alas! There was not a drop of water in the pond. So the Brothers returned to the Grand Temple. The Gods accepted this as a ritual fast and went to sleep.

The next day when the Brothers woke up from sleep long after daybreak, they could find no water to wash their faces.

'My wits have failed—what do we do now?' asked Balaram. 'We have spent the whole of yesterday without food. Today there is no strength in our body to walk one step. If we don't manage to get some cooked rice from somewhere today, we will not be able to remain alive.

'Let me have your attention, dear,' Balaram continued.

'Let's go and beg inside our kingdom so that we can save our lives.'

So the Brothers draped themselves with upper apparels reduced to rags and sacred threads. They carried tumbledown parasols and set out. They did not get water to prepare a paste of sandalwood, to draw tilak on their foreheads, which would identify them as Brahmin mendicants. Wherever they went asking for water, they were taken for purloiners and prowlers and were threatened with assault and chased away. And thus the terrified Brothers fled the streets immediately.

'Let's go to the house of the Chief Servitor, Elder Brother!' suggested Jagannath.

So the Brothers, hand in hand, walked towards their Chief Servitor's house and reached his house. 'Two Brahmins have rushed to our quarters,' said the daughter-in-law of the house to her mother-in-law. The mother-in-law, a widow, could not recognize the brothers. She closed the doors on their face and howled: 'Gather round, with staffs and sticks; let's hound away these two bandits, or burglars, O women folk, or whatever.'

The terrified Brothers left the gates of the house and chanted hymns from the Sama and Yajur Vedas from a distance. With their hymns, the dried and dead shrubs and trees blossomed. The Brahmin widow realized that they were Brahmin mendicants and not thieves. So she called back the Brothers, made them sit and cooked with great attention some partly broken rice grains—all that she had. The two brothers collected two rolled banana leaves from inside a banana plant. They spread the leaves on the ground, sprinkled water on the leaves and waited for the food to arrive. The elderly Brahmin woman took a bronze bowl into the kitchen to get the cooked rice for the Brahmins.

What will she serve? Her cooking pot had disappeared from the hearth! *These two men have been disowned by Lakshmi*, the Brahmin woman realized. She returned from her kitchen and came to the two Brothers, held them by their hands and showed them out of the door. She rewarded them with her furore and consigned the Gods to the road. The Brothers became hopeless as they witnessed such conduct of the Brahmin woman; they moved on nevertheless and showed up in the lane of the Sufis.

Sufis were only part Hindus and did not offer cooked food to Brahmin mendicants. *These two are starving Brahmins,* so the Sufis realized and fetched for the mendicants five measures of popped rice.

Now Lakshmi the lotus-faced Goddess knew of the episode with her insight. She summoned the Wind God right away and ordered forthwith: *Dear Wind God, make haste and blow away the popped rice of a few measures from the plates of the Brahmin brothers that they have received as alms.*

The Wind God raced bearing the summons of the Goddess. And up went the rice flakes in the wind as the Lords of the universe watched. *Do you hear, Jagannath?* says Balaram, the Elder Brother, *when our life threatens to walk out of our bodies why consider the caste and roots of the donor? Let's go to the pond of lotuses; we can feed on the lotus tubers there and save our lives. We can also feast on the flowers and their piths; and if we get a lot of these edibles we can store the surplus.*

So contemplating the brothers moved; they entered the pond where lotuses of many petals blossomed. The lotus pond had waters of seven fathoms. Alas! Came a command from Goddess Lakshmi and the water turned to slush, of seven fathoms.

What do we do now? says Jagannath, the Lord of the Universe. *There is no water in the pool and it is full of slush under the orders of Lakshmi, also known to be with a face of the lotus. How will we get here lotuses?*

The two Brother Gods proceeded further seeking food. The Gods trudged along. On the way they met a mendicant, a yogi who had no house or abode. Lord Jagannath said: 'O mendicant! We are hungry; do give us some rice from your plate.'

The eternally blissful mendicant looked at Lord Balaram and Lord Jagannath and said: 'You brothers have invited the curse of

Lakshmi, the Goddess of Wealth. My mendicant's bowl was filled with fine rice cooked in milk. As soon as you asked me for a share the bowl was drained of the kheer I had collected. You will get nowhere, so it looks, either rice or water; therefore rush to the sea at once, both you brothers. I had been to a house by the sea and the patron had given me kheer, my bowl was an extensive and endless buffet where you could eat and carry food home.'

Thus the truthful and the blessed directed the Brothers along the way. *We'll surely go there,* the Brothers resolved and straightened their waists.

Balaram hurried along and reached the portal—the Lion Gate of Lakshmi, the lotus-faced.

He entered the Lion Gate of the palace of Lakshmi, and called out for the Master of the House; his voice was loud and the housemaids surfaced with the noise.

One maid said to another:

'I've never seen another destitute like this beggar at our door. There was one fatso like him who had once hounded our Goddess Lakshmi from the Great Temple.'

The maidservants gossiped so, and they gripped Balaram by the neck and shoved Him out to the road.

Lord Balaram returned thoroughly insulted and met his brother Lord Jagannath on the way. 'The maids shooed me away, Kanhai.' He grieved before his brother.

'What do we do now?' said the Lord of the Universe. 'How do we manage to survive? Let's go there again, Brother, and humble ourselves before the maids. *Give us some cooked rice*: let's say in our prayer.'

'Then you must lead from the front,' the Elder Brother announced, 'you must beg the maids for cooked food and let me stand at your back and be your support.'

Lakshmi was lounging on her four-poster when she heard the chanting of the hymns from Lord Jagannath. 'I have got deliverance,' she cried to herself, 'I've been redeemed of my transgression and the accumulated sins of a billion rebirths have washed away today.'

Then she said aloud: 'Go, maids, and find from the two brothers what it is that they want.'

The chief lady-in-waiting darted to the portal and asked: 'Dear Brahmins, feel free to say what you want? What are you begging for.'

Lord Jagannath looked at the chief lady-in-waiting and said: 'Can you give us a fistful of cooked rice?'

The waiting maids went to the inner quarters and rapidly narrated everything before Lakshmi.

When the Goddess heard the maids, she relented: 'I've earned this calumny myself, the lowly woman, I am at the root of this ridicule of the Great Brothers. I have caused such hardship for them.' Then she said aloud to her maidservants: 'Go and ask the Brahmin brothers, how will they have cooked food from the kitchen of an untouchable woman? How will they take food in my house? Make it fast. Won't they shoulder the curse and calumny of having taken food from a chandaal woman, who has been ostracized from their society because of her lower caste? Moreover when I give them food from my house I have to touch the food. How can I pollute their food knowingly?'

The servant girls dispersed from near the Goddess and appeared before the Brahmins and narrated before them the discourse of Lakshmi. When He heard the words of the maids, the hungry Balaram said: 'Can you then give us new earthen cooking pots and utensils and raw ingredients? That will enable us to cook and eat food here.'

The servant girls carried the message before Lakshmi. The brothers themselves will cook their food and eat, said the girls.

The great Goddess was pleased to hear this. She dispatched ten pots with the servant girls. She sent twenty quintals of raw rice grains. She sent the brothers a bunch of spinach, yam, tubers, plantains, aubergines. She also arranged for milk, yoghurt, cottage cheese and sugar. 'Now cook and eat as much as you want to,' she mumbled.

The Goddess then dispatched her chambermaids to the brothers with fragrant massage oil. The maids asked: 'Dear Masters, is your food cooked or not? Use this oil for massage and have your bath fast.'

'The water does not heat up,' said Lord Jagannath. 'How can we cook? It's late now!'

'Listen, dear,' says Balaram. 'Tell me quickly if the rice is cooked.'

'Do you hear, Great Brother, the water is not even warm, how can the rice cook?'

'What do we do now?' asked Balaram.

'I can't see a way out,' replied Jagannath, 'My body is wasting away in hunger.'

'Then listen to me, brother,' said Balaram. 'Let us opt to lose our caste and eat in her house. If we do not accept a few morsels of cooked rice from this house, death will come upon us Brothers.'

The chambermaid rushed indoors and conveyed the message to Lakshmi. The maid told the Goddess how the Brahmins broke their cooking pots and threw away the broken pieces. So Lakshmi brooded over the events: 'How much the two Lords have suffered—the Lords who are known as benefactors of the poor.'

And then She, Lakshmi Devi, the Goddess, picked up a golden ladle and set off for the cooking quarters. The Goddess cooked coarse brown rice, roasted moong lentil cooked with gravy, vegetables sweet and sour, the sweet, fragrant porridge of milk and fine rice, a tangy dish of vegetables boiled in buttermilk, spinach cooked with mustard and cumin powder; sliced green plantains stir-fried in butter, inner caulis of banana plant cooked with several spices; she cooked as much food as was offered to the Lords in the Temple every day; the coarse brown rice she cooked was a miracle.

The Mother prepared pancakes of rice powder and homemade cheese dipped in thick milk; and pancakes deep-fried in clarified butter, dipped in cream saw her special care.

She cooked the items as the Brahmins would relish them.

She cooked a curry of sweet tuber, roasted sun-dried balls of black gram paste, and spiced with cumin and poppy seeds paste.

She cooked a thousand items in as many pots and placed the pots in appropriate order.

She prepared a drink of camphor, home-made cheese and brown sugar made from palm juice, and filled the potion into sixty huge pots.

She prepared a drink of tender coconut water and dumplings of cottage cheese with condiments of jaggery and crushed ginger roots.

How can I describe the culinary expertise of the Mother?

She readied all these items in a few moments. She readied the plates with one dish of each item; for the dessert she kept the cake made of powdered rice and black grams, raisins, nuts, coconut gratings, wrapped in green banana leaves and roasted on burning charcoal.

'Esteemed worshippers of Mother Cow! We will give you an oil massage and then you have a full bath.'

The Brothers relished the massage from the maids and bathed in fragrant water. They were given hand-made towels to wipe and robes of yellow silk to wear. The Brothers cleaned, and attired in new clothes, looked graceful, like Themselves.

'Brother Jagannath, why this honour suddenly?' asked Balaram. 'There is not a single man seen in this household. I think we will be executed—before a person is executed, he is given such sumptuous treatment. Let's flee from here immediately or else we shall lose our lives in a while from now.'

Lord Jagannath said: 'Now listen to me, Great Brother! Today you shall be the Lord of this household.'

'Dear younger brother, it is not proper on your part to talk like this.'

Lakshmi cleaned the whole palace with her own hands.

She sprinkled the house with camphor and oil of sandalwood.

She assembled for her guests utensils all made of gold: platters, plates, quarter plates, bowls and quarter bowls.

She too arranged basins for the rinsing of the hands.

And tubs for washing the feet, as is the practice with the Two Lords, when they are offered the *bhog*.

She made and laid out two sitting mats made of pure gold, where the brothers will sit and have their food.

Then the Mother pleaded with her maids:

'Go and usher in my Lords, dear ladies, and make it fast.'

The servant girls carried out the orders of the Goddess and appeared before the Brahmins. With humility, they entreated: 'Please O venerable Brahmins, do condescend to enter the palace as your humble dinner is ready.'

'Jagannath, you are a simpleton,' says Balaram. 'Lend me your ears. Here I can see only women. We do not see a single man in the entire palace. Would it be proper for us to enter the house? Go and fetch two banana leaves and let's eat here outside the palace.'

'Now listen to me, Great Brother,' says Lord Jagannath. 'Today we shall be the masters of this home. Why are you so restless and insecure? The giver is giving away; must we forsake that?'

A petrified Balaram stayed put in his seat firmly and he had to be taken by the hand by his younger brother, the husband of Lakshmi. Balaram refused to be seated on the seat of gold set up for the banquet, and Jagannath forced him to take the seat of gold.

Lakshmi told her kitchen maid Tulasi, a Brahmin woman: 'Girl! The older Brahmin Balaram is the elder brother of my husband; how can I serve food to him? It is taboo for a woman to come too close to her husband's elder brother. Therefore I'll pass on the dishes from the kitchen through you. You must find out who is elder and who is younger. You must serve food to the elder brother first.'

The housemaids brought in a thousand stacks of ripe banana. They brought in a beverage made of nuts, cheese, sugar, fruits and milk in sixty vessels. The Gods were treated to delicacies in keeping with their taste, as Goddess Lakshmi sent over the food dishes one after another.

After the elaborate dinner, Balaram said: 'The food is delicious, like the food cooked by Goddess Lakshmi.'

'Can I ever find a wife like Lakshmi, Great Brother?' lamented Jagannath. 'You berated her and hounded her out of the Temple. She went off to the abode of her choice.'

Then the brothers were treated with podapitha—the cake made of rice and lentil paste, nuts and raisins and roasted over cinders wrapped in banana leaves.

'Great Brother Balaram,' Jagannath continued, 'Lakshmi knew my mind; she always served podapitha as the last dish of my meals.'

The brothers finished eating and performed the ritual of thanks-giving by sipping in some water from their cupped palms. Then they relished cones of betel leaves stuffed with nuts and spices, and ambled to the portal. Lakshmi was observing them out of her window.

She said to her maids: 'Dear girls, ask if the brothers are married.'

The maids rushed out and asked the Brahmins: 'Do you have sons and wives, Brahmins? Do you have homes of your own? Which country are you from? Where is your abode and what is your occupation?'

'Listen to me, O Ladies-in-waiting,' replied Jagannath. 'I have no possessions, no sprawling estates with orchards, and who will marry me? I have chased away a wife like Lakshmi from our household. We two brothers roam around like this bearing the misfortune and fate—a result of our karma—since the day we drove out Lakshmi.'

'Have you gone off your heads, O Brahmin mendicants?' countered the waiting maids. 'Does a man become poor if he forsakes his woman?'

'Do me a favour,' said Jagannath. 'What kind of wife harbingers ever-growing prosperity? What kind of wife causes the family to be annihilated without leaving an heir? What kind of woman deprives you of even a pot of stale gruel? What kind of woman heralds in the good luck of beautiful attires and gold bracelets? What kind of ill-omened wife disintegrates the family? Do me a favour, go and ask these questions to the lady of the house on our behalf.'

'Your garrulousness is unbecoming, O venerable mendicants!' replied the girls. 'You had been starving and were given a sumptuous meal. Now satiated, you want to parley with the lady of the house?'

'Dear Jagannath, go near the Great Lakshmi,' said Balaram. 'Hold her hands and seek her forgiveness. Tell her that everything was our errancy. She can go anywhere she likes and we'll never object to that.'

With such orders from Brother Balaram Lord Jagannath rose with grace and set out for the inner quarters. He, the Yellow-Robed Deity, sauntered along the corridors and reached Lakshmi in the inner palace.

Lakshmi, the weaver of great miracles, continued to chide: 'Now, dear Husband, tell me what brings you here.' Jagannath remained pensive for a long time and then said:

'Give up your hubris, O Mother of Creation.
You chide and reprimand us,
O the cohort of my life-force without sufficient reason.
We plead before you to return to our Temple.
Though we are more powerful gods,
You vanquished our arrogance.
You assured that your glory shines on through all the aeons under the sun.
Because we forsook you
we endured agonizing suffering and pain.
The whole world learnt that
the two Brothers went begging for food.
The glorious account of your triumph is now resounding in the universe: that you gave us food and saved the lives of the famished gods.
Anyone listening on a Thursday
to this Holy Scripture,
will earn atonements for his sins of this life,
and the sins he has committed in lives before.
A woman who recites the verses
on the day dedicated to the worship of Lakshmi,
will be righteous in this life
and will find a place in heaven.
If a woman makes an oral exegesis of this glorious Scripture,
who can ever measure the virtues she earns for herself?'

Lord Jagannath ordained these proclamations and took her hands again.
But Goddess Lakshmi did not relent.
'First you must make a pledge, O Lord of the Universe,' she said.
'That the chandaals as well as the Brahmins and people from all caste and class shall feed each other inside the Temple.

After feeding each other
they shall not wash their smirched hands with water.
People from the highest caste and class
shall take food from
the fists of people from lowliest castes,
whose mere touch would
otherwise have defiled them.
After sharing the Holy Rice no one will rinse his sloshy palms,
and instead,
everyone will clean his hand by wiping it on the top of his head.
Inside the Temple everyone
must share the holy offerings
irrespective of the caste to which they are born.
Only when you concede to my stipulations
O Lord,
I shall enter Your holy abode.'

Jagannath, the-Lord-with-great-arms, solemnly agreed to the conditions imposed by Goddess Lakshmi and ordained: 'Let it be, dear Lakshmi, and let your magnificence shine through the aeons.'

31

THE DARKER SIDE OF FORTUNE[*]

TRANSLATED BY N.A. DESHPANDE

Padma-purāṇa is one of the Upa-purāṇa. The text is dated between 900 and 1400 AD. It is a vast compilation of chapters with subjects such as creation, *bhakti*, *tirtha* (pilgrimage), incarnation of Viṣṇu, etc.—Editors

The sages said:
1. O Sūta, how has this Aśvattha tree become untouchable, and similarly how has it become fit to be touched on a Saturday? Please tell us all this in detail.

Sūta said:
2–3. Out of the gems that the lordly gods obtained after churning the ocean, the gods gave Lakṣmī and Kaustubha to Viṣṇu. When

[*] Padma Purana, Chapter 116.

he accepted Lakṣmī as his wife, she respectfully said to him having the disc in his hand.

***Lakṣmī said*:**
4–5. How will you marry me, the younger one, without getting this elder one married? Therefore, O Viṣṇu, having first married this Alakṣmī, my elder sister, take me. This is an old practice.

***Sūta said*:**
6–10a. Hearing these words of her, Viṣṇu, the creator of the world, gave according to his own words, to sage Uddālaka who had practised penance for a very long time, that Alakṣmī, of a big face, white teeth, having a bright body, tall, having red eyes, and having rough and tawny hair. That sage, in accordance with Viṣṇu's words, accepted her and he, knowing Dharma, brought her to his hermitage full of sounds of (the recital of) the Vedas, rich with the fragrance of sacrificial fire, and resounding with the sounds of (the recitals of) lores. Seeing that hermitage, she who was afflicted, said these words:

***Jyeṣṭhā said*:**
10b. This abode full of Vedic sounds is not proper for me. O Brāhmaṇa, I shall not come here. Take me somewhere else. Do not delay.

***Uddālaka said*:**
11. Why do you not come? What is here that you don't like? Tell me at which place an abode proper for you would be (found).

***Jyeṣṭhā said*:**
12–15. I shall not stay there where the sound of (the recital of) the Vedas is heard, guests are honoured and sacrifices, etc., are (performed). So also I shall not stay there where a pair of lovers

live, and where the dead ancestors are honoured. I love a place where there are men engaged in gambling and taking away others' wealth, and where there live adulterers. I am interested in that place where cow slaughter takes place, drinking is indulged in, so also where sins like the killing of a Brāhmaṇa take place.

Sūta said:
16–17. Hearing these words of her, sage Uddālaka's face was dejected; and recollecting Viṣṇu's words, he did not say (anything). He went here and there. Seeing his worship she said, 'I will not come.' Then through confusion, he too became very much afflicted. Then Uddālaka spoke these words to that Alakṣmī:

Uddālaka said:
18. O Alakṣmī, stay for a moment at the root of this Aśvattha tree till I return after finding a place for (our) stay.

19–21. Thus keeping her there, Uddālaka went (away). When she who was waiting for him for a long time did not see him, she, afflicted due to being forsaken by her husband, wept piteously. Lakṣmī, in her abode in Vaikuṇṭha heard her weeping there. Then with her mind dejected, she respectfully said to Viṣṇu:

Lakṣmī said:
22. O lord, O kind one, my elder sister is afflicted due to being forsaken by her husband. If I am dear to you, then go to console her.

Sūta said:
23. Then Viṣṇu, full of compassion, came there with Lakṣmī, consoled that Alakṣmī, and said these words to her:

***Śrī Viṣṇu said*:**

24–25. O Alakṣmī, being in possession of this Aśvattha tree, be stable. I have made from my portion this abode for you. May this younger sister of you be stable with those householders who every day worship you, the elder one.

***Sūta said*:**

26–28. Those who listen to and recite this (account of) the greatness of Kārtika, would live in Viṣṇu's city till the final deluge. There is on the earth no other (vow) than that of Kārtika, dear to Viṣṇu, which removes diseases, which destroys sins, which is a great giver of intelligence, which is a means of getting sons, wealth, etc., which is the cause of salvation. What is the use (the need) for going to and resorting to holy places for the man who, with restraints, observes the Kārtika vow which is dear to Viṣṇu, which destroys all sins, which brings about prosperity in the form of good sons and grandsons, wealth and grains?

32

VRATA KATHAS FROM LAKSHMI: THE REBEL

BIDYUT MOHANTY

THE STORY OF KOJAGARI LAKSHMI PUJA

THE MOST IMPORTANT story of Bengal's Lakshmi Vrata Katha is the story of Kojagari; or, Lakshmi and Alakshmi who have been depicted as two sisters. Lakshmi is represented as dharma and prosperity but Alakshmi represents poverty. So in the Vrata Katha, when the King buys the iron idol of Alakshmi, to honour his dharma, all the other forms of Lakshmi leave him. The story also depicts that the wife should not be trusted; hence, the King left her on the bank of a river. But, finally, the wife worships Goddess Lakshmi and prosperity returns.

Many important messages become clear—the most important message in all these versions is women's agency within several contradictions. First of all, the term Alakshmi means women who supposedly don't bring good luck! It is an abuse also. In other words, adhering to the patriarchal principle, the story depicts that women may bring bad luck! Thus, the story represents patriarchal influence as well as women's agency.

Yet another aspect of the same story is that the king understands the language of animals and that of insects. It gives the message of an integral relationship between nature and the human world. The story also has introduced various nomenclatures of Goddess Lakshmi, viz., Rajlakshmi, Kshetralakshmi, Kulalakshmi, etc.

There is yet another version of Kojagari Lakshmi Vrata Katha, which depicts that the wife is not obedient and so the husband worships Goddess Lakshmi and becomes rich, then the wife welcomes him! In this version, the wife is considered to be Alakshmi but later on she changes. The plot could be interpreted as depicting women's independence subjugated by the use of wealth or Lakshmi.

In another version of Kojagari Lakshmi Puja , the king buys the idol of Alakshmi but he is not willing to throw away the same to save Lakshmi since it would hurt the creative skill of the artisan. The role of the wife is limited to worshipping Goddess Lakshmi and bringing back the prosperity. The King did not leave her, nor is there any mention of animal or insect. Yet another story shows that the mother had to make a supreme sacrifice for the sake of her son. Here also, one notices both women's agency and patriarchal influence. The characters are limited to royal or rich families unlike that of the Odia *Lakshmi Purana.*

THE STORY

In the land of Banga, there was a very virtuous king, who was well known for his observance of the dictates of dharma. He was also always respectful towards the wise and the learned. A market used to be held in front of his palace and, in accordance with the dictates of his dharma, he used to buy up whatever was left over at the market at the end of the day's exchange. He did it so that no seller ever had to sustain any loss.

One day, Goddess Lakshmi resolved to test the king's commitment to dharma. She asked God Dharma to disguise himself as a seller and take an iron statue of Alakshmi to the King's market to sell. The divine sculptor Vishwakarma made a statue of Alakshmi and Dharma took it to the market. At the market, the people asked him the name of the Goddess whose statue he was trying to sell. At this, Dharma addressed the public loudly so everyone could hear and said: 'This is the statue of Alakshmi and I am ready to sell it for a thousand rupees.' On learning that it was a statue of Alakshmi, the angry buyers turned away from him. Dharma then carried the statue on the streets and loudly announced his intention to sell it. On hearing his announcement and according to his dharma, the King bought the statue of Alakshmi to keep in his house since no one else was ready to buy it.

That night the King woke up from his sleep upon hearing a woman cry. When he went out to investigate he saw an extremely beautiful woman crying as she walked out of the palace. When the King asked her who she was and where she was going in the dead of the night, the woman said that the she was the Rajlakshmi (the Lakshmi of the Kingdom). Since the King had given shelter to Alakshmi in his house, Rajlakshmi could no longer stay under the same roof with her. She could stay only if the King were to agree to throw Alakshmi out of his house. However, since she was very fond of the King she was ready to grant him a boon, which was that the King would from now onwards understand the languages of all animals and insects. The King politely addressed the Goddess: 'Oh Mother! I do understand your anguish. But I have no option. I stand by my dharma, and according to its dictates, I must keep the statue of Alakshmi in my house. I am ready to withstand anything, even the loss of my life, to be true to my dharma. Though the departure of the Rajlakshmi worried the King a great deal, he still stood by his resolve. On the following night, he once again woke up on hearing a woman crying and this time found the Bhagyalakshmi (the Lakshmi of good fortune) leaving the palace. Like Rajlakshmi, she too offered the King the alternative of throwing out Alakshmi to retain her, but as before, the King decided to stick to his dharma even at the cost of losing the Lakshmi of good fortune. The King went back to his bed even more worried. Once again, he heard a woman cry and went out to enquire. This time, he found the Jasholakshmi (the Lakshmi of fame and goodwill) leaving his house. He answered her in the same vein that, regardless of the consequences, he had to keep Alakshmi in his house to be true to his dharma.

Back in his bed, the worried King heard someone cry again. This time he found a man and a woman leaving the palace. The woman introduced herself as the Kulalakshmi (the Lakshmi of the lineage). Once again, the King declared his firm resolve to be true to his dharma and she left. Now the King looked at the man and asked him who he was. The man said he was the God Dharma. Since all the Lakshmis had left the King, he did not think it appropriate for him to stay on with the King. But this time, the King did not passively stand aside and let him leave. The King asked: 'Why, sir, would you be leaving me? All my life I have acted according to dharma. All the Lakshmis may leave me, but you have no reason to leave me and you should not. I will always be true to you.' God Dharma was pleased at this reply and agreed to stay back. However, he advised the King to perform the worship of Lakshmi on the full-moon of the Kojagari.

With all the Lakshmis of the palace gone, the King's situation went from bad to worse. Now, every day, when the King sat down to eat and the Queen served his food, some ants regularly gathered by the side of his plate for the leftovers. As the King's situation deteriorated, he became very depressed and started to lose his appetite. One day, he told his Queen that she should instruct the cook not to put any ghee in his food. Next time, when the King sat down to eat, the ants which came for the leftovers did not taste any ghee in it. Then the leader among the ants told the others: 'You see, the King has fallen upon such hard times since buying that Alakshmi that he cannot even afford ghee in his food any longer.' Since the King could now, with the grace of his Rajlakshmi, understand the language of the insects, he understood what the ants were saying among themselves and laughed. However, his Queen, who knew nothing about it, was surprised at his laughter for no apparent reason and asked him. At this, the King answered that he could not tell her because if he did he would be sure to die. The Queen persisted. Finally, the King gave in and agreed to tell her the reason, sitting on the side of the river Ganges. When they went to the banks of the Ganges, the King heard a he-goat and a she-goat talking among themselves. The she-goat requested the he-goat to get her some grass that was floating down the river. At this, the he-goat answered that the grass was floating on deep water and he would surely drown if he were to try to get it. He was not so stupid or crazy like the King that he would lay down his life at the words of a woman. On hearing these words of the he-goat, the King came back to his senses. He left the Queen behind in the forest and went back to his palace and applied his mind to the duties of running his kingdom. He never gave any thought to the Queen or what situation she might be in.

The Queen, while wandering around in the forest, heard some auspicious conch-shell blowing accompanied by other music. Following the sound, she came to a place where she found the daughters of the sages in the forest worshipping an image of Goddess Lakshmi made of some dough of flour. On being asked by the Queen who they were worshipping, they told her that it was the day of the Kojagari full moon and therefore an auspicious day for worshipping Goddess Lakshmi. If one were to worship Lakshmi on this day, then that woman would get anything she desires by asking the Goddess. Worshipping Lakshmi on this day also throws Alakshmi out of the house and one gains prosperity. On hearing this, the Queen took some flour dough from the women, made an image of Lakshmi and worshipped her with full devotion and the appropriate rites. Then she ate the prasada with the women sages and stayed up the night with them.

From that day, all the forms of Lakshmi who had left the King came back to the Queen. Alakshmi, thus defeated by Lakshmi, left the house of the King. Then the God Dharma gave the King the good news that Alakshmi had left his house since his Queen had worshipped Goddess Lakshmi on the full moon of the Kojagari. On hearing this, the King went to fetch his Queen back with great love and respect. From that time, the King prospered from day to day by worshipping Goddess Lakshmi on the full-moon night of the Kojagari. Here ends the story for the month of Ashwin (the sixth month of the lunar calendar) and let us all sing in chorus the name of Hari!

(Translated by Dulari Nag)

THE LAKSHMI VRATA FROM MAHARASHTRA is observed in the month of Margashirsha and on Thursdays. Women of the household observe it in the hope of getting material wealth. The central message of the story is how a wife teaches her husband a lesson by showing him the relevance of salt. The story has some similarities with that of the Vaibhava Lakshmi Vrata, which is observed in northern India: five unmarried girls are invited and are given haldi-kumkum. The influence of both women's agency and patriarchy is noticed here as well.

STORY OF SHRI LAKSHMI VRATA

Attention! Please listen to the story of Shri Lakshmi Vrata. This is the story of Thursday. What is the benefit of listening to this story? It will eliminate sorrows and poverty, and give you ample wealth and money. It will fulfil your wishes quickly.

Shri Lakshmi has different forms and names. Lakshmi, who resides at Mount Kailash, is known as Parvati, daughter of the ocean, or Sindhukanya. She is Maha Lakshmi in Swargalok, Lakshmi on the earth, Savitri in Brahmalok, Radhika and Rajeshwari in Vrindavan, Chandra in Chandavan, Viraja in Champakvan, Padmavati in Padmavan, Malati in Malativan, Kundadanti in Kundanvan, Sushila in Ketakivan, Kadambamala in Kadambavan, and Rajalakshmi in Rajgruha, and the Lakshmi who resides in every house is known as Grihalakshmi.

This is the story of Maha Lakshmi. In Dwapar Yug, King Bhadrashrava was the ruler of Saurashtra state. He was very brave and courageous. He had thorough knowledge of the four Vedas, six shastras and eighteen puranas. Suratchandrika was the queen of the state. She was a very beautiful and dutiful lady. They had eight children, seven sons and a daughter. Their daughter's name was Shambala. Once, Shri Lakshmi thought that she should stay at the king's palace. She thought that if she stayed in a poor man's house, he would not spend his money on anyone else.

Shri Lakshmi changed her appearance; she became an old lady and went to Queen Suratchandrika's palace. One of the servants asked her who she was and whom she wanted to meet. The old lady said, 'My name is Kamala. My husband's name is Bhuvanesh. We stay in Dwaraka. In her previous life, your queen was the wife of a businessman. Both of them were never happy together. She left home in distress. She was wandering in the forest without eating any food. After seeing her condition, Shri Lakshmiji felt very bad for her. She told her about the Shri Lakshmi Vrata. After listening to the story, she started the vrata. Shri Lakshmiji gave her a lot of money and prosperity. She returned home and they lived a happy life for many years. Now, they are here as your king and queen. But the queen does not remember her vrata. I want to remind her.' The queen's servant asked her about the vrata, and the old lady explained what it was. Thanking her, the servant went inside the palace to convey the message.

The queen was very proud of her money and wealth. She was also very arrogant. She insulted the old lady and gave her a punishment too. Because of the queen's bad behaviour, Shri Lakshmiji did not stay there. While walking away, she met Shambala, the daughter who had come to know about the incident. She apologized for her mother's behaviour. Shri Lakshmiji told her about the vrata. That day was a Thursday in the month of Margashirsha. Shambala followed the vrata with devotion. With Lakshmiji's grace, she got married to a wealthy prince, Maladhar, son of the great King Siddeshwar. She was very happy.

Because of Lakshmiji's anger, King Bhadrashrava and Queen Suratchandrika lost their kingdom and wealth. They became very poor. One day, the queen advised the king to visit their daughter's state and seek help from her.

Bhadrashrava came to his daughter Shambala's kingdom. He was sitting near a river, where some servants from Shambala's palace had come to fetch water. They saw King Bhadrashrava and asked him, 'Who are you? Why are you here?' The king narrated his story. When the servants learnt that he was Queen Shambala's father, they hurriedly went back and told her. Shambala brought her father to her palace most respectfully. She offered him sweets and a pot full of money and gold, etc.

King Bhadrashrava returned home, and the queen felt very happy. She opened the pot curiously but was disappointed because it was filled with coal and soil, and not with money or gold.

Some time later, Shambala came to her parents' home. But Suratchandrika held a grudge against her, as Shambala had presented a pot full of coal to her father. So no one cared for Shambala. When she was returning home she took some salt with her. Back at the palace, her husband asked, 'What things have you brought from your parents' home?' She told him that she had brought 'sar' (salt) of the whole kingdom. He did not understand the meaning of her words.

Next day, Shambala ordered food to be prepared without salt. When her husband said the food was tasteless she gave him some salt, and the food became tasty. It was then that her husband understood the meaning of her words.

After some months, Suratchandrika came to her daughter's house. That was the last Thursday of Margashirsha. Shambala was observing Shri Lakshmi Vrata. She told her mother to observe the same vrata. When Suratchandrika returned home she was surprised. She had got her wealth, property and lost glory back. It happened due to the blessings of Shri Lakshmi.

So whoever will perform Shri Lakshmi Vrata with full devotion, they will get the blessings of Shri Lakshmi. They would get peace and prosperity throughout their life. The only thing you should remember is that once you get money and wealth, you should not forget to perform the vrata regularly. One should read the story of the vrata every Thursday. This vrata would bless everyone.

33

LAKSHMI TESTS KHIRI

SUNITA PANT BANSAL

LAKSHMI IS THE most popular goddess in India. Travelling across the length and breadth of the country, it is clearly visible that gods like Shiva, Vishnu, Ganesh and Hanuman are worshipped more, or less, in different regions. The same is true with goddesses such as Parvati, Durga, Kali and Saraswati, but Lakshmi is a constant. Her popularity remains undisputed. Why?

For a layperson Lakshmi represents good fortune and prosperity, material wealth or simply—money. And as they say, money makes the world go round. No wonder then, there are countless myths and legends associated with Lakshmi. The following one comes from Bengal.

'Esho Maa Lokkhi bosho ghore' or 'goddess Lakshmi come and stay in my home' has been a prayer uttered by the lady of the house in Bengal from time immemorial, and so is the story that I am narrating here.

Ages ago, there was a young, widowed queen who ruled the hearts of the people of Bengal. She was as generous as she was beautiful. Her name was Kalyani. Kalyan means 'welfare' and Kalyani, true to her name, looked after the welfare of her people in numerous ways.

Queen Kalyani held court every day where anyone could come, talk about their problems and seek help from the queen. There would be property disputes amongst fathers and sons, uncles and nephews, or just brothers. Marital disharmony or squabbles of mother-in-law and daughter-in-law or even daughter-in-law and sister-in-law were common, and the aggrieved parties would seek the queen's intervention. Kalyani's wisdom would help the families find peace amongst themselves.

Not only was Kalyani generous in sharing nuggets of her wisdom, she was so with her wealth too. She would gift gold and silver to young girls for their bridal trousseau and give money to their families to help with marriage expenses. Widows and orphans were given refuge in the royal palace. This particular trait of hers was appreciated by everyone except her chief maid Khiri.

Khiri was a mean-minded woman who helped herself to her mistress's jewels and brought in her numerous near and distant relatives to the palace to live off the queen's generosity, but could not tolerate anyone else doing the same. 'Here they come with their tall tales to swindle my queen!' would be her exasperated refrain every time she saw Kalyani listening patiently to the stories of her people. On seeing Kalyani disbursing money and jewels, Khiri would storm into her quarters in anger.

'Why is the queen so foolish! Why can't she see through the people who cheat her! Their husbands are sick forever or they continue to die over and over again . . . Such lies! All of them are liars and cheats. Why does Goddess Lakshmi bless such fools with fortune!'

People leaving the palace would hail the large-hearted queen, praying for her long life, chanting, 'Long live Kalyani, the most kind-hearted and generous queen in the world.' And this would make Khiri cringe even more.

One such day, as Khiri was sulking in her room, she heard a knock on her door. In no mood to talk to anyone, she told the person to go knock on the queen's door, as she was the one with a patient ear and a large heart. When the knocking persisted, she yelled at the person to come in. To Khiri's surprise, it was a beautiful, well-dressed woman who did not in the least look indigent.

'I have nothing to give! Had I even a fraction of Queen Kalyani's fortune, I would be doing some actual help instead of wasting it on undeserving scoundrels . . . Go to her!'

Khiri was still in a grumpy mood, though her tone had softened a bit by now.

'Tathaastu!' was the response from her unusual guest. And in a flash, everything changed. Khiri found herself in an ostentatious palace surrounded by dozens of maids. She was a queen now. It had actually happened—her prayer had been heard by Goddess Lakshmi.

Queen Khiri loved to dress up in fine silks and jewels, which she changed every few hours. She loved to eat fine cuisine, but alone. She did not share her table with even her own relatives, whom she employed as managers to keep an eye on the other servants. Since she was a queen now, needy people came to Khiri's palace too, looking for succour. She would give them advice readily but never share anything from her wealth. In fact, she would go as far as to punish those who asked for material help.

Surrounded by splendour, one would assume that Khiri would be happy with her life. But not so. She was always concerned about her wealth, especially her jewels, getting stolen and kept the managers on their toes. She was paranoid about her servants eating the leftovers of her lavish meals, so much so that she would rather eat everything herself. This resulted in her feeling sick most of the time.

One day Queen Kalyani visited Queen Khiri. Having undergone a stroke of misfortune, Kalyani had lost all her wealth, including her home. She requested Khiri for refuge, which the latter refused, saying that her palace was so full of servants that accommodating a guest would be impossible. Kalyani left and Khiri gloated. 'See! This is what happens when you waste your wealth on all and sundry who walk in with their sob-stories. I know how to look after my own fortune.'

Just then, an old impoverished-looking woman entered Khiri's court. Before she could say anything, Khiri shooed her away, saying, 'My palace has no place for the likes of you. Go away . . . go to Kalyani.' The old woman responded, 'I will do just that,' and to everyone's surprise, changed into a beautiful woman, the same one who had visited Khiri a while back in her room.

'I am Lakshmi. You wanted wealth and I gave it to you. But contrary to your claims, you do not know how to look after it. Hence, I am going back to Kalyani.'

Aghast at the startling turn of events, Khiri started crying uncontrollably. After weeping copious tears, when she opened her eyes, she was back in her old quarters at Queen Kalyani's palace. Rushing straight to the royal court, Khiri touched Kalyani's feet, hailing her generosity. The queen, though a little bewildered, continued listening to the problems of her people and sharing her wealth with them. Khiri sat down to assist her.

34

LAKSHMI AND ALAKSHMI: THE DICHOTOMY EXPLORED

TRANSLATED BY PARTHA SARATHI GUPTA

ONCE UPON A time there was a fight between Laksmi and Alaksmi. Laksmi said, 'I am more powerful than you are because I can shower riches on anyone who is poor!' Alaksmi argued, 'You may fill up any coffer, but remember, my single glance can wipe a coffer dry and reduce the same man to rags!' The argument seemed endless. However, to test their skills the goddesses descended on earth.

In a village nearby, an old widow lived with her son. His name was Ramanna. Ramanna was lazy and good-for-nothing. Throughout the day he either loitered around the village paths or spent his time sleeping. That was his routine.

But how long would the poor old widow continue to feed two mouths? She told her son: 'Son, you aren't young anymore. You have grown up in years. So you have to assist me at work. From tomorrow, you shall have to earn your wage in the fields.'

The following morning, Ramanna was out in the field owned by the village headman. But he had never held a plough in his hands! Despite all his efforts, he failed to plough the field. The village headman snubbed and scolded him. He was later sent back home. As soon as he reached home, his mother's fury was waiting to greet him. In exasperation, he said to his mother, 'From tomorrow, I shall go out to a faraway village to find work. You please pack up a bundle of rice for me for my afternoon meal.'

His mother was only waiting for this response. She wanted her son to realize his duties. The following morning, his mother prepared his *butti*, or rice wrapped up in a wet cloth. Ramanna then set out on his journey to a distant village.

Do you know what happened in the meantime? Ramanna was about to cross the same path on which descended the two warring goddesses: Laksmi and Alaksmi! They saw Ramanna walking along with eyes fixed onto the ground. Laksmi spotted him and instantly knew what went on in his mind. She told Alaksmi, 'See, the poor fellow is a pauper. He has no work. I'm going to make him rich. You just watch.' Alaksmi quipped, 'I'll see how you do that!' No sooner had the boon emanated from Laksmi's lips than a pot of gold lay in Ramanna's path! Alaksmi, with a sly chuckle, shot back: 'Now watch my trick!' And she gazed at Ramanna.

Ramanna spotted the pot from a distance. He could see the shining gold coins inside. He was delighted at the discovery and said to himself: 'Our days of misery shall now be over forever!' But by that time, Alaksmi's gaze had already fallen upon Ramanna. Ramanna, overwhelmed with excitement, decided to shut his eyes and approach the pot of gold. A little later when he opened his eyes, much to his dismay, he realized that he had crossed the pot of gold behind him. Exasperated, he decided not to turn back towards it anymore and continued walking. Alaksmi's spell worked and she laughed out aloud. Laksmi's face fell. A little later, Laksmi threw a gold necklace on his path. Alaksmi cast her spell once again. But this time Ramanna was wiser. He picked up the jewel as soon as he spotted it.

Laksmi was overjoyed. She said, 'See, Ramanna's fate has embraced him! You could do nothing!' Alaksmi retorted, 'Wait. The game is not over yet!'

The two sister-goddesses waited eagerly in the skies to watch the fallout of the discovery. A little while later, Ramanna returned home to find that his mother was out. She was busy in the field of the village headman. Ramanna hung the necklace on a pole in the courtyard and went out to call his mother. As soon as he saw his mother in the field, he called out to her, 'Mother, I've got a gold necklace. Let's return home. Our days of misery are over. We need not work anymore.'

The old woman was overjoyed and rushed back home. But to her dismay, there was no gold necklace. A *cheel* had by that time carried it away on its beak. Mother blasted Ramanna. However, what was done could not be undone. Misery greeted their fates again. She then went back to work in the field.

The following morning, Ramanna once again packed his butti and left home in search of work.

Once again, Laksmi showered a few gold coins on his path. Ramanna picked them up as usual and returned home with renewed joy. As usual, he found the door shut and knew that his mother was in the field. But this time he felt that he needed to be smarter. So he began to search for a secure place to keep the coins. He found the place at last. He went to the corner of the courtyard where an oven had been prepared. He dug up the ashes in it and placed the coins inside, and covered them up with the ashes. Assured of their security, he rushed to the field to let his mother know of the developments that day. His mother was reluctant to leave the field as she suspected that her son must have been fooled once again. However, on Ramanna's repeated insistence, she obliged. When they returned home, Alaksmi's spell had already worked by then. As Ramanna dug up most of the ashes, his face went pale. The coins had disappeared. He wondered where they might disappear.

In the meantime, while Ramanna was away in the field, an old lady from the neighbourhood had arrived in the courtyard to light a fire from the hidden embers in the ashes under which the coins lay hidden. She was spellbound to unearth, not sparks, but gold coins, from the embers. Quietly, she took them away without a word.

Here, Mother was furious for having been duped by her son's stupidity once again. She returned to the field promptly. Ramanna was crestfallen.

Ramanna left home the next day once again with his butti. Alaksmi and Laksmi were on the vigil from above. Alaksmi said, 'As long as my spell is active, you cannot do anything.'

Laksmi argued, 'Man grows wiser by the day from his experiences. With each passing day, Ramanna will grow wiser. Let me see what he does today.'

Laksmi scattered a few coins on his path again. Ramanna was overjoyed to be blessed with good fortune again. But this time as he returned home with good news and found his mother away, he did not keep his treasure away. He tucked them in his own cloth and rushed to the field. His mother was first suspicious. But then as the coins shone in front of her eyes, she became ecstatic. Their happiness knew no bounds after that. They returned home. The next day, Mother explained how Ramanna should start a trade with the coins. Ramanna did as he was told. And as days passed, the family grew richer by the day.

Then Laksmi said to Alaksmi, 'You see, your gaze shall not work at all times. There will come a day when wisdom shall teach man the art of dodging your gaze.' Left speechless, Alaksmi bowed her head down in reverence.

35

THE ASHTA LAKSHMI STOTRAM AND THE KANAKADHARA STOTRAM

R. MAHALAKSHMI

Sumanasa vandita sundarī mādhavī candra sahodarī hemamaye
Munigana mandita moksa pradāyinī mañjula bhāsinī vedanute
Pankaja vāsinī deva supūjita satguna varsinī śāntiyute
Jaya Jaya He Madhusūdana kāminī Ādilaksmī sadā pālayamām

(Ashtalakshmi Stotram, verse 1)

(O Primeval Lakshmi, you are the one I send this heartfelt prayer to, you are the beautiful one, the embodiment of spring, the sister of the moon, and golden-hued. You are worshipped by the sages and hordes of followers, provide deliverance, are beautiful and recite the Vedas. You dwell in the lotus flower, are worshipped by gods, shower manifold virtues and bestow peace. Praise be to the goddess who is the desire of the destroyer of the demon Madhu [Vishnu]. May she always protect me.)

RELIGIONS ARE NEVER static and numerous streams of thought come up at different points of time. Some of these streams have acquired a pan-Indian presence while others have remained popular in the regions where they evolved. Interestingly while we assume the roots of religion lie only in the ancient past, there are many innovations and transformations that have been taking place all around us even in the twentieth century. The Vaishnava tradition has expanded, like others, in such a manner that the distinctions that were held so dear by the sectarian denominations within the tradition remain in name alone, except in orthodox circles. Even here, the migration of less orthodox beliefs and practices to other non-Hindu-majority nations obviously causes further adjustments and transmutations. Also, new-age gurus have consciously undertaken the task of reinventing Hinduism, drawing from various local and textual traditions.

There are a number of *stotramalas,* literally, garlands of eulogies, that have been compiled over the past two centuries to help ordinary worshippers retain their religiosity in a world where time is scarce. The compilers pick certain hymns in honour of certain deities, for instance, Vishnu, Lakshmi, Devi, and provide the source of the hymn as well as the manner in which these stotrams have to be read as part of a ritual offering.

Thus, instructions that *pushpa* or flowers be offered to the deity after every incantation, *jalabhisheka* or water be poured on an image and *dhupa* or incense be offered intersperse the text. With the advent of the electronic media, this has been simplified even further and cassettes, CDs and videos detailing rituals, mantras and festivals are the main source of religious knowledge. The Ashta Lakshmi hymn is very popular particularly in south India. The Kanakadhara Stotram, given its legendary composer Adi Shankara, is an integral part of any prayer book on the Devi.

Ashta Lakshmi Stotram

In the 1970s, Shri U. Ve Mu Srinivasavaradacharyar Swamigal composed a poem called the 'Ashta Lakshmi Stotram', which drew on earlier notions and conceptualizations of the goddess Lakshmi and strung these together to provide a composite view of different forms of this goddess. In a manner that would appeal to the devotee most, the poem is based on an understanding of the attributes of the goddess and the fruits of devotion to her. The earliest such inspiration for the savant may be traced to the famous Shri Sukta hymn in the Rig Veda.

> *Putra Poutra Dhanam Dhānyam Hastyaśvāśvatarī Ratham*
> *Prajānām Bhavasi Mātā Āyuśmantam Karotu Me* (SS, verse 20)

Here, the goddess as mother is invoked and asked to bless the devotee's sons, grandsons, wealth, grain, elephants, horses, beasts of burden, chariots and subjects with long life. Some of the conceptualizations among the eight Lakshmis indeed draw upon the benefactions that the goddess is seen as bestowing in this ancient Vedic composition.

The 'Ashta Lakshmi Stotram' has an important place among the many offerings that are today considered a part of the daily worship routine of Hindu women. As the name indicates, there are eight different forms in which this goddess is venerated. Each of these forms is seen as representative of a quality, characteristic or virtue attached to the goddess, and the worship of this form of the goddess is seen as bringing the same virtues in the form of blessings into the lives of her devotees.

The first form of the deity to be venerated in the composition is the primordial one—Adi Lakshmi. The stotram states: she is to be worshipped from the heart (*sumanasa)*. She is the beautiful one (*sundari*), the desire of Madhusudan, Madhavi and the sister of the moon *(Chandra sahodari).* She bestows liberation on her devotees (*moksha pradhayani),* is worshipped by the gods, dwells in the lotus flower and rains down virtues on those around her. Adi Lakshmi is the root cause of all existence, without whom creation is inconceivable. This concept brings the Samkhya understanding of prakriti and purusha very clearly to mind. In her aspect of Adi Lakshmi, it is not just the goddess as Lakshmi who is invoked but also Sriman Narayana of the Srivaishnava tradition. Just as purusha is incomplete without prakriti, and mind without matter has no meaning, Lord Narayana is seen as incomplete without Lakshmi, and this is why she is Adi Lakshmi.

Other interpretations about this stotram have become current, such as the rising of the goddess from the ocean during the great churning, showing her primeval nature. What is significant about the invocation of Narayana with reference to Adi Lakshmi is that it presents the primacy of the goddess on the one hand and the complementarity between the male and female principles of creation on the other.

The second verse is in praise of Dhanya Lakshmi—the goddess of grain—a typical earth goddess representation. Ironically, she is first praised here as the personification of the Vedas, then as the home of the mantras. She is born of the milky ocean and the devas and *ganas* ('flock', generally the followers of Shiva and Durga) reside at her feet. The signature last line again praises her as Madhusudana Kamini. What is essential to note about this form is that grain or dhanya is made out to be so important in the lives of people—the notion of food sustaining life is reiterated in this concept. And who better to symbolize this than the great mother who herself produces and reproduces life?

Secondly, women are traditionally seen as the managers of the household, and no household can run without the plentiful availability of grain. The wonderful thing about such a conceptualization is that the goddess Dhanya Lakshmi also encompasses in herself other conceptualizations such as that of the goddess Annapurna, the goddess of food. In fact, it is said that among the different kinds of charities a householder may engage in, *anna danam* or the donation of food brings the greatest blessings. In a predominantly agrarian society, where hard toil and heavy labour characterize the annual cycles of sowing, reaping and harvesting, the fruits of that labour are dependent on the vicissitudes of nature. A drought, cyclone or pest attack can demolish all the best efforts. In such circumstances, Dhanya Lakshmi is seen as providing a rallying point for her worshippers, assuring them of a plentiful supply of grain.

The third conceptualization is of Dhairya Lakshmi—the goddess of strength. She is referred to as Vaishnavi, Bhargavi, the embodiment of mantras and the means to attain victory. She is also the one worshipped by the gods and divine beings, and readily gives her blessings to those who worship her. She helps them overcome their fears and provides absolution from sins. According to this verse, she provides shelter to learned people and her followers, and contributes to the growth of knowledge and understanding of the religious scriptures—the Shastras—by her devotees. She is also referred to as Vira Lakshmi, and by alluding to the idea that her worship will provide a path to the Vedas, it is indicated that she personifies not merely physical courage, but also the mental power to overcome all strife. The Shastras, as the fount of all knowledge, in this understanding, help the believer in overcoming the illusions of the material world.

In the next form, as Gaja Lakshmi, the goddess destroys the misery of her followers and they are granted the fruits of their devotion. The stotram states: *Harihara Brahmā Supūjita Sevita Tāpanivārani Pādayute.* Gaja Lakshmi is worshipped by the trinity—Hari, Hara and Brahma—and redeems the vows of those who seek her.

Scholars have shown that the earliest archaeological evidence of Lakshmi is found in Kushana period coins, where elephants flank the goddess, who is seated on a lotus. It is possible that some earlier tribal deity (deities?) whose totemic symbol was the elephant and/or lotus was gradually assimilated into the Brahmanical pantheon of deities. Philosophers and theologians, however, have interpreted this form of the goddess in other ways. According to some, elephants symbolize royal power and the goddess affirms power structures and authority. At another level, she may be seen as the protector of her devotees, just as the king looks after the well-being of his subjects. At the local level, various myths explaining the Gaja Lakshmi icon have gained currency. At the Thirunavay temple, a sacred Vaishnava site in Tamil Nadu, it is said that the elephant king Gajendran offered flowers to Lord Narayana here, but was unable to provide enough flowers to the goddess Lakshmi. To remove the dejection of his devotee, Narayana drew Lakshmi unto himself and became Lakshminarayana, so that together they could be propitiated with the flowers brought by the elephant king. As the elephant king worships her, she is known as Gaja Lakshmi. Such stories reveal how sacred landscapes emerge in disparate regions by incorporating some indigenous traditions with Puranic themes, essentially localizing the deity and claiming the centrality of that particular place or temple in the sacred geography of the religion.

In her fifth form in the stotram as Santana Lakshmi, the goddess is seated on a white crow and is described as attractive (Mohini), as the source of all melody and the centre of Being (Chakrini). She is said to be at the heart of the universe, home to virtues and devotees and adorned with the *sapta svaras* (seven notes). All the gods, demons, learned men and humanity venerate her. This is a very significant form as it brings one of the core needs of the devotee to the forefront—a lineage to carry forward his/her name. As *santana pradhayini,* the goddess offers women the boon of bearing and rearing healthy children. (The Hindu patriarchal family structure privileges women in the family primarily as mothers. In such a setting, the birth of a child is obviously something that both men and women cherish. There are many local legends at particular temples that assure the worshipper of a child if due worship is offered to the goddess Lakshmi.)

The sixth form of Lakshmi in the stotram is Vijaya Lakshmi, the goddess of victory, seated on a lotus, who provides knowledge and directs her followers to the right path. She is decorated with *kumkum* and other unguents every day, adorned with jewels and given her seat. She is the receptacle of prosperity and homage is paid to her by singing the 'Kanakadhara Stuti'. In this verse, some interesting allusions are made: on the one hand, the goddess symbolizes victory, and on the other, she directs her devotees to follow a certain path. Here, the emphasis is on ethical and moral values that need to be followed even on the battlefield. Secondly, the goddess is not merely the vanquisher of enemies, but also of illusion. This is why her association with knowledge is referred to. The Kanakadhara hymn is in praise of the goddess of prosperity and it is said to bring health, wealth and success to those who chant it after seeking a blessing from the goddess. Victory, in this sense, is also over poverty, misery and circumstance. By separating the goddess of strength from the goddess of victory, the composer appears to be stressing the need to realize victory in material and emotional pursuits, as symbolized by the goddess in her pursuit of demons like Mahisha as Jaya Lakshmi. This is an interesting example of intertextuality, very common in Sanskrit literary traditions, where one text recommends that another has to be read along with it.

The next form discussed in the 'Ashta Lakshmi Stotram' is Vidya Lakshmi, the goddess of learning and the leader of the gods, Bharati and Bhargavi. She is the gem-studded one who destroys all suffering. She is radiant with jewels, has a smiling countenance and provides peace of mind to her worshippers. She offers new opportunities and removes evil and malice from the path of her worshippers.

This form has a great significance for the young and old, particularly in modern times. Education is seen as a liberating force, moving people beyond their caste and class denominations. By worshipping the goddess as Vidya Lakshmi, the devotee is assured of her blessing in educational pursuits. At the philosophical level education can be viewed as an unending quest for true knowledge, and the more knowledge one acquires, the greater is the freedom from material shackles. It is in this sense that the goddess destroys suffering and gives peace to her worshippers. There are many stories of great men like Kalidasa and Tenali Rama who achieve phenomenal success and attain true wisdom due to the grace of the goddess.

Finally, the stotram describes Dhana Lakshmi, the goddess of wealth, who is praised for her resounding dance of prosperity. This appears to be a play on the *Natya Shastra*'s categorization of five *tandavas* or dances of Shiva. The dance of bliss/prosperity is well known as the *anandatandava,* and so the goddess is depicted as engendering prosperity with her dance. She is also the triumphant conch that blows the auspicious notes that symbolize wealth and health. She is the object of worship in the Vedas, Puranas and *Itihasas*, and is the one who firmly establishes the Vedic tradition among her followers. The goddess also performs a triumphant dance signifying her aggressive aspect, implying the total empathy of the goddess with the welfare of her devotees.

The Ashta Lakshmi concept is a very new one, but has found many takers. Amongst the many stotras and *stutis* recited at home every day, this one finds an important place. It is now a part of popular iconography as well. Silver pots used for rituals often have the Ashta Lakshmis depicted on them, as do printed and framed pictures of deities available at shops lining temple streets. A beautiful stone temple in the typical Dravida style, dedicated to the Ashta Lakshmi, and specially conceptualized and consecrated by the pontiff of the Kanchi Kamakoti Peetham, has been built on the beach at Besant Nagar in Chennai. The goddess is placed here with her back to the ocean so that she will not be drawn to it, remain on terra firma and keep granting benefactions to her devotees.

Kanakadhara Stotram

This hymn is said to have been composed by the first Brahmin monk to have attempted to unite the subcontinent by establishing four *mathas* or monasteries, Shankara. The monasteries are believed to have been founded at Shringeri in Karnataka, Dwaraka in Gujarat, Jyotirmatha in Uttarakhand and Puri in Orissa. Shankara most probably lived in the eighth century CE, and the exact details of his life are a matter of great controversy. At any rate, from medieval accounts, all bearing the title *Shankara Vijayam,* it is clear that the brahmanical tradition attributes its rejuvenation and propagation to this savant.

There are many hymns that have been ascribed to Shankara, and the 'Saundaryalahari' and 'Kanakadhara Stotram' are notable among these. The former is a mystical poem in praise of the goddess who is the consort of Shiva, and the embodiment of beauty and power. The latter honours the goddess Lakshmi, and was reported to have been uttered by the monk as a benefaction for a pious woman who gave him the remaining fruit in her kitchen when he went to her door begging for alms.

In the stotram, a simple refrain of the worshipper is that the goddess should turn her attention, symbolized by a momentary look, at him, her devotee. It is believed that even a simple glance from her will lighten up the life of the devotee singing her praises. There are many mythic allusions that are made in this prayer. The first is that of the goddess emerging from the ocean and choosing

Hari as her spouse (verses 1, 2). The second is her unswerving faith towards her lord (verses 2, 3). A third motif is her restoration of the power and strength of the lord of the heavens, Indra (verse 7). The Devi Mahatmya, Devi Bhagavata Purana and other texts include myths about the deaths of the demons Madhu and Kaitabha, on whom the goddess merely cast her beautiful eyes to divert their attention from Vishnu. This is alluded to in verses 6 and 7.

From verses 8 to 12, the goddess Lakshmi is conceptualized as the root of all power, knowledge and prosperity. Finally, the goddess is addressed by her many epithets, each signifying her many associations and powers. The signature verse sums up the purpose of this stotram:

Stuvanti ye stutibhiramū bhiranvaham,
Trayīmayīm tribbuvanamātaram ramām,
Gunādhikā gurutara bhāgya bhāginō,
Bhavanti te bhuvi budha bhavitaśayāh

The person who recites these verses in praise of the pleasing one, the embodiment of the three Vedas, and the mother of the three worlds, will be blessed with good virtues, fortunes and intellect, which will be praised by the learned of the world.

This particular hymn is part of the recently compiled *shlokamalas* or books of shlokas that are meant to be a part of everyday prayers, particularly on Fridays, in Hindu homes.

36

THE GODDESS OF WEALTH BY MANY NAMES

SWAMINI ATMAPRAJNANANDA

THROUGHOUT HISTORY, PEOPLE have worshipped gods and goddesses associated with wealth to escape poverty, make more money (yoga) or protect their earnings (*kshema*). Many cultures feature gods of wealth and prosperity as part of their mythology and folklore. A number of ancient civilizations worshipped multiple gods and goddesses of wealth while some had only one. Occasionally, some gods who were worshipped in one religion were transferred to another.

The Greeks had Core, the corn goddess, who was known to the Romans as Demeter. The Egyptians had Isis, the Sumerians had Inanna, the Babylonians had Ishtar, the Persians had Anahita and the Vikings had Freia. Shri Lakshmi is the goddess of wealth and prosperity in the Hindu pantheon. In fact, in India, not only Hindus, but even Jains and Buddhists worship Lakshmi for her blessings. Jainism and Buddhism are primarily monastic orders that turned away from Vedic rituals about 2500 years ago. They could not, however, abandon this goddess of wealth and prosperity.

In the most popular account of Lakshmi's birth, she rose from the churning of the ocean of milk—an important event in Hindu mythology—seated on a lotus and holding another lotus blossom in her hand.

Lakshmi is the divine power that transforms dreams into reality. She is prakriti, the perfect creation, self-sustaining, self-contained nature. She is maya, the delightful delusion, the dreamlike expression of divinity that makes life comprehensible, hence worth living. One can say about her, 'She whose mercy turns a dumb person into an eloquent orator and enables a lame person to cross the mountain.'

Various Manifestations of Lakshmi

Lakshmi, also known as Shri, is one of the principal goddesses in the Hindu pantheon. She is the goddess of wealth, prosperity, good fortune, power, beauty and fertility and is associated with maya (illusion). Along with Parvati and Saraswati, she forms the Tridevi of the Hindu pantheon. Her omnipresence is demonstrated clearly by the widespread use of the symbol Shri, which represents her and material blessing. She is seen as the consort of Lord Vishnu, the Preserver, and her avataras accompany many of his incarnations. Lakshmi is said to have taken different forms to be with him in each of his incarnations. Thus, when he was the Vamana, she appeared from a lotus and was known as Padma or Kamala, both of which are synonyms for lotus. When he was Parashurama, the destroyer of the kshatriyas (the warrior class), she was his consort Dharani (mother earth). When he was King Rama, she was his queen, Sita. In Krishnavatara, she incarnated as Rukmini.

Time and again, Lakshmi is also seen to have taught valuable lessons to Vishnu. The following story of Lord Narayana acknowledging defeat from Lakshmi is an amusing one narrated by my Guru, Swami Dayananda Saraswati, during an evening *satsang* gathering.

The Bet: A Story

Once, there was a bet between Lord Vishnu and Lakshmi as to who is more popular in *martyaloka* or earth. Lord Vishnu took the form of an old *kathakar* or storyteller and started the Bhagavata Katha in a temple. Many devotees came to listen to him. Suddenly, there appeared an old woman who seemed to need help. A few people approached her and asked if they could assist her in any way. The old woman asked for some water. When they got up to fetch drinking water, the old woman said, 'But I drink only from my own glass.'

She took out a bejewelled gold glass from her *thaila*, bag, and asked them to pour the water into it. The bhaktas fought with one another to bring her water. After she drank a glassful she asked for more water and said, 'I do not use a glass twice.' She threw away the bejewelled glass on the floor and pulled out another one from her bag. There was a mild stampede to pick up the glass she had dropped.

Devotees started leaving the narration of the Hari Katha and surrounded the old lady. Lord Vishnu was quite perturbed and uneasy. Finally, the entire audience left Lord Vishnu and started offering water *seva* to the elderly visitor. The wise Lord Vishnu surrendered to the old lady and said, 'Amma! I apologize. I am fully convinced that you are the most powerful in this world, and this world sustains because of you.'

Alakshmi

It is important to remember Alakshmi as the antithesis of Lakshmi. In the religious tradition, her name is not uttered as she is the deity of misfortune. The two places where she is referred to in the Shri Sukta, the lines are chanted with caution.

तां प॒द्मिनीमी॒ं शर॑णम॒हं प्रप॑द्येऽल॒क्ष्मीर्मे॑ नश्यतां॒ त्वां वृ॑णे ॥५॥

I worship you so that my Alakshmi* may be destroyed by you. (5)

क्षुत्पि॑पा॒साम॑लां ज्ये॒ष्ठाम॑ल॒क्ष्मीं ना॑शया॒म्यहम् । ॥8॥

I will eradicate from me that elder one, inauspiciousness/misfortune, uncleanliness in the form of hunger and thirst, poverty and lack of progress. Destroy all that from my house. (8)

Ashta Lakshmi

Most of us are aware of the eight facets of Lakshmi-tattva, or Ashta Lakshmi. The specific attributes as spelt out in the Ashta Lakshmi Stotram are spirituality, material wealth, agriculture, royalty, knowledge, courage, progeny and victory. The earliest source of her different aspects appears to be in the Shri Sukta, a supplement to the fifth Mandala of the Rig Veda.

सि॒द्धल॒क्ष्मीर्मो॑क्षल॒क्ष्मीर्ज॒यल॑क्ष्मीस्स॒रस्व॑ती।
श्रीलक्ष्मीर्व॑रल॒क्ष्मीश्च॒ प्र॒सन्ना॒ मम॑ स॒र्वदा॥—श्रीसूक्तम् 29

Variations such as the following came later in the 1970s, when the Ashta Lakshmi Stotram was composed:

Adi Lakshmi: the primal one
Dhana Lakshmi: wealth

* Orthodox Hindus do not utter this word because Alakshmi denotes the absence of all that Lakshmi denotes, in both explicit and implicit ways.

Dhanya Lakshmi: foodgrains/food in all forms
Gaja Lakshmi: elephant wealth
Dhairya Lakshmi: courage and patience
Santana Lakshmi: followed by progeny
Vijaya Lakshmi: victory in all fields
Vidya Lakshmi: knowledge = Saraswati

Lakshmi Sahasranama

Shri Lakshmi is invoked by 1000 names that are carefully enunciated as the Lakshmi Sahasranama (though several of her names or epithets are similar). The Sahasranamas comprise three groups. The first reveals the truth about Ishvara, whether one reads the Lakshmi, Saraswati or Devi Sahasranama. Another group denotes the gunas or attributes. Yet another cluster presents specific lilas that may be different with reference to each deity. When Ishvara is invoked as goddess, the names are in the feminine gender.

a) Epithets based on Svarupa unfold the essence of Vedanta
Most of the words in the Sahasranamas are words that reveal the truth of the goddess. Since that truth is only One, the words are bound to have the same meaning. The various natures of the goddess are symbolized through the epithets focusing on the svarupas.

Luminous self: ॐ स्वप्रकाशस्वरूपिण्यै नमः ।
Eternal joy: ॐ नित्यानन्दायै नमः ॥
Purity: ॐ शुद्धायै नमः ।
Truth: ॐ सत्यायै नमः ॥
Soul of love: ॐ प्रणवात्मिकायै नमः ।

b) Epithets based on Gunas

Another group of words describe the gunas of the goddess, the One who has created this world and is also manifest in the form of this world/universe. From this standpoint, we can see the goddess as:

One who creates everything: ॐ ब्राह्म्यै नमः ।
One who sustains everything: ॐ वैष्णव्यै नमः ।
One who takes back everything unto herself: ॐ शिवायै नमः ॥

These names are not svarupa but gunas of the goddess with reference to the entire *jagat* or the world, which includes the body–mind–sense complex. It is everything that is known and unknown. Alluding to jagat, these words describe the One who is in the form of the sun, space, earth, fire and other such elements.

There are also guna words and names describing her qualities. We see in the goddess several aspects that we admire and would like to emulate. We have these qualities to some extent, but the goddess has them in absolute measure. These qualities include auspicious attributes like the *kalyana* gunas of Devi. The objective is to imbibe qualities such as these in the devotee's self.

Blesses her devotees: ॐ भक्तानुग्रहकारिण्यै नमः ।
Fulfils desire: ॐ कामदायै नमः ।
Power behind action: ॐ क्रियाशक्त्यै नमः ।
Makes all mantras yield results: ॐ सर्वमन्त्रफलप्रदायै नमः ।
Destroyer of all troubles: ॐ सर्वोपद्रवनाशिन्यै नमः ।

c) Epithets based on Lila describe the Goddess's incarnations

The third set of words reveals how the goddess actively participates in answering the devotee's prayers. Some of the lila names are Sita, Rukmini, Parvati, Chandika and Chamunda, and her forms may denote the cycle of creation, the power to destroy evil and to be manifest in shakti rupa.

One who lives in the oleander flower: ॐ करवीरनिवासिन्यै नमः ।
One born from a lotus: ॐ कमलोद्भवायै नमः ।
One who rides on a swan: ॐ हंसवाहिन्यै नमः ।
The earth goddess: ॐ धरण्यै नमः ।
Shakti of the Narasimha (Vishnu): ॐ नारसिंह्यै नमः ।

Resolving a Few Apparent Contradictions

Lakshmi, Saraswati and Parvati are typically conceptualized as distinct in most of India, but in states such as West Bengal and Odisha they are regionally believed to be forms of Durga. In Bengali Hindu culture, Lakshmi and Saraswati are seen as the daughters of Durga and are worshipped during Durga Puja.

The goddess who is endless and is forever: ॐ अनन्तनित्यायै नमः ।
The goddess who shines permanently: ॐ नित्यप्रकाशिन्यै नमः ।
The goddess who is naturally shining: ॐ स्वप्रकाशस्वरूपिण्यै नमः ।
ॐ महालक्ष्म्यै नमः ।

When we chant ॐ महालक्ष्म्यै नमः we feel we are worshipping Maha Lakshmi and will be blessed with wealth.

ॐ महाकाल्यै नमः । She is Maha Kali also. The goddess who is the great Kali, the goddess who is black in colour.
ॐ महाकन्यायै नमः । She is Devi Durga also, though Durga is presented in our scriptures as an unmarried goddess (a *kanya*).
ॐ सरस्वत्यै नमः । She is Saraswati too, though *artharthi* devotees seek not the goddess of learning but the bestower of wealth.
ॐ शिवायै नमः। Parvati, consort of Lord Shiva, has come in here because Lakshmi is the same Shakti in the form of Parvati.

ॐ वाग्देव्यै नमः । प्रहसन्निव Shastra says: The one you are worshipping is Vagdevi Saraswati also.

ॐ महाराल्यै नमः । Hail Mother Kali (goddess of deluge). The ferocious-looking Goddess Kali is also another form of the Devi I am trying to worship, Shastra says.

ॐ कालरात्र्यै नमः । The One who is known as Kalaratri is also Lakshmi who is worshipped on Sharat Purnima, which comes after Kalaratri Diwali.

ॐ हरिप्रियायै नमः । The devotee is worshipping the beloved of Shri Hari. The same concept is repeated in 918. ॐ विष्णुपन्यै नमः । Salutations to the consort of Shri Vishnu.

ॐ पार्वत्यै नमः । Worship to the daughter of the mountain. Lakshmi is no different from Parvati.

ॐ अरूपायै नमः । Arupa: the goddess who does not have any form.

ॐ बहुरूपायै नमः । The goddess who takes several forms.

ॐ विरूपायै नमः । The goddess who has a gigantic form.

ॐ विश्वरूपिण्यै नमः । The goddess whose form is the universe.

ॐ अकारादि-क्षकारान्त-मातृकायै नमः । ॐ अकारादि-क्षकारान्त-सर्ववर्णाकृत-स्थलायै नमः । The one who is the beginning as well as the conclusion of the Sanskrit alphabet, alluding thereby to the whole of Sanskrit literature as well as all the literature in the world.

ॐ ब्रह्म-विष्णु-शिवात्मिकायै नमः । One who is the essence of Lord Brahma, Lord Vishnu as well as Lord Shiva.

ॐ इडा-पिङ्गलिका-मध्यमृणालितन्तु-रुपिण्यै नमः । In the discipline of knowledge, Ida, Pingala and Susumna are the three imaginary lines in yogic philosophy. Lakshmi is the presiding deity of yoga.

ॐ अमावास्यायै नमः । One who is the new moon.

ॐ पूर्णिमायै नमः । One who is the full moon.

ॐ सूर्य-चन्द्राग्नि-नेत्रायै नमः । She is manifest in the form of the sun, the moon and the fire—they being her three eyes.

ॐ ग्रह-नक्षत्र-रूपिण्यै नमः । She is also manifest in the form of the planets.

ॐ सहस्राक्ष्यै नमः । Salutations to the one with a thousand eyes.

ॐ सहस्रभुजपादुकायै नमः । Salutations to the one with a thousand arms and a thousand feet (omnipresent), referring to the Purusha Sukta.

ॐ प्राणदायै नमः । The One who gives life.

ॐ गतये नमः । She also takes away the life.

ॐ विद्याधिदेवतायै नमः । Lakshmi is worshipped as the presiding deity of all disciplines of knowledge.

ॐ मंत्र-व्याख्यान-निपुणायै नमः । She is proficient in Vedic and Puranic literature.

ॐ ज्योतिशास्त्रैकलोचनायै नमः । She is also the presiding deity of the science of astrology.

ॐ पुराणन्यायमीमांसायै नमः । She is manifest in three systems of philosophy, and more: Nyaya, Purvamimamsa, Shruti as well as Purana and Dharmashastra.

ॐ कृत्तिकादि-भरण्यन्त-नक्षत्रेष्ट्याचितोदयायै नमः । She is manifest as the twenty-seven *nakshatras* (constellations) in our zodiac.

ॐ वेदानाम्समन्वयायै नमः । She reconciles the four Vedas.

ॐ वेदानामविरोधायै नमः । She shows the non-contradiction in the content of the four Vedas.

Goddess Lakshmi stands as a symbol of profound significance in Hindu mythology and culture. As the embodiment of wealth, prosperity and good fortune, she symbolizes the essential aspects of a fulfilling and harmonious life. Her significance extends beyond material wealth, emphasizing the importance of inner abundance, spiritual growth and the pursuit of righteousness. The diverse manifestations and cultural interpretations of Goddess Lakshmi highlight her adaptability and universal appeal. Whether through elaborate rituals, vibrant festivals or personal prayers, devotees from various backgrounds find relief and inspiration in her divine presence. The devotion and rituals dedicated to Goddess Lakshmi reflect the timeless pursuit for balance and well-being in our lives. Lakshmi's association with virtues such as compassion, generosity and knowledge serve as a reminder that true wealth lies not only in riches but in the richness of character and the capacity to share one's blessings with others. Lakshmi's multiple appellations and attributes bear testimony to her infinite power.

108 NAMES OF LAKSHMI

ALKA TYAGI

1. Om Prakṛtyai namaḥ
Aum salutations to the Goddess who is of the form of Nature

2. Om Vikṛtyai namaḥ
Aum salutations to the Goddess who is of the form of modifications of Nature

3. Om Vidyāyai namaḥ
Aum salutations to the Goddess who is of the form of Knowledge

4. Om Sarvabhūtahita pradāyai namaḥ
Aum salutations to the Goddess who bestows welfare on all beings

5. Om Śraddhāyai namaḥ
Aum salutations to the Goddess who is of the form of Faith

6. Om Vibhūtyai namaḥ
Aum salutations to the Goddess who is Supreme Power

7. Om Surabhyai namaḥ
Aum salutations to the Goddess who is Celestial

8. Om Paramātmikāyai namaḥ
Aum salutations to the Goddess who is of the form of Supreme Self

9. Om Vāce namaḥ
Aum salutations to the Goddess who is of the form of Speech

10. Om Padmālayāyai namaḥ
Aum salutations to the Goddess who resides in the lotus

11. Om Padmāyai namaḥ
Aum salutations to the Goddess who is of the form of lotus

12. Om Śucaye namaḥ
Aum salutations to the Goddess who is of the form of Purity

13. Om Svāhāyai namaḥ
Aum salutations to the one who is of the form of *Svāhā*, auspiciousness

14. Om Svadhāyai namaḥ
Aum salutations to the Goddess who is of the form of *Svadhā*, inherent Power

15. Om Sudhāyai namaḥ
Aum salutations to the Goddess who is of the form of Nectar

16. Om Dhanyāyai namaḥ
Aum salutations to the Goddess who is of the form of Fortune

17. Om Hiraṇmayyai namaḥ
Aum salutations to the Goddess who is of Golden hue

18. Om Lakṣmyai namaḥ
Aum salutations to the Goddess of Wealth

19. Om Nityapuṣṭāyai namaḥ
Aum salutations to the Goddess who eternally gains Strength

20. Om Vibhāvaryai namaḥ
Aum salutations to the Goddess who is Radiant

21. Om Adityai namaḥ
Aum salutations to the Goddess who is radiant like the Sun

22. Om Dityai namaḥ
Aum salutations to Goddess *Diti*

23. Om Dīpāyai namaḥ
Aum salutations to the Goddess who is of the form of flame of a lamp

24. Om Vasudhāyai namaḥ
Aum salutations to the Goddess who is of the form of Earth

25. Om Vasudhāriṇyai namaḥ
Aum salutations to the Goddess who is bearer of the Earth

26. Om Kamalāyai namaḥ
Aum salutations to the Goddess who emanates from the Lotus

27. Om Kāntāyai namaḥ
Aum salutations to consort of Viṣṇu

28. Om Kāmākṣyai namaḥ
Aum salutations to the Goddess who has charming eyes

29. Om Krodhasambhavāyai namaḥ
Aum salutations to the Goddess who has potential for Anger

30. Om Anugrahapradāyai namaḥ
Aum salutations to the Goddess who bestows Grace

31. Om Buddhaye namaḥ
Aum salutations to the Goddess who is of the form of wisdom

32. Om Anaghāyai namaḥ
Aum salutations to the Goddess who is free of Sin

33. Om Harivallabhāyai namaḥ
Aum salutations to the Goddess who is beloved of Hari

34. Om Aśokāyai namaḥ
Aum salutations to the Goddess who is dispeller of Sorrow

35. Om Amṛtāyai namaḥ
Aum salutations to the Goddess who is source of Immortality

36. Om Dīptāyai namaḥ
Aum salutations to the Goddess who is Bright

37. Om Lokaśokavināśinyai namaḥ
Aum salutations to the Goddess who destroys sorrows of the world

38. Om Dharmanilayāyai namaḥ
Aum salutations to the Goddess who is the abode of dharma, eternal law

39. Om Karuṇāyai namaḥ
Aum salutations to the Goddess who is of the form of Compassion

40. Om Lokamātre namaḥ
Aum salutations to the Goddess who is mother of the universe

41. Om Padmapriyāyai namaḥ
Aum salutations to the Goddess who loves the Lotus

42. Om Padmahastāyai namaḥ
Aum salutations to the Goddess with hands like Lotus

43. Om Padmākṣyai namaḥ
Aum salutations to the Goddess with eyes like Lotus

44. Om Padmasundaryai namaḥ
Aum salutations to the Goddess who is Beauty of Lotus

45. Om Padmodbhavāyai namaḥ
Aum salutations to the Goddess who emerges from Lotus

46. Om Padmamukhyai namaḥ
Aum salutations to the Goddess whose face is Lotus

47. Om Padmanābha priyāyai namaḥ
Aum salutations to the Goddess who is beloved of Padmanābha

48. Om Ramāyai namaḥ
Aum salutations to the Goddess who pleases the Lord

49. Om Padmamālā dharāyai namaḥ
Aum salutations to the Goddess who wears the garland of Lotuses

50. Om Devyai namaḥ
Aum salutations to the radiant Goddess

51. Om Padminyai namaḥ
Aum salutations to the Goddess who is of the form of Lotus

52. Om Padma gandhinyai namaḥ
Aum salutations to the Goddess who has fragrance of Lotus

53. Om Puṇyagandhāyai namaḥ
Aum salutations to the Goddess who exudes divine Fragrance

54. Om Suprasannāyai namaḥ
Aum salutations to the Goddess who is ever Cheerful

55. Om Prasādābhimukhyai namaḥ
Aum salutations to the Goddess who emerges to grant Joy

56. Om Prabhāyai namaḥ
Aum salutations to the Goddess who is radiant like Sun

57. Om Candravadanāyai namaḥ
Aum salutations to the Goddess who is Moon-faced

58. Om Candrāyai namaḥ
Aum salutations to the Goddess who is Moon

59. Om Candrasahodaryai namaḥ
Aum salutations to the Goddess who is sister of the Moon

60. Om Caturbhujāyai namaḥ
Aum salutations to the Goddess with four arms

61. Om Candrarūpāyai namaḥ
Aum salutations to the Goddess who is of the form of Moon

62. Om Indirāyai namaḥ
Aum salutations to the Goddess who is queen of Heaven

63. Om Induśītaḻāyai namaḥ
Aum salutations to the Goddess who is cool like the Moon

64. Om Āhlādajananyai namaḥ
Aum salutations to the Goddess who is source of Happiness

65. Om Puṣṭayai namaḥ
Aum salutations to the Goddess who is of the form of Health

66. Om Śivāyai namaḥ
Aum salutations to the Goddess who is Auspicious

67. Om Śivakaryai namaḥ
Aum salutations to the Goddess who makes everything Auspicious

68. Om Satyai namaḥ
Aum salutations to the Goddess who is of the form of Truth

69. Om Vimalāyai namaḥ
Aum salutations to the Goddess who is extremely Pure

70. Om Viśvajananyai namaḥ
Aum salutations to the Goddess who is Mother of the universe

71. Om Tuṣṭayai namaḥ
Aum salutations to the Goddess who is source of Contentment

72. Om Dāridryanāśinyai namaḥ
Aum salutations to the goddess who Destroys poverty

73. Om Prītipuṣkariṇyai namaḥ
Aum salutations to the Goddess who is a pool of love

74. Om Śāntāyai namaḥ
Aum salutations to the Goddess who is of the form of Peace

75. Om Śuklamālyāmbarāyai namaḥ
Aum salutations to the Goddess who wears sky as white garland

76. Om Śriyai namaḥ
Aum salutations to the Goddess who is Wealth

77. Om Bhāskaryai namaḥ
Aum salutations to the Goddess who is radiant like Sun

78. Om Bilvanilayāyai namaḥ
Aum salutations to the Goddess who makes Bilva tree her home

79. Om Varārohāyai namaḥ
Aum salutations to the Goddess who is ready to offer Boons

80. Om Yaśaswinyai namaḥ
Aum salutations to the Goddess who is Illustrious

81. Om Vasundharāyai namaḥ
Aum salutations to the Goddess who is daughter of the Earth

82. Om Udārāṅgāyai namaḥ
Aum salutations to the Goddess who has beautiful Limbs

83. Om Hariṇyai namaḥ
Aum salutations to the Goddess who is of the form of Female Deer

84. Om Hemamālinyai namaḥ
Aum salutations to the Goddess who has Golden garlands

85. Om Dhana-dhānyakaryai namaḥ
Aum salutations to the Goddess who bestows grains and wealth

86. Om Siddhaye namaḥ
Aum salutations to the Goddess who is of the form of *Siddhi* (special Powers)

87. Om Straiṇasaumyāyai namaḥ
Aum salutations to the Goddess who bestows grace of Women

88. Om Śubhapradāyai namaḥ
Aum salutations to the Goddess who grants Auspiciousness

89. Om Nṛpaveśmagatānandāyai namaḥ
Aum salutations to the Goddess who loves to reside in Palaces

90. Om Varalakṣmyai namaḥ
Aum salutations to the Goddess who bestows Bounty

91. Om Vasupradāyai namaḥ
Aum salutations to the Goddess who bestows Wealth

92. Om Śubhāyai namaḥ
Aum salutations to the Goddess who is Auspicious

93. Om Hiraṇyaprākārāyai namaḥ
Aum salutations to the Goddess who circles the Golden womb

94. Om Samudratanayāyai namaḥ
Aum salutations to the Goddess who is daughter of the Ocean

95. Om Jayāyai namaḥ
Aum salutations to the Goddess who is Victory

96. Om Maṅgaḻādevyai namaḥ
Aum salutations to the Goddess who is most Auspicious

97. Om Viṣṇuvakṣassthalasthitāyai namaḥ
Aum salutations to the Goddess who resides on the chest of Viṣṇu

98. Om Viṣṇupatnyai namaḥ
Aum salutations to the Goddess who is consort of Viṣṇu

99. Om Prasannākṣyai namaḥ
Aum salutations to the Goddess with Cheerful eyes

100. Om Nārāyaṇasamāśritāyai namaḥ
Aum salutations to the Goddess who seeks refuge in Nārāyaṇa

101. Om Dāridryadhvamsinyai namaḥ
Aum salutations to the Goddess who destroys Poverty and Misery

102. Om Devyai namaḥ
Aum salutations to the Radiant Goddess

103. Om Sarvopadravavāriṇyai namaḥ
Aum salutations to the Goddess who is dispeller of all kinds of Distress

104. Om Navadurgāyai namaḥ
Aum salutations to the Goddess who is of the form of nine Durgas

105. Om Mahākāḻyai namaḥ
Aum salutations to the Goddess who is Mahākāḻī

106. Om Brahmā Viṣṇu Śivātmikāyai namaḥ
Aum salutations to the Goddess who is of the form of Trinity of Brahmā,Viṣṇu and Śivā

107. Om Trikāḻajñānasampannāyai namaḥ
Aum salutations to the Goddess who possesses knowledge of Time in three forms—past, present and future

108. Om Bhuvaneśvaryai namaḥ
Aum salutations to the Goddess who is Sovereign of the universe

AFTERWORD

NAMITA GOKHALE

AS A YOUNG woman, I was deluded into thinking that Lakshmi, the goddess of wealth, and Saraswati, the goddess of learning, had to be approached through different trajectories that could never be reconciled. I cast my lot with the latter and shall remain loyal to her all my life.

As I approached the Biblical span of three score and ten, the belated realization dawned upon me that the two goddesses, the contemplative Saraswati and the dynamic Lakshmi, representing between them wisdom and abundance, were emanations of the same force. Some texts cast them as sisters, daughters of Goddess Durga. In other versions Lakshmi, Saraswati and Ganga are sparring co-wives of Lord Vishnu. Epic and myth mention them in different familial configurations but they are invoked together. Devotion to knowledge and material aspirations are not conflicting paths.

From the ancient rice goddess, the symbol of plenitude and fertility, to the modern icon of luxury and material wealth, the goddess of abundance has undergone countless incarnations and interpretations. In today's world, where tangible assets are not counted just in oxen and elephants, and reside not only in gold but also in virtual and digital equity, access to knowledge is an essential aspect of wealth.

Who is Lakshmi? In all her aspects—Shri, Kamala, Gaja Lakshmi, Padmavati Bhargavi and so many more—the goddess fulfils a fundamental need within all of us across the world. Different cultures and religious constructs project the universal human desire for security and good fortune on to their deities. Ancient Greece had Tyche, capricious goddess of fortune and prosperity. The Roman goddess Fortuna was an oracular divinity, represented holding the cornucopia of plenty and a rudder to steer the path of destiny. Freyja, the Norse goddess of fertility, like Fortuna, held the power of prophecy. The ability to pierce the veil of the future was common to both Fortuna and Freyja. Vasudhara is the Tibetan goddess of wealth and well-being. Benzaiten, the Japanese goddess of good fortune, the only feminine figure among the seven lucky gods, is also the goddess of wisdom, deriving from Saraswati and the spread of Buddhism into Japan.

The complex Hindu system of belief is not bound by any single book, text or decree. It nurtures a multiplicity of understanding and interpretation. Our anthology delves into the enigma of Lakshmi, her secrets, her treasures, her many blessings. The stories and essays, poems and hymns and meditations that we have collated here carry myriad interpretations of the elusive goddess of good fortune. She is fickle and restless. She is Prakriti, the nurturing and creativity of the natural world. She is Maya, the delusion and deception of wealth and attachment. She is Shakti, the boundless power and energy of the divine. The goddess with a thousand names reveals different facets to her devotees, divergent even within their own hearts. She contains multitudes.

Worshipped in every part of India in various forms and manifestations, Lakshmi was born of the churning of the ocean, the epochal Samudramanthan, a monumental event akin to the tectonic collision of the continental crust of the Indian plate thrusting into the Eurasian plate about 50 million years ago. Geo-mythology depicts Lord Shiva as consuming the poison, the toxic halahala, produced by this churn, to maintain cosmic harmony. Goddess Lakshmi and her elder (Jyestha) sister Alakshmi, symbolizing between them the polarities of the auspicious and the inauspicious, were born from this Samudramanthan. Both represent the duality of fortune in its positive and negative aspects and are part of the cycle of a larger unity, with different roles and attributes.

Lakshmi, the wife of Lord Vishnu, is the very symbol of marital and familial harmony. Her sister Alakshmi represents all that is unfortunate, ill-starred and lacking in auspiciousness. Alakshmi is also known as 'Jyestha' or the older, senior presence, and as 'Daridra' or poverty. Alakshmi is ill-spoken and lazy and brings jealousy and malice in her trail. She was thrown out from his ashram by her husband, Rishi Uddalakh.

Yet, Lakshmi's compassion and sorority, and her understanding of polarities, extend to her elder sister, Alakshmi. She herself was birthed and blessed by the nectar, the Amrit that rose from the mythic churning of the ocean. Her shadow self Alakshmi was born of a drop from the lethal poison halahala and its noxious residue.

To the patriarchal gaze, Lakshmi's sister would have appeared a subversive, undomesticated and dangerous figure. After Alakshmi was abandoned in the forest under the shade of a peepal tree, she was ostracized and kept outside any societal interaction. Yet, her sister, Lakshmi, did not abandon her and continued to visit her on Saturdays in her refuge under the peepal tree to give her comfort.

The lonely figure of Alakshmi has always filled me with both deep sympathy and a superstitious awe and trepidation. The Hindu pantheon accommodates rebels and outliers, and

Alakshmi is also associated with the widow Dhoomavati, the seventh of the ten wisdom goddesses, the Mahavidyas. Lakshmi's standing by her wild sister only strengthens my respect for her, for the compassionate goddess who gives.

Hindu cosmology is said to have 33 *koti* (330 million) gods and goddesses. The feminine divinities in this bewildering pantheon are distilled into the Dash Mahavidyas, the ten wisdom goddesses. Shri Lakshmi in her form as Kamala or Kamalatika is the last and ultimate representation of the great wisdom goddesses.

These goddesses are divided into the 'Ugra' or wrathful and 'Shanta' or sublime manifestations. The first of these Mahavidyas is Kali in her fierce or Ugra aspect as the destroyer of ego and negativity. The final culmination of the collective wisdom of the ten great goddesses lies in the sublime aspect of Kamala, who represents both cosmic spiritual wisdom and the joy and treasures of our living, material world.

Contemporary Hinduism as understood in popular private and public practice devolves from several strands of layered ritual and philosophical understanding. Kamala represents the spiritual essence while Lakshmi incorporates those aspects of worship that have to do with material boons and well-being.

The word Kamala, signifying the lotus, literally means 'robed in water'. 'Ka' in Sanskrit denotes the summit, the head, the waters. 'Mala' comes from *malla dharane* which means 'to wear'. Water is the life-giving essence of life and creation.

Puranic texts describe Kamala as *kshira sagarakanyaka*—daughter of the milky ocean. The Greek goddess Aphrodite, and the Roman Venus, who represent love and fertility, were also ocean-born. Kamala/Lakshmi arose from the epic churning of the Samudramanthan and brought forth the treasures of the deep.

The Vishnu Purana describes Kamala as the daughter of the divine sage Bhrigu, one of the Sapt Rishis or seven sages, and his wife, Khyati. Bhrigu, who authored the great predictive text of the *Bhrigu Samhita*, is believed to have passed on the gift of foreknowledge to his daughter Lakshmi/Kamala, contributing to her ability to grant good fortune. Since understanding the contours of the future helps us to embrace good luck and avoid misfortune, Bhrigu is known as the father of fortune, and his daughter Lakshmi, also known as Bhargavi, is goddess of all that is auspicious. Like the oracular Roman goddess Fortuna and the prescient Norse goddess Freyja, Lakshmi's knowledge of astrology and her intuitive understanding of the future is a crucial part of her powers.

Indic culture is deeply material, celebratory and rooted in the here and now while simultaneously remaining consistently spiritual. It worships the *nirgun* or abstract non-manifest truths while making them accessible to laypersons in the dimension of *sagun* or manifest knowledge. It is of the world and affirmative of life in its philosophy while also deeply invested in the path of the renunciate.

The complex Hindu system of belief is never monolithic. It is not bound by any single book, text or decree. It is full of paradoxes and contradictions, and nurtures a multiplicity of understandings and interpretations.

Shri, in her many manifestations, is the symbol not only of material wealth but also of abundance, of family and community, of dharma and societal equilibrium. Shri Lakshmi represents the order, stability and harmony of the universe. She is, through her various forms and emanations, born of Prakriti, of nature, and is the feminine incarnation of agriculture, husbandry and rich harvests. She is the wife of Dharma, the very embodiment of righteousness and ethical conduct. She resides symbolically in the lotus, both as diagrammatic representation as in her *yantra*, and in the Padma, the Kamala and other such emblematic representations of her many-petalled, sacred abode, and of Mahalakshmi's mystic Mahamaya. She is ever *sumangal* (auspicious) and *subhaga* (fortunate).

As Kamala, Lakshmi is a personification of the lotus. Her yantra is of very special and specific significance. The multi-petalled lotus is an iconographic symbol of the manifest universe and is found in some aspect in every yantra. Literally meaning 'instrument', a yantra is a meditative tool and visual invocation representing a specific plane, dimension or cosmic vibration. There is a specific geometry and discipline to every yantra, and each representation is a composition of concentric circles, triangles and squares radiating from a central point or *bindu* and encompassing a lotus. The sacred Lakshmi yantra has geometric forms of interlocking triangles encircled by eight lotus petals, which help in meditative practice to unleash her essential energies.

The lotus, rising above the muddy water, is an abiding symbol of purity, enlightenment and transcendence, and an essential part of Shri Lakshmi's iconography. Her esoteric energies are said to be centred in the astral zone of the Manipur Chakra, situated three fingers above the navel. The Beej Mantra or seed syllable of Shri Lakshmi is श्री (Shrim). Recitation of this sound is said to draw her blessings, granting generosity and contentment.

Another important part of Lakshmi's iconography is the figure of her familiar, the owl, Uluka. The vahanas or vehicles of Hindu divinities are their totemic or spirit signifiers. The vahana or mount of Lakshmi, Uluka symbolizes intelligence and wisdom and has the ability, like Lakshmi, to foresee the future. In other mythology the owl is associated with Minerva, the Roman goddess of wisdom.

Lakshmi, the goddess of fortune, is notoriously capricious. She is described as *chanchal* or restless. When propitiated, she is *karm prabhav prakashak*—she who illuminates the fruits of good actions. When displeased, she is quick to withdraw her favours from her devotees. In the daily superstitions of popular religion, householders are advised never to have the goddess of wealth placed near a depiction of the owl as this might prompt her to mount Uluka and fly away with him.

The abiding images of Shri Lakshmi in the collective consciousness of most Hindus are derived from the vastly popular oleograph prints from the Raja Ravi Varma Press, dating from 1894, when the press was established. These are based on a sequence of oil paintings Ravi Varma worked on for royal patrons. Lakshmi is depicted draped in a red sari. She is seated upon a red lotus and holding red lotus flowers in two hands. The other two hands are spread out in postures signifying blessings and boons.

The cover image for this volume diverges starkly from the prevalent Raja Ravi Varma–inspired visualizations. Sourced from an old print from the Chitrashala Press, Pune, it depicts a powerful and resplendent feminine figure draped in yellow, wearing a golden crown festooned with pearls, a gold tilak on her forehead, long earrings, a dazzling Maharashtrian nose ring and a profusion of gold necklaces. Her gaze is direct and piercing, and there is a force field of strength and energy that she exudes.

We are deeply grateful to Aman Nath for his generosity in locating cover images for all three books in our Goddess trilogy: *In Search of Sita*, *Finding Radha* and *The Treasures of Lakshmi*. This one, of Maha Laxmi Gouree, illuminates our efforts with her grace.

Both Sita and Radha are incarnations of Lakshmi. Each anthology is a quest for the hidden narratives and feminine energies behind these three goddesses. Of these, Lakshmi is said to be the most fickle, inconstant and enigmatic. The wealth of material, which Dr Malashri Lal and I have uncovered while searching associated stories, legends and hymns, is a timeless treasure.

Working on each of these goddesses has been accompanied by difficult learnings and hard-won insights. In the essay 'Sita: A Personal Journey' from *In Search of Sita: Revisiting Mythology*, I observed that mythology in India is not just an academic or a historical subject but a vital and living topic of contemporary relevance, and that Sita's exile was a collective wounding in the psyche of Indian women. In the introduction to *Finding Radha: The Quest for Love*, I wrote: 'Radha, the bucolic milkmaid, follows the instincts of her heart, of her passion, to seek union with her innermost self. The enigma of Radha and the example of Radha coexist and are both contained in the apparent paradoxes and composite unity of the Hindu religion.'

The essays in this collection explore different facets and interpretations of Shri Lakshmi over millennia. They also examine other allied figures from the religious and mythic spheres, such as Kubera and Alakshmi, to understand the evolution of the goddess as she is known and worshipped in our times. The signs and symbols of Lakshmi have changed and adapted through the ages, but at the seat of it is the power of the feminine, as allied with the plenitude of Prakriti, with nature and creativity and abundance, and with the wise husbandry of that abundance. Yet, the goddess of wealth is not averse to risk-taking, and during the festival of Diwali gambling is indeed encouraged as auspicious.

The collective consciousness that irradiates Indian myths, legends, folktales and religious texts constantly yields multiple layers of meaning. The reinterpretation and re-assimilation of these by successive generations creates a sense of both continuity and movement.

Salutations and obeisances to Sita, Radha and Lakshmi, to Kamala and Mahamaya, to Shri and Saraswati, and all the mighty goddesses and feminine deities and energies around the world. The timeless perspectives and contemporary interpretations across this anthology have provided profound insights and learnings. This book has been a journey and a quest. It is in its small way a tribute to Lakshmi from her sister Saraswati.

NOTES ON CONTRIBUTORS

Alka Tyagi, a poet, researcher and translator, teaches English at Dyal Singh (Evening) College, University of Delhi. Her research areas are Bhakti movement, ancient Indian literatures, Upanishads, Yogic studies and Kashmir Trika Śaiva Tantras. Her doctoral thesis is on medieval Bhakti poets, Andal and Akka Mahadevi. Her recent book, *Reconstructing Devotion through Narada Bhakti Sutras*, was published by DK Printworld. A former fellow at IIAS, Shimla, she completed her monograph on *Bhavana* (Creative Contemplation) and *Bhairava* (Supreme Reality) in Kashmir Trika Shaivism. Dr Tyagi has been an ardent practitioner of yoga for forty years. She continues to imbibe higher practices under the guidance of her spiritual masters at ashrams in Munger and Rikhia. Website: www.tantravimarsha.com.

Arunava Sinha is associate professor of creative writing at Ashoka University. He earned his bachelor of arts (English honours) from Jadavpur University. He translates classic, modern and contemporary Bengali fiction and non-fiction into English, and from English into Bengali. Over eighty of his translations have been published so far. He has conducted translation workshops at the British Centre for Literary Translation, UEA, University of Chicago, Dhaka Translation Centre and Jadavpur University. Besides India, his translations have been published in the UK and the US in English, and in several European and Asian countries through further translation.

Ashutosh Garg is the author of renowned Hindi novels, *Ashwatthama*, *Indra*, *Kalki* and *Kuber*. He is proficient in Hindi and English , has dictionaries and books for children to his credit and has translated over thirty bestselling books. He is a post-graduate in Hindi literature and writes regularly for magazines and newspapers. A senior officer in the Government of India, Garg has been conferred the National Award (2016) by the former President of India, Dr Pranab Mukherjee, and also the prestigious Bhasha Bandhu Alankaran (2022) by Amar Ujala Foundation for the Hindi translation of *The Last Girl*, authored by the Nobel Peace laureate Nadia Murad.

Bibek Debroy is a noted economist in the Government of India, but for scholars of classical Indian literature, he is an outstanding Indologist with prolific translations of ancient Sanskrit texts into English. His books constitute a ready reference for scholars in search of literary material on the epics, mythology, Puranas, Vedas and many other shastric discourses. Bibek Debroy has translated the unabridged version of the Mahabharata into English, in a series of ten volumes. He has also translated the Bhagavad Gita, the Harivamsa, the Vedas and Valmiki's Ramayana (in three volumes). He has translated the Bhagavata Purana, the Markandeya Purana, the Brahma Purana, the Vishnu Purana and the Shiva Purana. He was conferred the Sir Ramakrishna Gopal Bhandarkar Memorial Award in July 2023 by the Bhandarkar Oriental Research Institute.

Bidyut Mohanty is head of women's studies and senior fellow at the Institute of Social Sciences (ISS) in New Delhi. She has been a visiting professor in the Global and International Studies programme at UC Santa Barbara and is a fellow of the Orfalea Center for Global & International Studies at UCSB. She is the coordinator of the ISS and UNDP project on Capacity Building of Elected Women Leaders in Local Government in India, and of the project sponsored by the National Commission on Protection of Child Rights. She has coordinated projects sponsored by UNIFEM (UNWOMEN), UN AIDS and FINISH (through the ISS). Dr Mohanty is a specialist on famine, agrarian history and decentralization studies with a focus on gender, culture and development. She combines grassroots activism with research and writing.

Constantina Rhodes is a professor of religion, workshop facilitator and certified intuitive consultant. With a specialty in the goddess and tantric traditions of India, her best-known book is *Invoking Lakshmi: The Goddess of Wealth in Song and Ceremony*, based on her original translations of Sanskrit invocations. Constantina serves on the faculty at Hunter College of the City University, New York. She also teaches at the New York Open Center and in various yoga teacher training programmes, where she leads workshops on prosperity consciousness, yoga philosophy and intuitive development.

Devdutt Pattanaik writes on mythology, which he defines as cultural truths revealed through stories, symbols and rituals. He lectures on the relevance of both Indian and Western myths in modern life. In the last twenty-five years, he has authored and illustrated over fifty books, including *The Book of Ram* and *Dharmic Leadership*. Known for his TED talk and TV shows such as *Devlok* and *Business Sutra*, he is a regular columnist for reputed newspapers like the *Times of India* and *Dainik Bhaskar*. A medical doctor by training, Devdutt spent fifteen years working in the pharma and health-care industry, but over the past decade he has been fully immersed in exploring mythology and sharing its wisdom with the world.

G.V. Tagare, a former member of the Maharashtra Education Service, retired as professor of education from the Government Secondary Training College, Kolhapur. A versatile scholar, untiring researcher and prolific author, he has written on diverse themes of Indology, linguistics and education. In addition, his published works include translations of Mahapuranas, critical editions of Sanskrit texts, and histories of Prakrit, Pali and Assamese literatures. Dr Tagare is also known for discovering several old, unpublished manuscripts: in both Marathi and Sanskrit.

Jawhar Sircar, a retired civil servant with over four decades of experience in administration, is currently a member of the Indian Parliament. He has served as India's culture secretary and, thereafter, as the CEO of India's public service broadcaster, Prasar Bharati. Sircar, till recently, chaired the board of governors of the Centre for Studies in Social Sciences, Kolkata, one of India's premier research and teaching institutes. He has been actively involved in research on the intersection of politics and religion. His book on this subject, written in Bengali, has found wide acceptance and his earlier work on the emergence of the Hindu identity in medieval western Bengal has been quoted by social historians. He is a social and political commentator who regularly contributes to leading media publications.

Lipipuspa Nayak is a Bhubaneswar-based academic, freelancer and translator. She translates literature from Odia to English, specializing in translations of classics. A particular text she has translated is *Lakshmi Purana,* dating back to the sixteenth century CE, presumed to be the first feminist literary text in an Indian language. With fifteen published English translations of Odia fiction, poetry and plays, she is a recipient of the National Culture Fellowship of Government of India. She reviews books for prestigious magazines and newspapers, has made a documentary film on the lesser-known temples of Odisha and filmed a story adaptation for the national television.

Malashri Lal, professor in the English department (retd) and former dean, University of Delhi, has authored and edited seventeen books. These include *In Search of Sita*, *Tagore and the Feminine* and *Finding Radha*. *Betrayed by Hope: A Play on the Life of Michael Madhusudan Dutt* (2020), co-authored with Namita Gokhale, received the Kalinga Fiction Award. Malashri Lal's latest book is *Mandalas of Time: Poems* (2023). She has received research and writing fellowships at Harvard University, Bellagio and Newcastle. A senior consultant to the Ministry of Culture, Lal has also been a member of the international book award juries. She is currently convener, English Advisory Board of the Sahitya Akademi. Among other recognitions, Lal received the Maharani Gayatri Devi Award for Women's Excellence in 2022.

Meghnad Desai is an economist by profession and taught at the London School of Economics for forty years, where he is Emeritus Professor of Economics. He has authored more than fifty books and 200 articles. His recent books include *Marx's Revenge: Resurgence of Capitalism and the Death of Statist Socialism*; *Nehru's Hero: Dilip Kumar in the Life of India*; *Development and Nationhood: Essays on the Political Economy of South Asia*; *Rethinking Islamism: The Ideology of the New Terror*; and a novel, *Dead on Time*. Meghnad

Desai was a member of the British Labour Party from 1971 to 2000. He was made Lord Desai of St Clement Danes in 1991 and was awarded the Bharatiya Pravasi Puraskar in 2004 and the Padma Bhushan in 2008.

Menka Rai is an assistant professor (history) at Amity Law School, Noida. She has also worked on a project dealing with violence against women in the development sector. Her PhD research work is 'Representations of Women in the *Mahāpurāṇas*: Through the Lens of Family, Caste and Class (c. 3rd to 8th centuries C.E.)', where she explored different social themes from a gendered perspective. She has published and presented papers on themes such as the cult of sixty-four yoginis, polyandry in Brahmanical tradition in early India, asceticism for women in Brahmanical religion, violence against women, public policy in ancient India, etc.

N.A. Deshpande is regarded as a pioneer scholar of Indology. One of his important contributions to the field includes the translation of Padma Purana (I–X volumes) in the series Ancient Indian Tradition and Mythology.

Namita Gokhale is the author of twenty-three books, including twelve works of fiction. She has co-edited the anthologies of the Goddess trilogy on Sita, Radha and Lakshmi with Dr Malashri Lal. Her acclaimed debut novel, *Paro: Dreams of Passion*, was published in 1984. Recent works of fiction include *The Blind Matriarch*. The edited anthology *Mystics and Sceptics: Searching Himalayan Masters* was published in 2023. Gokhale is co-founder and co-director of the Jaipur Literature Festival. She has been recognized both for her writing and her commitment to multilingual Indian literature and cross-cultural literary dialogue. She received the prestigious First Centenary National Award for Literature in 2017 and was a

Sahitya Akademi awardee for 2021. She has been honoured with the Nilimarani Sahitya Samman 2023.

Niharika K. Sankrityayan holds a PhD in ancient Indian history from Centre for Historical Studies, Jawaharlal Nehru University, New Delhi, India. As a postdoctoral fellow in the School of Humanities and Social Sciences, Indian Institute of Technology Mandi, she worked on 'Sixteenth Century Renaissance in South India'. She was awarded the Charles Wallace Fellowship in 2016, where she worked more closely on Brahmanical iconography of the Deccan in London. She is a published writer of articles and book chapters on diverse themes of South Asian culture, most notably 'Emblems of Faith, Monuments of Authority: Brahmanical Iconography in the Western Deccan' in R. Mahalakshmi's edited book *Texts, Contexts and Visual Representation in Ancient and Early Medieval Art and History*.

Nilima Chitgopekar is an associate professor, Department of History, Jesus and Mary College, Delhi University. She has authored seven books and edited one, along with several articles and essays on Hindu gods and other related matters. Her latest book is *Shakti: An Exploration of the Divine Feminine*. She has been the recipient of prestigious fellowships, including the Oxford Centre of Hindu Studies, Charles Wallace India Trust Fellowship and USIS fellowship at Boston College, and has lectured widely in India and overseas, most recently at Harvard University. Dr Chitgopekar has featured in and worked with BBC documentaries and radio programmes. In her attempt to take Hindu mythology to a far larger audience, she has been involved in making several online films. These films of her lectures have sold worldwide, covering topics like the history of a god, the iconography and more current themes, such as gender roles in the celestial world, mythology and personal development.

P.P. Joglekar is director (Academic Development Programme), Bhandarkar Oriental Research Institute, Pune. He formerly worked as professor of archaeology at Deccan College Post-Graduate and Research Institute, Pune. His research specialization is in the field of bioarcheology. Prof. Joglekar combines field archaeology and bioarcheology to understand the faunal remains from past societies and their role in emergence and sustenance of human cultures. He has published eleven academic books, two edited volumes, 238 research papers and twenty-seven popular articles.

Prasanna K. Dash is a retired civil servant and author of eleven books, including short-story collections, poems, translation, literary criticism, essays and stories for children. Some of his notable books are *Tell a Tale and Other Stories, Invisible Poet and Other Stories, The Mysterious Ladies and Other Stories, Kathapur Tales, River Song, O Krishna, O Son: Yashoda's Sublime Song of Sorrow*. He has translated from Sambalpuri, Odia, Sanskrit and Urdu to English. He is also a prolific blogger on diverse subjects, including scriptures, micro-stories, current affairs, crypto-currencies and AI.

Reba Som is an acclaimed author, academic, historian, singer and a cultural ambassador. She was the recipient of the prestigious Jawaharlal Nehru Fellowship from 2000 to 2002 and served as the regional director of the Rabindranath Tagore Centre, ICCR, Kolkata, from 2008 to 2013. Her publications include *Gandhi, Bose, Nehru and the Making of the Modern Indian Mind* (2004), *Rabindranath Tagore: The Singer and His Song* (2009), *Margot: Sister Nivedita of Swami Vivekananda* (2017) and *Hop, Skip and Jump: Peregrinations of a Diplomat's Wife* (2023). Som is a trained singer of Rabindra sangeet and Nazrul Geeti.

Renuka Narayanan is a commentator and columnist on religion and culture. She was arts editor, the *Indian Express*, with a column on religion; editor, religion and culture, *Hindustan Times*; and the start-up director of the Indian Cultural Centre, Embassy of India, Bangkok. Her published books include *The Book of Prayer, Faith: Filling the God-Sized Hole* and *The Little Book of Indian Wisdom.*

R. Mahalakshmi is a professor at the Centre for Historical Studies, Jawaharlal Nehru University, New Delhi. She specializes in the history of ancient and early medieval south India. She has authored many books and research articles on religion and society, art and architecture, gender studies and political economy. Some of her publications are *The Book of Lakshmi, Making of the Goddess: Korravai Durga in the Tamil Traditions* and *Art and History: Texts, Contexts and Visual Representations in Ancient and Early Medieval India*. She has also held the position of general secretary of the prestigious Indian History Congress (2018–21).

Robert Chalmers, 1st Baron Chalmers, GCB, PC (Ire) (18 August 1858–17 November 1938) was a British civil servant, and a Pali and Buddhist scholar. In later life, he served as the Master of Peterhouse, Cambridge. In 1882, he began his career as a civil servant in Her Majesty's Treasury, but he did not abandon his classical studies, as he wanted to perfect his knowledge of ancient languages. In almost forty years, he translated more than 2000 Buddhist texts.

Sanjukta Dasgupta is an Indian feminist scholar, poet, short-story writer, critic and translator with twenty-one published books to her credit. She is professor and former head, Department of English, and former dean, Faculty of Arts, Calcutta University, and has been the recipient of a number of fellowships, including the Fulbright postdoctoral fellowship and Fulbright Scholar in Residence grant, Australia–India Council fellowship and the Gender Studies fellowship grant, University of British Columbia. She is president, Executive Council, the Indian Poetry and Performance Library, ICCR, Kolkata, and was the convenor of the English Advisory Board of the Sahitya Akademi. Her awards include the IWSFF Women Achievers Award, Kolkata (2019) and the WEI Kamala Das Poetry Award (2020).

Sunita Pant Bansal, a storyteller and mythologist, has been creating different forms of media for over four decades. Apart from heading publishing houses, founding–editing newspapers and magazines, Sunita has written numerous articles, stories, poems, created board games and produced short films. Her forte is to decode Hindu scriptures to show their relevance and application in today's times. Sunita has authored twenty-eight books for adults and young adults, and a thousand books for children, which are sold in multiple languages globally. Amongst Sunita's recent bestsellers are *Krishna the Management Guru*, *Everyday Gita, Puranas: The Origin of Gods and Goddesses* and *The Return of Vikram and Betaal.*

Swami Vijnanananda (born Hariprasanna Chattopadhyaya; 30 October 1868–25 April 1938) was born in an upper-class family near Dakshineswar and was a direct disciple of Ramakrishna. He was an engineer and worked as the district engineer in the erstwhile state of United Provinces, India. He was a great scholar of Sanskrit with expertise in religio-philosophical works, astronomy, civil engineering, etc. He spent considerable time in Allahabad (Prayag) centre of Ramakrishna Math. He became the president of Ramakrishna Mission in 1937. It was under his presidency and direct supervision that the Ramakrishna Temple at Belur Math was constructed and consecrated.

Sukumari Bhattacharji (12 July 1921–24 May 2014) was a Sanskrit scholar, author (Bengali and English) and Indologist. Born in Kolkata, Bhattacharji initially studied English but later pursued a master's degree in Sanskrit. She joined Jadavpur University as a professor and was known for her proficiency in multiple languages. Bhattacharji's most notable work, *Indian Theogony: A Comparative Study of Indian Mythology from the Vedas to the Puranas*, was based on her doctoral thesis and published by Cambridge University Press. As a social activist, she co-founded Sachetana in 1982 to aid underprivileged girls.

Swamini Atmaprajnananda Saraswati is a PhD in Sanskrit, and an MBA in finance and marketing, XIMB. She is a published author of eight books—*Daśaśānti* (2008), *Rūpasiddhi* (2008), *Nomenclature of the Vedas* (2012), *Ṛṣikās of the Ṛgveda* (2013), *Om: The Sound Symbol* (2014), *Vision of Vedanta in Taittirīyopaniṣad* (2016), *Bhagavadgītā: A Study* (2020), *Sūktas and Stotras* (2021). She has convened and directed thirteen National Conferences since 2009 on various Indological topics. She was a speaker at the Jaipur Literature Festival in 2018. She has written around 140 blogs in *Speaking Tree* (*Times of India*) and was conferred the title 'Vedanta Shiromani' by them in 2017.

Tamalika Chakraborty was born and raised in Kolkata. A teacher by profession, she connects with children and adults alike, and her poems are often a reflection of the society we live in and life's greatest teachings.

Tanashree Redij currently serves as an assistant professor at Amrita Darshanam (International Centre for Spiritual Studies) at the Bengaluru campus. She holds a doctoral degree in archaeology from Deccan College Post-Graduate and Research Institute, Pune. Having a background in archaeology and Sanskrit, she is working on the rituals of Goddess Jyeṣṭhā from the sociological, historical and anthropological point of view to get into the complexities of the ritual and the possible reasons behind it. Her extensive ethnographic fieldwork in various parts of Maharashtra has given her good insight into understanding the various layers of cultural beliefs and their possible reasons supporting the textual and historical dynamics of rituals.

COPYRIGHT ACKNOWLEDGEMENTS

Grateful acknowledgement is made to the following for permission to reprint copyrighted material:

Aparna Sharma of DK India for 'Tulsi: The Sylvan form of Devi', originally published in *Shakti: An Exploration of the Divine Feminine*.

Bidyut Mohanty for 'Vrata Kathas', originally published as 'Vrata Kathas from States: Varying Representations' from *Lakshmi: The Rebel.*

Bibek Debroy's translated extract from *The Bhagavata Purana*, published by Penguin.

Dr Pramod Pandey, vice chancellor, Deccan College, Pune, for 'Alakshmi—Symmetry and Asymmetry', originally published as 'Origin and Development of Alakṣmī and Alakṣmī Concept' in *Bulletin of the Deccan College Post-Graduate and Research Institute*, Vol. 70/71.

Devdutt Pattanaik for 'Decoding Lakshmi', published in the Diwali Issue of *Deccan Herald* in 2009.

Dr K. Srinivasarao of Sahitya Akademi for 'Lakshmi and Alakshmi: The Dichotomy Explored', originally published as 'Lakshmi and Alakshmi', in *Indian Folk Narratives*, Sanjukta Dasgupta and Ramkumar Mukhopadhyaya (eds).

K. Jaikumar of The Theosophical Publishing House for extracts from the *Saubhagya Lakshmi Upanishad.*

Lipipuspa Nayak for 'Manabasa Lakshmi Purana: The Redeemer of the Poor', originally published as *Lakshmi Purana* by Balaram Das.

Malerie Lovejoy of SUNY Press for 'Invoking Lakshmi', originally published as 'Living the Powerful Life: Lakshmi of the Tantric Traditions' and 'The Power of Tantric songs' in *Invoking Lakshmi: The Goddess of Wealth in Song and Ceremony.*

R. Mahalakshmi for 'The Ashta Lakshmi Stotram and the Kanakadhara Stotram', originally published in *The Book of Lakshmi.*

Shri Ravindra Jain of Motilal Banarsidass, (http://www.mlbd.co.in/) 41-UA Bungalow Road, Delhi, for sections from the *Skand Purana*; 'Agastya's Prayer to Lakshmi', 'The Glory of Lakshmitirtha' and 'Lakshmi Cursed to Turn Elephant-headed'. Also, 'The Darker Side of Fortune' (Alakṣmī's Episode) from the *Padma Purana* by N.A. Deshpande.

Shri Nandu Ji from Sanskrit Documents (https://sanskritdocuments.org/) for extracts from Kanakdhara Stotram of Adi Shankaracharya.

Sri Swami Padmanabhanandaji of The Divine Life Society for extracts from Shri Suktam.

Veenu Luthria of Orient Blackswan Private Limited for 'Bali's Sacrifice', originally published in *Legends of Devi.*